THE JOY OF ANTIQUES

THE JOY OF ANTIQUES

Ronald Pearsall

DAVID & CHARLES
Newton Abbot · London

FRONTISPIECE: *Large Canton
vase of about 1750, the kind of
object found in large country
houses open to the public for the
disposal of sweet-papers and often
worth many thousands of pounds.*

British Library Cataloguing in Publication Data

Pearsall, R
        The joy of antiques.
        1. Antiques. Collecting.
        I. Title
        745.1′075

ISBN 0-7153-9217-4

First published 1988
Second impression 1989

Typeset by Character Graphics Taunton Somerset
and printed in Portugal by Resopal
for David & Charles Publishers plc
Brunel House Newton Abbot Devon.

CONTENTS

INTRODUCTION

Antiques are a gateway to days gone by. Take an old stool, for instance, rather battered, but firm and solid because it is made of oak, and oak resists woodworm. It has survived more than four hundred years, and will last another four hundred.

Since then it has been through a lot. When it was made ordinary people did not sit on chairs – chairs were much too grand for them. They sat on stools and benches and shivered, for houses were austere and draughty. The stool has only three legs. Was this because three-legged stools were easier to make? No, it had three legs because the floors were so uneven that stools of this kind were more stable.

Furniture developed in a haphazard way. No one knows who

An antique shop set out as a dining room in a most imaginative manner.

An antique as an object of beauty. Two South Staffordshire enamel nécessaires, open and closed.

first thought of the idea of putting a box within a box, and inventing the drawer, but it was a short step then to fitting drawers one on top of the other, and making, naturally, a chest of drawers.

Everything from the past has about it something special, and it does not have to be the distant past. Looking at some of the china of the 1920s and 1930s it is easy to imagine it set down in some drawing-room while the gramophone plays and the bright young things dance the Charleston. Equally evocative is the blue and white china from the eighteenth century, the days when Dr Johnson held sway in one or other of the two thousand or more coffee-houses in London, when taking tea was an elaborate ceremony. Looking around, it appears that there are fewer teacups than coffee-cups. Have the teacups been broken over the years? No – tea was drunk from bowls. It was very expensive, which is why teapots were so small and tea-caddies were equipped with locks so that the servants could not help themselves.

All this is living history. It does not need much effort to conjure up these days gone by. And there is no need to just look at these objects in museums. Buy them, look at them, cherish them for the unique objects they are.

Everyone of course has different tastes. There are some who find Victorian furniture heavy and oppressive, while others think the elegant Georgian furniture spindly and cold and much prefer to curl up in one of those massive armchairs of the 1860s, made comfortable by the invention of such a mundane device as the spiral spring. There are some who want to furnish their homes in one style, while others want just one extra-special item.

The Joy of Antiques – that really sums it up. And of course the whole business of antiques – their survival, the way they move around from dealer to dealer, through the auction rooms, or just handed down through generations – is endlessly fascinating.

HOW IT ALL BEGAN

In the early history of the trade, collectors were far more important than dealers. Collectors bought from the source or used agents, and the antique dealer is the direct descendant of these agents. The heyday of collecting was probably between 1770 and 1830 when the English gentleman was more affluent than his continental contemporaries, and capitalised on this. England was calm, while Europe was in a state of flux. Great collections were broken up, museums were ransacked, all was available to the Englishman with a long purse, and even the treasures of the Vatican were not inviolate.

Because the English gentleman had been nurtured on the classics, his primary demand was for antiquities, but the necessity to undertake the Grand Tour of Europe brought him face to face with furniture, paintings, and miscellane-

ous ill-identified objects that had nothing to do with ancient Greece and Rome. Some of the tourists found these a good deal more interesting than the antiquities.

Furniture was not regarded highly; dealing in it was common trading. No single piece of furniture was valued at more than an average painting. The gap between picture dealers and general dealers was mirrored by the social chasm between collectors and dealers of all kinds, but to some extent this ceased to exist when the new industrial middle classes began to come into prominence in the nineteenth century. The tastes of the old aristocracy were predictable; not so those of the new rich, falling victim to pathetic forgeries, but also plunging into the shifting world of modern art.

The new class evolved a new lifestyle, demanding a different environment. The elegant Regency

The ideal bedroom in the 1920s, chintzy, unpretentious, and largely without character.

and Georgian furniture was dismissed into the servants' quarters, mahogany went out, walnut was rediscovered, and rosewood came in. Opulence replaced refinement, collecting became accumulation, and from the 1850s there was an increasing demand for art objects of all kinds, necessitating a structure for buying and selling.

In the 1870s and 1880s the Americans entered the market for a share of the world's antiques, and were eager to buy the best at any price, relying heavily on experts who scoured Europe on their behalf.

Competition for the Americans came not only from the British collectors, but also from the German museum and art-gallery curators who had a lot of money to spend. The British 'shopocracy' – men who had made their money in trade – were lavish buyers, and credulous with it, so that they often built up expensive collections which turned out to be worth very little.

By and large, antique-dealing was a leisurely business. Except for a few select establishments in the West End of London, dealers were lowly characters, quaint, smelling of snuff, and a bit crafty, so that they had to be watched. Only the well-off bought antiques, invariably for use and display, never for investment.

After World War II there was a self-conscious vogue for Victoriana, and it was considered by those who doted on G-Plan and the furniture of Ambrose Heal that this was proof of some aberration. When it was found that demand regulated prices, that there was money to be made in bric-à-brac and curios, the affluent society of Harold Macmillan's era became an acquisitive society, and the exposure given to antiques on radio and television, and in the newspapers and the many journals that sprang up, catered for naked cupidity. The bargain-hunters came out in force from their surburban houses with their 'heirlooms' under their arms, antique shops and markets sprang up and trade boomed, with

For many the shop is still the obvious outlet, particularly where furniture or specialised items are concerned.

Since the 1960s antique fairs have grown in popularity. A fair near Plymouth, January 1988.

everyone an instant expert. The dealers expanded, took over huge warehouses, and began exporting in bulk to America and Australia, making use of the new transport facility, container vessels.

And that would be the end of it, except for the occasional hiccup, the oil crisis, rocketing local-authority rates which killed off the old type of junk-dealer, and the antique price spiral. In 1969, when the antique markets were opening as fast as supermarkets and Portobello Road was swinging like mad, a Davenport desk in the trade was £20 ($35), to be resold to shippers or private 'punters' for £25 ($43.75). Today the same item would be in the £800–£1,000 ($1,400 – $1,750) bracket. A music box at £50 ($87.50) could now be worth £1,500–£3,000 ($2,625– $5,250). The trade spiral almost killed off the amateur dealer – but not quite. He or she went downmarket, but having been bitten by the antique-dealing bug there was no going back to a life of stability and sanity.

FURNITURE

Pieces of furniture are the most personal of all antiques; they are lived with and used, and they take on a personality of their own; they are loved despite (or even because of) their imperfections. For true antique furniture is never flawless; and that is part of its appeal.

In the early days furniture was far less important than the tapestries and hangings that relieved the austerity of the great houses and castles. The basic requirement was that furniture should be portable; when the great moved from stronghold to stronghold their furniture went with them.

Before the seventeenth century houses were sparsely furnished. The most common item was the coffer, which held everything, and the aumbry or hutch for food. The rich had four-poster beds, not because they looked imposing, but because they served to display costly draperies – and, just as important, they could be curtained to keep out the draughts, which swept through ill-fitting doors. Ordinary people slept in beds not far removed from boxes.

Most of the furniture that survives from the seventeenth century and earlier was made from oak, which was easily worked and took the kind of decoration that was popular, done with gouge and chisel.

Chests were the most important pieces of furniture. The earliest form was a hollowed-out tree trunk, but by the thirteenth century chests were made with simple carved decoration and hinged lids which could be locked. The sides could extend past the body of the chest and act as legs. In the late fifteenth century thin panels were set loosely in the chests (to reduce the impact of shrinkage of wood). The ornamentation on these panels is known as linen-fold, because they were carved to imitate folded cloth.

Towards the end of the seventeenth century chests were made with drawers. They were beginning to develop into something else.

Chests were also used to sit on, and so were stools – three-legged or four-legged. Some stools are known as joyned or joynt; this is because they were made by joiners. For from an early stage workers in wood were differentiated. In the thirteen and four-teenth centuries chairs were unwieldy and cumbersome, made from solid planks. The person who sat on a chair was important: the chairman still is to this day.

The main early table was of the trestle type, quite narrow, sometimes 25ft (7.5m) long, and dismantled when not in use. The diners sat on long benches. Small tables with fixed tops were used in the private rooms.

The best furniture was imported, and the immigration of re-

Knocked Down

One day a dealer of repute called at a house by appointment to see a table. He was shown into a room in the centre of which was an ugly draw-leaf table, probably of Edwardian vintage, if that. 'How much will you give me for that, young man?' asked the lady of the house coyly. It was not the kind of table the dealer had expected to see. 'Has it got the handle?' he asked. Yes, it had the handle. 'Six pounds', said the dealer. '*Six pounds?*' echoed the woman aghast. She looked at him piercingly. 'How long have you been an antique dealer, young man?' she asked, 'Are you *really* an antique dealer?' The dealer, irritated, answered that he was indeed an antique dealer, and had been one for eight years. 'It seems to me that you don't know very much about furniture', said the woman sardonically, 'that table is worth' – and she paused dramatically – '*eight hundred pounds!*'

And then the story came out. A knocker had called, and had abased himself before the table. 'Lady', he said humbly, 'I simply haven't enough to buy your table. I would like to, but …'

He then acquired a set of Edwardian chairs, six dining-room chairs and two carvers, for £12, plus a few other odds and ends, including a smattering of gold and silver.

fugees from religious persecution brought new ideas of what constituted taste to Britain. More important was stability; when the lords and major personages no longer had to trek from castle to castle with their belongings or raise armed bands to fight their neighbours they could begin to think about comfort, about armchairs and large static pieces of furniture, such as the court cupboard, which could display treasures and valuables such as plate.

In the sixteenth century the 'framed' table was introduced. Heavy turned legs are set into a framing at the corners. The draw-top table, with leaves that could be put in and out, was a useful innovation and this was followed in due course by the gate-leg table. There were only a few major developments to follow in table design – such as the drop-leaf on pull-out supports and the table on a central pillar.

In many kinds of furniture there are few significant alterations that can be made once the basic form has been established. Once the form of the chair had been established, for example, it only remained to refine it, prettify it, and make it more comfortable, the culmination of which process was the invention of the spiral spring in the nineteenth century. It may appear that much of the furniture before, say, 1700 was unbearably uncomfortable. But the earlier furniture was fitted out with cushions and a form of upholstery, and indeed the materials used were regarded as far more important than the chairs themselves.

Furniture construction depended on the means available. Until

An early nineteenth-century yew, elm and beech Windsor chair.

George I walnut bureau.

Mistaken identity

Not every book on antiques is completely accurate. In a book on refurbishing antiques the writer illustrated a 'Hepplewhite Shield-Back Chair' – with springs in the upholstery. Hepplewhite died in 1786, more than fifty years before the invention of spiral springs.

the sixteenth century glue was simply not strong enough to hold very much together, and the uniting of timbers depended on the mortise-and-tenon joint (the tenon is the tongue that slots into the square or oblong mortise). By drilling a hole through the mortise and the tenon, a peg could be pushed through, making a rigid unbreakable fixture of the pieces of wood. The timber of contemporary houses was held together in this way. In the seventeenth century two pegs instead of one gave the mortise-and-tenon even more strength.

For a time, two types of hinges were popular, the wire hinge (two interlocking loops of wire) and the strap-hinge, made in two parts – a short broad part on the wood which remains stationary, and a long often ornate tongue on, for example, the lid of a chest. Strong and reliable, the strap-hinge continued to be used after the wire-hinge had been dropped, and for substantial articles has not been bettered since. For more delicate use, the butterfly hinge came in at the end of the seventeenth century, concurrently with a new way of joining two pieces of wood at right angles, the dovetail, which consisted of interacting wedges, best seen in the construction of drawers.

Periods of exuberance followed periods of restraint. During the time of Cromwell, chairs were austere – short-backed, with simple bobbin turning in the uprights. The backs and seats were covered by strips of leather held in place by large brass-headed nails. With the Restoration of Charles II there emerged the upholstered wing armchair and the use of extravagant decoration in the form of cherubs, crowns, foliage, flowers and birds. Heavy oak furniture was out of fashion.

The furniture of the revolutionary designer Ernest Gimson in a cottage setting. He was more than fifty years ahead of his time.

About 1670 floral marquetry furniture began to come in from Holland and was imitated by British craftsmen. Walnut was everywhere preferred to oak, though some preferred the lacquer work imported from Japan, which was also imitated. Japanese motifs mostly garnered from engravings in travel books were used, giving the British an insight into the mysterious East.

The bookcase was invented, the first recorded mention being by Pepys in 1666. It was tall, plain and at first made of oak, with wide glazing bars to minimise the use of expensive glass. As English furniture was still considered appropriate to the rude peasantry but few others, elegant gilded furniture was imported from France, the European cultural centre.

As women became more important in society, they began to demand more in the way of custom-made furniture, and dressing-tables which had consisted of a simple table with drawers became more sophisticated and genteel. For ladies of a delicate constitution day-beds or couches were very popular, but being made of walnut or beech most of them have not survived.

What oak has survived from this and early periods? Is it all in museums or private collections?

Early chests are plentiful and, considering their age, cheap. They range from about £400 upwards, and even those at the bottom of the range are replete with marvellous decoration. Oak settles can also be bought for £400 or so, their size and chunkiness keeping the price down. The prices of chairs vary enormously, with some single Charles II chairs fetching only £200 or so, and armchairs of the same period £600 plus.

To many, old oak is the furniture without equal: honest, straightforward, enjoyable, with the wear and patina of three hundred or more years.

Two seventeenth-century oak stools, still available at modest prices.

The end of oak as the favourite wood, except in the country, where it never went out of fashion, coincided with the introduction of veneers, glued on the 'carcase' of various types of furniture. Veneer was hand-sawn, and the thicker it is ($^{1}/_{16}$–$^{1}/_{8}$in [1.5–3mm]), the earlier. The use of dovetail joints instead of mortise-and-tenon meant that the timber used in furniture could be thinner (the mortise-and-tenon joint needed wood that was at least 1in [2.5cm] thick, maybe 2in [5 cm], while dovetailing could be used in timber ¾in [20mm] thick). This was a great help in making drawers. Before about 1680 draw sides (known as linings) were nailed. The grain of the wood on the bottom of the drawer ran from back to front, not side to side, and this feature, useful as a dating guide, lasted until the middle of the eighteenth century. That is why you see furniture dealers taking out drawers to examine them.

The close of the seventeenth century saw further innovations. In accessories, the earliest attachments to drawers and doors had been wooden knobs. Sometimes there was only a key grasp. Iron handles were used subsequently but towards the end of the century brass was used. The favourite type of handle proved to be the pear-shaped drop. Articles of furniture which had been in use for some time were smartened up; in the old gate-leg table there had been a gap between the leaves, but by making a 'rule joint', so that two leaves did not meet in an absolute right-angle, the gap disappeared. This is the weakest part of an antique gate-leg

Regency rosewood games and work table, sold in January 1986 for £2,500.

table, and even with one in good condition generally there may be damage at this crucial point, where the leaves abut.

Walnut was used as veneer and in the solid, and great quantities were imported. Chests of drawers in veneered walnut were inlaid with holly, boxwood and sycamore in strict geometric patterns, and often stood on handsome stands. To many the style seemed alien, far removed from the no-nonsense oak. Chairs were lighter and more fragile, and proliferated in a number of styles, some awkward, some elegant and foreshadowing things to come. Typical of these was a narrow-back chair with a curved shape, with a central splat and cabriole legs in the front, unashamedly based on French and Italian models.

Different kinds of feet were used on chairs, hoof-shaped, scrolled, club, and the ball-and-claw, believed to be an echo of Chinese designs. Richly upholstered stools, often with drop-in seats, were popular, and high-backed luxuriously padded settees, often covered with lavish embroidery, made their appearance. In the country there was not the same concern for the little extras of civilised life. Caned furniture was still much used, and plain oak settles were staple features of the yeoman's farm or house.

With the fashion for totally panelled rooms wardrobes could be built into the walls, and open cupboards were also fitted into the panelling for the display of china and curios brought back from foreign parts. Corner cupboards made their appearance in the 1690s, sometimes with mirror glass for display; these could hang or be full-length, and some had a half-dome 'umbrella' on top.

Amongst the most varied types of furniture were side tables, useful, ornamental, sometimes topped with marble or its cheaper substitute, scagliola (a blend of marble, granite, porphyry, alabaster, plaster of Paris and glue). Amongst the most impressive pieces of furniture were the huge two-stage writing cabinets, the top part fitted with small drawers and a multitude of pigeon-holes, the bottom part a bureau with a fall-front for writing on. The upper part was sometimes used for books – the classic bureau-bookcase, one of the most desirable and expensive of all antiques.

What, it may be asked, of mahogany? In 1709 there was a harsh winter. The walnut supplies were cut off, and in due course foreign governments forbade its export. Wood from the British colonies was freed from heavy import duties, and this included mahogany. Although mahogany had been known as a novelty it was now valued as a substitute for walnut, and from 1725 it supplanted it, though walnut furniture continued to be made after supplies had been restored, especially in the provinces.

What was special about mahogany? Workers in wood liked it. It was strong, did not easily mark, was easily polished, did not easily warp or crack, and was resistant to woodworm (which has eaten its way through much walnut furniture). It permitted finer carving, and because of its strength it did not need bolstering up. Chairs did not need stretchers for support; the gate of a table could be cut down in size or made more delicate.

Carving, which fashion had rejected in favour of veneers, was introduced once again, and mahogany was very suitable for a variety of decorative mouldings. Flat surfaces became bowed and

---

Ahead of its time

The most famous antique in Britain is perhaps the Great Bed of Ware, which is boldly dated 1463. Yet it is generally agreed that it was not made until about 1580. Dates on anything are not necessarily true.

elongated. Lion masks and other designs could be carved onto any furniture terminal. The tripod table made its appearance.

Glass had now reached a stage where it was possible to make large mirrors, and some of these were ornate and asymmetrical, influenced by the styles fashionable in France, which otherwise had little effect on English taste except amongst certain rich aristocrats with a taste for the meretricious and the monumental. The item most characteristic of this furniture was the console table, with its massive top on heavy supports.

In many cases buyers did not know what they wanted until they had got it. With Thomas Chippendale's *Gentleman and Cabinet-Maker's Directory* of 1754, makers, sellers and purchasers were provided with a book of patterns and a guide to what was in fashion. Later Hepplewhite and Sheraton were to provide further books on similar lines, all immensely influential.

Certain trends were encouraged: curved, bowed, serpentine shapes in all furniture; delicate carving; elegance above all, espe-

---

Investment in tea chests

In the 1950s a dealer on one of his calls between Brighton and London was offered several tea-chests full of wooden bits. He was told that when reconstituted the result would be a William and Mary bureau-bookcase. He was asked £75, a good deal of money in the 1950s, but he bought the tea chests, gave them to a restorer, and *thirteen years later* he was presented with a William and Mary bureau-bookcase. Shortly afterwards he was offered £25,000 for the masterpiece, which he turned down, though he admitted that this was above the market price, which he put at around £12,000.

Georgian sideboard with a pair of fine decanters and a rococo gilt mirror.

cially if it could be spiced with influences from China or could mirror the current enthusiasm for the Gothick, a prettified version of the Gothic. This meant neat little pointed arches and pinnacles incorporated into the furniture. The taste for the Chinese style resulted in fretwork in the form of ornamental railings or geometric piercing, and friezes in low relief ('card cut').

The neo-classicism associated with the name of Robert Adam made an appearance in the 1760s. Classical ornament (ram's heads, corn husks, vases and medallions), light-coloured wood, and marquetry, were all combined in the new style, along with ormolu mounts set against mahogany.

Specialities of Adam and his followers were the sideboard flanked by pedestals and urns, chairs with tapered legs and round, oval, shield- and kidney-shaped backs. The style was airy and graceful, and was carried on by Hepplewhite, who endeavoured, as he said himself, 'to unite elegance and utility and blend the useful with the agreeable', though he is best known for his variations on the shield-back chair and his use of Prince of Wales feathers. He also introduced the Pembroke table, a delightful drop-leaf table, and revived japanning.

No legs!

A dealer was offered a black painted table-top for £7, and although it had no legs there was something about it that he liked. He gave it to his restorer, who removed *twenty* layers of paint, and three years later handed the dealer a Queen Anne lowboy worth about £700.

A William and Mary japanned (lacquered) cabinet on chest, the upper part containing ten drawers.

P. E. GANE
(Late TRAPNELL & GANE)

Highly Artistic Bedroom Furniture of First-class Workmanship,
. . . at moderate cost. . .
CARRIAGE PAID TO ALL STATIONS.

No. 918c.—Quaintly designed Bedroom Suite, comprising 6 ft. wardrobe, 4 ft. dressing table, 4 ft. washstand, pedestal cupboard, three upholstered chairs, in Fumed Oak, American Walnut, or Chippendale Mahogany.

. . . For Prices see New Catalogue, post free. . .

38a, 39 & 40, College Green, Bristol. *Branches:* 38 & 41, Queen St., Cardiff.
161 & 162, Commercial St., Newport, Mon.

A nightmare scene of 1902, art nouveau at its most debased.

Sheraton refined even Hepplewhite. Simple clean lines, compactness, and furniture that could be used for a variety of purposes. Square chair backs were favoured, upward sweeping arms, and tapered legs. 'Stringing', delicate line-inlay in contrasting woods or brass, was an ideal form of unostentatious decoration for such furniture.

There is certainly nothing excessive about the best-known country chair of all time, the Windsor, of which the first recorded mention is in 1724 and which continued in a multitude of varieties. No doubt London modes were duly transmitted to the provincial furniture-maker, but the country maker, equal to the best with oak and local woods, was at a loss with classical motifs, ormolu and the new imported woods.

From about 1700 imports of pine from America became an important source of timber. The best pine furniture was made before about the middle of the nineteenth century but little can be confidently dated earlier than about 1780. Country-made pine took as its models the respectable furniture in other woods but took on its own distinctive character.

The gap between town and country was not lessened by the arrival of the nineteenth century. Strictly speaking the Regency period ran from 1811 to 1820 but stylistically it has been allowed to spread backwards and forwards, sometimes nudging a once well-defined reign, that of William IV, out of sight.

What characterises Regency furniture? First of all the use of woods such as rosewood, amboyna, zebra wood and calamander, many of them having exotic figurings. Rosewood had been used to a modest extent between about 1660 and 1685, but now it was used in bulk and in the solid and it remained a very popular wood until the 1860s. A strong-looking unmistakable wood with its black streaking, it was ideally suited to the phase of Regency furniture which favoured straight lines, unbroken surfaces, and low height.

These woods were used in association with lion masks, lyres

Pieces of Chippendale

Many years ago a sharp city dealer was out in 'the sticks'. He went to a shop and saw a Chippendale chest. He hid his excitement claiming that he only wanted it for the drawer linings (the draw sides), so that he could repair the good furniture he had in stock. He remorselessly beat the dealer down from £7 10s (£7.50) to £3 10s (£3.50), regardless of the fact that the chest, even then, was worth several hundred pounds. Very pleased with his acquisition, he went to get his car and have a celebratory drink on the way. When he got back he found that the other dealer, eager to please, and believing implicitly in the fable of drawer linings, had smashed the chest up, taken out the linings, and neatly wrapped them up in brown paper.

Pair of ebonised and ormolu French display cabinets.

and neo-classical motifs in brass and other metals, and Egyptian motifs such as sphinxes and lotus patterns, very modish since the British and French involvement in Egypt culminating in the Battle of the Nile in 1798. Typical of Regency furniture are low angular bookcases with trellis doors, behind which was silk curtaining; chiffoniers (elegant cupboards with shelving, often with a brass gallery); sofa tables, designed to run alongside a sofa but used in lieu of dining tables on account of their more compact size; and heavy and spectacular round tables with central pillars, sometimes with brass claw feet. There was also the exquisite 'Carlton House' table, modelled on furniture in the French style created for the Prince of Wales in 1783 for his official residence. This was basically a writing table with nests of drawers on top at the back and on the sides.

Ancient Greek influence could be seen in couches and chairs. The sabre leg made it appearance, square-sectioned and curving in an arc. Supplies of some of the new woods, such as zebra wood from Brazil, were soon exhausted, but fortunately mahogany continued to hold sway. There were new styles in decoration, with an emphasis on bold patterns in fabrics and wallpapers – 'Regency stripe' retains its appeal.

There was considerable contempt for the furniture of the past, a conscious rejection of the old-fashioned; this coincided with the discovery in 1815 of French polishing. French polish is shellac dissolved in spirit; it imparts instant durable gloss, far more impressive than the time-honoured way of rub, rub, rub with beeswax, turpentine and oils. There was also a new interest in Chinese styles, lacquering enjoyed a revival, and bamboo was imitated in other woods.

Fashionable diseases such as gout had their own furniture – the gout stool, for example – and gadgetry was welcomed, such as the library steps hidden in the bowels of tables or springing from innocuous-looking stools and chairs. Furniture with an X-frame construction was popular, as was the delightful bergère suite with cane backs and sides.

Among the smaller pieces of furniture so typical of the Regency and made throughout the nineteenth century were nests of tables, cheval mirrors, and work tables fitted with suspended bags, often of pleated silk. Sheraton had illustrated a number of designs, and some of the work tables had fire-screens incorporated in them. These work tables, used for embroidery or for games (in which case there was often a folded top, one side for draughts or chess, the other for backgammon), could be set on a four-legged base or on an elegant tripod. In the 1850s the design was modified: the top was circular and the silk bag was replaced by a funnel, tapering down to the tripod legs.

Tea-caddies, often of sarcophagus shape, are still very reasonably priced, especially in mahogany. Some caddies were made in the shape of fruit, the apple being especially popular. In the Regency period the caddy was set on a stand and called a teapoy. One of the most useful pieces of furniture which persisted with variations from 1795 was the Davenport desk, neat, compact, with drawers at the side, often with an ornate brass gallery.

There was an accent on comfort and a degree of clutter. Ladies of romantic temperament, nurtured on the fashionable Gothic novels, could loll on couches. The couch, simple or ornate, could go under a variety of names – *chaise-longue*, *récamier*, *confidante*, *veilleuse*, *lit de repos*, *duchesse*, *turquoise*, or rest-bed or day-bed. If these ladies suddenly woke up and were upset by the utter ghastliness of the things around them they could look at the fashionable circular convex mirrors set in gilt. This eliminated 'the coarseness of objects by contracting them'. These convex mirrors enjoyed renewed popularity in the 1930s, when the coarseness of objects was a good deal more apparent.

Many of the types of furniture, forms, wood preferences, and styles persisted well into the rest of the nineteenth century, sometimes throughout the century. Some furniture did not need further development. The heavy library tables, pedestal tables, couches and bookcases were as useful to Victorians as they had been to their parents and grandparents.

True, there was a search for novelty and a decline in the interest in classicism, but at the same time there was a determined search through past styles to see what the past had to offer. These were often misunderstood, and manufacturers enthusiastically grafted on ornament which they in their simplicity thought appropriate.

For many years it was supposed that the Great Exhibition of 1851 reflected Victorian taste, but not by anybody who had actually looked at the furniture as a whole or had had dealings with it.

Victorian inlaid walnut credenza sold in November 1987 for £1,050.

A George III mahogany kneehole desk on bracket feet, plain, functional, and utterly unspoiled.

Much of the large furniture that bedazzled the exhibition-goer, had a Gothic or Elizabethan pedigree. When it was decided in 1835 that the Palace of Westminster was to be Gothic and not classical a nationally accepted style was formulated. Its later flowering included St Pancras Station and later still Tower Bridge.

Much Gothic furniture was made from dark oak imported from Danzig. The Victorians associated dark wood with antiquity, and native oak was darkened by 'fuming', i.e. smoking in ammonia. Heavy items of furniture were also made with non-Gothic themes. Some of these individual pieces are famous, such as the Chevy Chase sideboard, exhibited in London in 1865.

An achievement of the Great Exhibition was to persuade people that furniture was not necessarily made from wood. Although papier mâché had been used since the eighteenth century, it was now employed for furniture. The marvellous painted trays inlaid with mother-of-pearl and the work-boxes demonstrate the material's potential.

In 1834 the manufacture of iron furniture began; it was mostly hall-stands and garden furniture, but the cast-iron bed was an important innovation, cheap and hygienic – and functional. By 1870 the wooden bed was thoroughly out of date. Elaborate brass beds with twisted rails, knobs and intricate tracery were preferred. They were often strengthened with iron.

There was good sense in much Victorian furniture. The balloon-back chair, gently curved for maximum comfort, was the standard dining- and drawing-room chair until about 1870. The cameo- and camel-back chairs were low, with short legs, and with small arms enabled women of the 1850s in their wide-spreading crinolines to sit comfortably. Another new chair was the prie-dieu or vesper, harking back to the high-back chair of Charles II but unmistakably Victorian, ideal for family prayers, tall enough for non-religious children to hide behind. These provided an excellent vehicle for fashionable Berlin woolwork.

If women had their chaise-longue, immensely popular in the 1860s when Empress Eugénie brought it back into fashion in France, the men had their Chesterfield, an enormous upholstered double-ended couch named after an Earl of Chesterfield, popular as club and study furniture from the 1880s and still made today. The drawing-room equivalent of the Chesterfield was the ottoman, originally a round upholstered seat, sometimes used in groups to put round a central feature such as a tall palm. The box ottoman was introduced in the 1880s, and provided storage as well as a seat. There was perhaps only one deliberately uncomfortable chair – the hall chair, angular, uncompromising.

The Canterbury music-rack reflected the interest in music; the work-boxes and games-boxes in walnut, rosewood and mahogany, the delight in recreation of all kinds. The piano was a very important piece of furniture, often the centre piece of a room. The 'cottage' pianos often had an ornate fretted front with a curtain behind, and candleholders in ornate brass. The imposing 'giraffe' piano was a grand piano set vertically. Rosewood and walnut were favourite woods. Towards the end of the century pianos were ebonised.

Pianos from an earlier period might well have remained because of their compact size, and large numbers of square pianos, introduced to Britain in about 1742, are still about, though many have been converted into writing desks.

It is worth remembering that the Victorians spent a lot of time music-making in the home, and larger houses had a music-room in which would be found the piano and probably the harp which was immensely popular with young ladies as they could look

A pair of William IV rosewood card tables with hinged baize-lined tops. Notice the characteristic reeded bun feet.

Pair of handsome Queen Anne chairs.

appealing as they ran their hands across the strings. If they could play the instrument, so much the better. There were several varieties of harp, the concert harps in Grecian or Gothic styles and the smaller Irish harp. Apart from the piano, the favourite instrument for men was probably the flute. The oboe was not so popular; invented in about 1660 it replaced the shawm. Towards the end of the century the banjo became the instrument of the young man who wanted to cut a dash.

Musical families often formed string quartets, and violins and other stringed instruments were produced on a huge scale, often bearing fake labels stating that the instrument was made by Stradivarius.

In some houses of a religious persuasion the piano was replaced by the harmonium or the American organ, characterised by its sweet voix céleste stop. These instruments have survived in re- markable numbers, many of them modernised by the installation of a vacuum-cleaner motor to save pedalling.

The familiar round piano stool in rosewood, mahogany or wal- nut with a wind-up screw mechanism was introduced in about 1860, and remains one of the most popular small pieces of Victo- rian furniture. Tables of every kind proliferated, as did easy chairs, low ones called nursing chairs and expansive club chairs in leather, and sideboards of every size, from small chiffonier types to heavily carved reissues of the court cupboard.

Fire-screens were made in all shapes and sizes, hand-held in the shape of a fan, chair screens for fixing on the backs of chairs, screens fixed to standing pedestals. And there were folding screens for keeping out draughts, often exquisitely painted, some made of leather, others plain, lending themselves to home adornment by the gluing on of scraps and cut-out illustrations. And, of course, there was the whatnot, tiered shelves on a wooden frame, often in walnut with elaborate inlay. The whatnot sometimes bore the name omnium, and was used for the display of the numerous oddments that filled, often infested, the drawing room.

Of course much furniture of an earlier age was retained, mingling with the latest styles. The quantity of foreign furniture was immense – Spanish cabinets with a multitude of small drawers, ideal for the Victorian collector of sea-shells and molluscs, heavy Dutch and German furniture, and gilt furniture from France, still the only possible choice for the very grand.

There was excessive carving on some furniture, billowing upholstery on couches that destroyed any lines. There were some who saw 'cheap enrichment' and vulgarity in everything around, and strenuously tried to promote the good and the honest. Simple country furniture was mooted as the ideal. Typical of this was thought to be the Morris or Sussex chair, introduced by the William Morris firm in about 1865, made of ebonised beechwood, rush-seated and straight-backed.

In about 1830 Michael Thonet of Vienna had discovered that moist beechwood could be steamed and bent into a circular shape, eliminating joints completely, and by the 1850s bentwood furni-

Regency papier-mâché tray about 1820. Except for chairs and small tables this material was far more suitable for smaller items.

A semi-lune card table of great quality and elegance, made in satinwood, harewood, and rosewood. Notice that nobody has tried to repair the cracks, wisely.

The Knocker

K is a knocker. That is his real initial but his anonymity must be respected. He started life in the East End, taking a ring to Sunday-morning jewellers in the Petticoat Lane area. He would show it to the jeweller, ask for a price, and when this was offered say he would think about it. At the door he would turn round and say that he accepted the offer. In the meantime he had switched rings, and the jeweller got a replica in paste. In due course K landed up in borstal, and eventually became a knocker and runner in the West Country. His gambit when he calls at a house to 'pull gear' is to ask 'Please, ma'am, how do you cook a chicken?' (He says that he has had unexpected guests descend upon him.) This rarely fails, and thus he gains entrance to the house. ▶

ture was immensely popular in England especially for use in restaurants, clubs and hotels. It was copied in metal for rocking chairs, and in the 1920s and 1930s the shape was revived in chrome and other polished metals.

In 1880 William Morris exhorted: 'Have nothing in your house that you do not know to be useful or believe to be beautiful.' This was the thinking behind art furniture. It paralleled art needlework and art pottery, made by a minority for a minority. Amongst its innovations were plain oak stained green, ebonised furniture, furniture with painted scenes, bright mahogany, imitation Japanese ornament. The favourite motif was the sunflower. The art-furniture movement produced masterpieces – the furniture made by William Burges – and ebonised furniture was taken over with enthusiasm by commercial manufacturers.

Some art furniture may have been beautiful, but not much of it was especially useful. And it was expensive, as was the furniture of the Arts and Crafts movement, instigated by William Morris. Typical of those involved in this movement was the Century Guild, formed in 1882. Much of its furniture, whether a chair, sofa, cabinet or desk, was characterised by the presence of a classical cornice of some type. Many of the makers worked outside London, and a school of furniture-making grew up in the Cotswolds.

The coming of the twentieth century was seen as symbolic, and there was a self-conscious urge to 'pass through decadence towards renaissance'. The Victorian period had seen a host of short-lived fads, such as Japanese lacquer, ebonised furniture, bamboo and imitation bamboo, and fumed oak, though the revival of the Sheraton style in the 1890s using satinwood and other delicate woods seemed to hold some promise for restrained useful furniture.

Alongside these retrospective styles was a new angular fashion, harking back to the Century Guild, with an emphasis on the vertical. Uprights and feet were provided with squat triangular caps, and stretchers were often only just above floor level. Carving was out and inlay was in, preferably not wood, but stained glass, enamel and especially pewter. Mottoes not only featured on walls and above mantelpieces of green-stained oak but were built into the furniture.

In 1898 Ambrose Heal issued his first catalogue of no-nonsense pleasingly simple furniture designs. His influence persists through the 1930s furniture of Gordon Russell, through the G-plan of the 1940s, into today, ageless, functional, but often forgettable.

This individual angular furniture existed alongside its polar opposite, sinuous formless furniture influenced by the French, called by critics the essence of worm and squiggle. This type of furniture was organic, and the protuberances and curious knobbly knuckle shapes reminded some of the bone-structures of prehistoric monsters. It was fiendishly expensive then, and is today.

There was a half-way house in which the lines were slightly bowed, and flat surfaces were pinched at the corners, and the whole design was slightly wavy, as though viewed through glass which was out of true. The commercial manufacturers took what they wanted from all these prototypes for the new century, and worked their will.

Chain-store art nouveau has few supporters. It is most seen in surviving part bedroom suites – the thin-panelled oak wardrobe with low-relief engraving of a lily or other representative motif, with maybe a token medallion of pewter or coloured enamel; the

▶ He regularly goes to auctions, and just as regularly spends £5,000 or so, money he has not got, so he has to dispose of the goods very quickly before his cheque bounces. He regularly covers three hundred miles or more a day buying and selling, taking goods from one shop to another, wheeling and dealing, working on a tiny profit margin, perhaps 10 per cent. He shows the auction receipts to his regulars, so that they know exactly what he is up to. His old battered van is often piled up with thousands of pounds' worth of real antiques, over which he clambers, occasionally putting a foot through some little treasure, which does not worry him in the slightest.

On a recent visit to one of his regulars he left a large Pears print in the gutter, having forgotten he had taken it out of the van. He had just sold a cabriole-leg chaise-longue; after he had gone it was discovered that it had three cabriole legs and one square leg. K was happy to take it back; he just had not noticed it when he had bought it at auction a couple of hours earlier. He owned two houses, and had put down £10,000 to buy a property in Spain. As with many of K's operations it was a complex devious deal, and he had to complete in a month or he would lose his deposit. Rather than give up his wheeling and dealing, even for a few days, he let it go.

Regency mahogany drum-top table with swivel top inset with tooled leather panel, with characteristic brass cappings on the feet and brass castors.

Furniture for practical use, without a modern-day equivalent – a partner's desk, an item of furniture almost without an upper price limit.

wash-stand with a curved back and side-pieces topped with the triangular cap, with a white marble top and coloured tiles extending along the back-board. There were also the small square tables with a quartet of coloured tiles in the middle, the plain oak bookshelves with heart-shaped holes in the uprights, and the simple bureaux. Some of the bookshelves were small, made to take the volumes of the Everyman Library, then published for the first time.

Furniture was cheap. A suite consisting of wash-stand, toilet table, chest of drawers, towel-horse and chair cost between £3 and £4.

The new-style furniture was welcomed in the suburbs and in

the garden cities, but the most fashionable style was reproduction Georgian in mahogany with satinwood stringing and inlay. Twenty years ago the traders were bringing it in by the lorry-load to Bermondsey market, but no-one wanted it. They do now, for it has gradually dawned on people that the quality is often superb.

Compared with the exuberance of the Victorian and the splendid cabinet-work of the Edwardian furniture, the furniture made after World War I was uneasy and unadventurous except for the first stirrings of modernism and the daring use of contrasting materials. Most attention seems to have been focused on the various ways in which the gramophone could be incorporated into furniture, and Georgian pieces were cannibalised to hold both the gramophone and the wireless set. The popularity of the game mah-jong created a craze for Chinese décor, and Harrods created rooms with an eastern atmosphere for earnest enthusiasts.

Spiral and bobbin-turned furniture was once again popular, and Victorian furniture was thrown out. Interiors were a medley of the old and the chintzy, with overstuffed sofas and chairs covered with bold rose-patterned material holding sway. There was far more interest in new labour-saving devices such as the vacuum cleaner and electrical gadgets than in creating furniture that was different.

The ideal sought was 'suggestive of quiet repose' and to help this Heal's brought out their floor-lounge, an armchair with a double sprung seat, part of which could be extended along the floor to form a bed. The Artesque receptacle seat was a long stool on four turned legs, with a drop-front to house 'all the things that otherwise are apt to clutter up your hall and spoil its appearance'. It cost £6 15s (£6.75).

Kitchen cabinets with a host of shelves and pigeon-holes; porcelain-topped kitchen tables; spindly tea-trolleys; vast wardrobes incorporating tie-racks, mirrors, drawers and stud-boxes; 'silky oak' bedroom suites of mediocre design set against busy floral wallpapers – it was as though style had died with the war. Garden furniture was more interesting, with basket wicker chairs and caned hammock-chairs such as 'Swyngsiesta', the title being illustrative of self-consciously cute furniture.

The meaningless clutter of the 1920s interior was a world apart from the modernist furniture initiated in Scandinavia and Germany. Bauhaus furniture (1919–33), based on mechanised production and the use of new materials, set a standard of creative design, with furniture stripped of ornament and brought down to its basic elements. Young designers learned the lesson, but had to soften the message, and stress the novelty of it all and its fashionability. Thus the furniture of art deco.

What *is* art-deco furniture? The best was made in France from exotic and unusual materials: wood covered with parchment; chrome and smoked glass; painted wood contrasting with lacquer in the same piece; expensive woods such as amboyna often inlaid in zigzag patterns; and materials previously not considered worthy of expensive furniture such as aluminium. Characteristic of this age of invention was bent plywood, harking back to the bentwood chairs of eighty years earlier.

There was no one path for these very talented designers in

A classic antique, the period bureau-bookcase.

27

Britain, on the Continent and in America. Some of their furniture was austere, geometric, in the finest and most tasteful of woods. Some was dynamic, with elements from cultures recently discovered or popularised such as the Aztec, best seen in the stepped sides of radio sets. There was a fascination with curved forms – semi-circular armchairs on a plinth, wide-bowed cabinets with horizontal stringing of bright metal to emphasise the curvature. And, for those enamoured of the jazz age, there was dashing streamlined glittery furniture which served no purpose but to startle.

Much of it was hand-made and it was expensive, even the simple structures in steel tubing, intended by the dreaming inventors to replace the three-piece suite in the ordinary family home. The public saw watered-down versions of these progressive designs in cinema foyers, in hotels and restaurants, and in high-class stores with a reputation for adventure. They also saw them in films. But what looked good on a film set did not necessarily fit into the home.

There was good art-deco furniture made but, although it makes astonishingly good prices in London, when it appears in the provinces it is largely disregarded. The best is plain, with woods such as bird's-eye maple, satinwood and rosewood as veneer often on a bent carcase of plywood, with fittings of plastic or other contrasting materials. Long low sideboards, cocktail cabinets with coloured mirrors, dumpy armchairs, S-shaped chrome-tube chairs, compact occasional tables often drum-shaped or angular with internal shelves – they have all survived because the quality of the workmanship was good.

World War II brought an end to adventure. And then a curious thing happened. The authorities banned the production of all furniture except one type – Utility. This was widely disliked; it was plain, functional and devoid of ornament, and lacked deep upholstery. Arts and Crafts furniture had returned by another name and been given an official stamp of approval. It was to be a powerful influence on post-war styles such as G-plan, and ultimately on Habitat, despite the encroachment of the new synthetic materials.

The streamlined furniture of the 1920s and especially the 1930s still has a powerful influence on furniture design, and reproduction Georgian and Regency furniture is always in evidence in furniture showrooms, too vapid to be taken as genuine. Some furniture is not reproduced; Victorian walnut and rosewood furniture would be far too expensive.

Is good furniture of whatever age beyond the reach of the person of modest means? Decidedly not. Some furniture does seem to be valued out of proportion to its merits; some is decidedly cheap. A large piece of high quality will often be worth less than a smaller mediocre item. If an article of furniture bears a designer's name the price can rocket. A pair of Arts and Crafts rush-seated oak armchairs of amiable appearance recently sold for £15,000 the pair because the designer was one of the doyens of the movement, C. A. Voysey. An exceptionally elegant satin-birch elbow chair in Sheraton style and of ambiguous date sold for £220. A marvellous George III mahogany serpentine-fronted sideboard

Aspidistras and pedestrian

House-sales can contain curious and bewildering items. At a sale at Wilton Lodge, Worksop, just after World War I one lot was 184 aspidistras. At another house-sale run by the same auctioneers one of the lots was a lady's bicycle. The auctioneer later said, 'It turned out to belong to a lady who was too bashful to say anything, and we heard next day that she had walked a mile home.'

A marvellous piece of furniture of 1862 vintage telling the story of Pericles.

made £2,200. An Arts and Crafts chair of stained oak made £15,000 because it was designed by the big name in Arts and Crafts, Charles Rennie Mackintosh. A magnificent Victorian or-molu-mounted cabriole-legged bureau went for £1,600. For £550 one could get a Georgian Pembroke table. But a Regency table in the Chinese style, quite plain, estimated at £500-£800 by the auctioneers, made £7,000. Why? Who knows? But if it had been bought at £500, someone would have had a bargain.

DEALERS

A fine example of a still climbing market – the doll's house, formerly called a baby house.

There are several types of dealer: those who join the family firm and have been indoctrinated into the trade from an early age; those who have clambered up from the lowly ranks of street traders; collectors who have begun by weeding out their collections to make way for something better and have been caught up in the fascination of buying and selling; those who move into it from other trades and professions; and those who think it is better than working. Some of them have rued the day. It is all very well having an outside stall in the Portobello Road and chatting about this and that to one's well-bred neighbours, actors who are resting or housewives looking for pin-money, but when the rains sweep down from Notting Hill Gate and the Baxter prints turning up at the edges with damp look like nothing, then the situation has to be reviewed.

Sometimes dealers new to the trade lack flair. If they buy something and sell it quickly for a reasonable profit, they will look around for something exactly the same, as if antiques were on the same stratum as sweets or tobacco.

Sometimes, aware of their lack of knowledge and experience, they will be reluctant to spend reasonable amounts of money and will buy bits of cheap nothingness, which are cheap because no-one wants them and not because they are bargains.

An immense amount of business takes place between dealers, and for many the private trade is unimportant. There are many dealers who only deal with the trade, and whose shops serve no purpose other than to store goods. Obviously the more affluent dealers buy from those a rung lower, knowing that they have better outlets and, as they have been more successful, they probably have rather more knowledge.

Dealers selling to each other aim to 'leave something in it', i.e. to agree a deal that allows both of them to make a profit. Selling between dealers keeps stock moving, and eventually it will go outside the area, perhaps to London, perhaps overseas via the shippers, perhaps picked up en route by a private buyer.

Shippers operate on small profit margins of the order of 10 per cent

A specialised field. Three mid-eighteenth-century Delft plates which obtained at auction £480, £440, and £320 respectively.

and rely on a huge turnover for their success. They do not have retail shops and never deal with the general public, but many of them employ quite a number of people, some of them renovating or smartening up the furniture, others covering the auctions – all the auctions. The isolated farm miles from the nearest decent road, the unlikely looking semi, if sales are being held there the shippers will have their representative on the site. Many dealers make their living selling to the shippers, knowing exactly what they will get for a certain object.

Dealers can move in from any other profession – double-glazing reps, the police, journalists and teachers – but with many employees taking early retirement or being made redundant in their fifties, an increasing proportion of people coming into antiques are doing so not because of a desperate need to buy and sell but as a hobby or a good way to invest redundancy money. In a current government scheme, by putting down £1,000 of their own some of them are eligible for a government grant of £40 a week. It is very easy for many of these middle-aged people to take it easy, to plod along playing safe, but the most successful dealers have been those who can jump in, working on a hunch, even over-extending themselves if they feel they are on to a winner or 'earner'. For it must always be remembered that the aim of the antique dealer is to buy something at the price he or she wants to pay, not the market price.

Many seasoned dealers prefer not to have shops. If they want to go to auctions they either have to shut the shop and risk losing a sale, or they have to employ somebody. Such help can cost more than wages. Assistants can be pressurised into taking cheques from suspicious characters, and at one time it was a fact that 50 per cent of carriage clocks, fairly anonymous and easy to pass on, were paid for with 'kites' (bad cheques). That was in the days before banker's

cards, but banker's cards only guarantee up to £50 (Eurocheque cards up to £100) [$175]. If someone buys something for £500, is a paid assistant going to ask the buyer to write out ten cheques for £50 each, or hope for the best and merely ask for an address? And many of the top dealers do not carry banker's cards, assuming that those from whom they buy will recognise their probity.

With the rise in shoplifting an assistant will not be so watchful as an employer, nor will he or she be aware of price-switching. This is taking the tag or label off one item and exchanging it with that on something less expensive, and

The quintessential dealer's piece – the country dresser.

Amongst the most desirable and recognisable of all small antiques are miniature globes. This one is celestial (the sky was better known than the land).

buying the expensive item at the lesser price. Unless the assistant is well versed in the trade, the odds are that the deception will work. Over-eagerness to do the best for a kind employer can work to the dealer's disadvantage. A typical case, minor but representative and repeated a thousand times a year over the country, occurred in 1966, when a dealer bought a Queen Anne box-mirror worth a considerable amount of money for 30s (£1.50). He took it back to his shop, religiously entered it in his buying book, and went out, returning to find that the girl who worked for him had been asked about the mirror, had looked in the book and, as she had been told that her boss made 100 per cent profit on most of the things he bought, sold it for £3. Assistants who make their own assessment of items which happen to be unpriced can equally dumbfound their employers.

It is customary for a dealer buying from another dealer to ask for the trade price, and the discount can vary from 10 per cent to 30 per cent or more, especially if more than one article is involved. The price tag offers a clue to this discount; it may be expressed as −10 or T10 if the trade price is £10 less than the ticket price. Today the general public often expects the trade price, and usually gets it. Some dealers put up signs stating that they do not give trade to any-

one, dealers or not, a practice not liked and an encouragement not to return.

If dealers do not have shops, how do they operate? They attend antique markets, often several a week in different places, and antique fairs. Some do weekly general markets. Others buy from various sources and place everything in auction, sometimes buying from one auction room and putting their purchases in an auction somewhere else. Some will take their purchases from dealer to dealer.

Why do dealers have shops, with all their disadvantages? One of the reasons is that a shop gives a dealer credibility. If a purchaser buys a fake or something that is not what it purports to be, he or she has a come-back. A shop is essential if the dealer is principally concerned with furniture, as a much larger stock can be held. And a dealer who has a shop has more chance than a marketeer of buying privately. This was once a major factor, but thanks to widespread publicity people with something of consequence to sell are more likely than was the case to take the item for sale to an auction room. Objects taken to the local antique shop now are often mediocre, perhaps refused by an auction room, unless the dealer has proved that he or she can be trusted, gives a good price and pays cash. This last item is sometimes important, as immediate money might be wanted, but it is too often the case that the kind of person in desperate need is the kind of person without antiques to sell.

Some dealers advertise that they clear houses. This might seem odd, but it is a way of acquiring articles that are fresh, that may never have been on the market. A price is offered for the entire contents of the house, and this means everything from soiled bed-linen and jars of rusty nails to the mouldering Georgian bureau used as a tool-chest in the garage. It is customary to subcontract the dirty work to someone else, just select-

A selection of 'trade goods' from a catalogue of 1902, with the possible exception of the fire screen. There is also a limited demand for Edwardian gongs.

At first glance these two tennis-playing figures seem to be bronzes and worth a considerable amount of money. Actually they are of spelter (zinc), and when they came up at auction they achieved a modest £140. But that was in 1979. If they reappeared today, their style and sporting interest would ensure a much higher price.

ing the more choice items. House clearances usually occur after a death, and some dealers are able to build up connections with solicitors so that if there is a house clearance they get first option.

A newcomer to the trade should be wary of house clearances; in the enthusiasm of the moment too much can be offered. But even old hands can trip up. Recently a runner cleared a house for £400 ($700); he packed it all in a lorry and sold it on for £650 to one of his dealers. The consignment included a set of eight chairs, two damaged, and a watercolour by Widgery. The dealer framed the watercolour and repaired the chairs. Finding himself short of stock to pass on, the runner returned, paid £500 ($875) for the chairs and £300 ($525) for the painting. The dealer made about £1,500 ($2,625) on the deal, without leaving his shop. But he had looked into the murky back of a lorry, looked at a mess of rain-sodden carpets, filthy blankets, and rusty tools, and had picked out amongst the rubbish enough to make a worthwhile speculation. Would a novice dealer have done the same?

CLOCKS AND WATCHES

A magnificent long-case clock veneered in burr walnut and made by George Graham about 1725.

A selection of superb quality French carriage clocks, many with rare subsidiary dials and features.

There is something appealing about the sound of a clock, whether it is the tick-tick-tick of a small timepiece or the steady pulse of the grandfather.

There are two types of traditional clock. One relies on the fall of a weight, the other on the recoil of a spring. It was found necessary to interrupt the action of the driving force at regular intervals, so that the indicator moved in steps rather than continuously. This is the function of the escapement, which periodically checks and releases the driving train.

The pendulum was invented in 1658, four hundred years after the first mechanical clock. It was soon discovered that the longer the pendulum the greater the accuracy, and once the distance the pendulum swung was regulated it was found possible to house all the works (or movement) in long relatively slender box.

The size of this case was sometimes determined by the requirements of the mechanism, but more important was the necessity to conform to fashions in furniture. The earliest cases are long and thin, made in oak and veneered with ebony, a wood which is not wholly black but has streaks of brown. These clocks dating from the 1670s are very rare; they had small brass dials and a short pendulum of no more than 10in (25cm) long. The shorter the pendulum the less it needs to swing and so the narrow case was suitable.

Although the best makers continued to use ebony others found a substitute in pearwood veneer which was similarly close-grained. The pearwood was blackened with a solution and then polished until it shone.

There were three major innovations in case decoration. Marquetry came in about 1680 – though ebony continued to be used for several decades – and continued until about 1720, when walnut veneer took over as the favoured form for about twenty years, except outside London where it continued longer. Lacquer finish was in its prime between 1725 and 1750, though it had been used in the seventeenth century.

Pendulums became longer, meaning a wider case, and the favourite length was 39in (1m). The marquetry was contained in small oval or circular panels arranged geometrically and the themes were usually floral. The basic shape was architectural, with the dial flanked by pillars, and the hood began to acquire an architectural form, first with a plain pediment and vase-shaped finials, later extremely ornate and impressive.

These top-knots are known as caddies, and as clocks were now up to 7ft (2m) in height they needed reasonably high rooms. When these marquetry clocks went out of fashion and found their

Clock works

A dealer in clocks was doing his rounds and in one of the shops something caught his eye in a dark corner. It was a bracket clock by a well-known maker, someone who was in 'the Book'. He knew it was worth somewhere between £4,000 and £8,000. The question was, did the owner know? The clock-dealer did not want to examine the clock too carefully in case the owner realised that he had something valuable on his hands, so he did not examine it at all, but ogled it from a safe distance. How much did the man want for it? Five hundred pounds was the answer. So the owner was not all grinning fool. The spring had gone, the clock man was told. That was nothing; repairing a spring was child's play. So he paid out, sped back home, and examined his treasure. His heart sank. Not only was there no spring at all, but the inside of the clock was a mess. There was nothing original at all. In the end the dealer sold it on for the case for £150, and was glad to get that.

way into humbler homes with low ceilings these caddies were removed or the bases were cut down, and this applied as well to the walnut-veneer clocks.

Clocks followed the trends set by furniture, and when mahogany came in in about 1760 it proved eminently suitable. The mahogany clock of this time is really the classic clock, elegant, restrained. The demand for a cheaper clock was met by pine and oak.

Fashion applied not only to the cases but also to the dials. The first were of brass, with a silvered brass ring about 2in (5cm)

A terrestrial globe combined with a clock, a very unusual item made in France about 1901. The open movement of the clock is also remarkable.

wide with Roman numerals for the hours engraved upon it. This is known as the chapter ring. Around the rim of this ring the minutes were usually marked, with Arabic numerals. From the 1770s the dials were brass all over. Earlier dials were smaller – 10in (25cm) square until 1690, 11in (28cm) square 1690–1700, and 12in (30cm) square to the 1720s, though country makers continued to use the large square dial long after it had been superseded in London by the arched dial. Before the all-over brass dial there was room outside the chapter ring for decorative corners, made in moulds and chased and gilded.

In about 1690 calendar circles showing the date were introduced, and at about the same time the centres of the dials were frosted and engraved. The London makers preferred restrained decoration featuring scrolls, but the provincial makers preferred flowers, birds and quaint heraldic devices.

The dial was a means of telling not only the time and maybe the date, but also the maker's name – but only the maker of the movement. The value of a long-case clock does not solely depend on the maker, but a known name carries a considerable premium. What is a known name? It is a clockmaker who appears in 'the book' – F. J. Britten's *Old Clocks and Watches and their Makers*. The result has been that the names of unknown makers have been erased from the dial and accepted names substituted.

Around 1710 there was a fashion for the arched dial and the semi-circular space was used for a variety of purposes: for a calendar; for the maker's name; or, using the movement, for displaying the phases of the moon by means of revolving moon-faces. Sometimes figures or ships were made to move.

Some early clocks had only the hour hand. Early minute hands were quite plain, but as the dial grew larger so did the decoration on the hands. Until about 1800 the hands were hand-made but it was found cheaper to stamp them out of thin steel by machinery.

In the 1770s the painted dial appeared, an event regarded with abhorrence by the connoisseur but not by modern collectors, for painted-dial long-case clocks are often the only type within their pocket, along with country-made eighteenth-century oak. The practice of replacing painted dials with brass dials where there happens to be a good eight-day movement has long been widespread.

The first painted dials were quite plain, just black and white. They were therefore a good deal more legible than the brass dial, and had a contemporary sparkle. Decoration was largely confined to the corners of the dial, an echo of the spandrels on brass dials. In the early nineteenth century Arabic numerals began to appear instead of Roman, and there was a wider use of decoration. In particular, much use was made of the semi-circle above the dial, for floral decoration or for all kinds of quaint fancies.

During the Victorian and Edwardian periods the dial was perhaps the most restrained feature. Monsters were built, often combining different woods such as mahogany and oak, with the traditional 'swan's neck' ornamentation on the hood being contorted into nightmarish shapes. They were designed to make an impression, and the proportions were often grotesque. Although long-case clocks had long been fitted out with musical movements,

A curious novelty, with a very ordinary timepiece made more interesting by the addition of cricketing accessories.

Cuckoo out for a duck

Sometimes antique stalls are masterpieces of compression. On one stall, built on the lines of the Taj Mahal, a heavy gilt-framed picture fell off a hook, hit a brass tray which flipped up, sending a circular glass paperweight hurtling across the room like a cricket ball. It hit a cuckoo-clock two stalls away; the cuckoo appeared, looked about in surprise (as it was upside-down) and expired. The stall-holder was none too pleased either.

Enamel and gilt chatelaine with verge watch by Thomas Betson, who worked about 1740 to 1780.

the Victorian and later clocks had tubular bells which played the Westminster, St. Michael and Whittington chimes. Some of the clocks incorporated large disc musical movements and these clocks could be more than 10ft (3m) in height.

Reproduction clocks with brass dials have of course been frequently made but they are easy to spot. Small long-case clocks are sometimes given the name 'grandmother clock' but there is no reason for this and it is not recognised by the clock trade. Exceptionally plain clocks with a superior movement are what are known as regulators. In a house with a number of clocks one specific clock was used to establish what the true time was, and all others were set by this.

The first domestic clock was made from iron, and is known as the Gothic clock. It was a small-scale version of the tower clocks so familiar in our churches, and the very basic movement was mounted in an open-work frame with posts at each corner.

The French and English successor of the Gothic clock was the lantern clock, popular throughout the seventeenth century and made mostly of brass. It had a bell on top which gave the appearance of a helmet. It was wound by pulling on cords or a chain which raised the weights, and it ran for thirty hours betweeen windings. Gothic and lantern clocks were variously known as birdcages, bedposts, and Cromwellian clocks.

The first domestic clock that could be moved from room to room (thanks to the use of the coiled spring) is known as the bracket clock, though it has no bracket, only handles for it to be moved. These were the standard clocks of the late seventeenth and the eighteenth centuries, and they reflect the styles of the long-case clocks. They are spring-driven pendulum clocks, and often incorporate not only striking mechanisms but alarm and repeating mechanisms. They were made with little change well into the Victorian period, and improvements in technology were applied as they came along. Some earlier movements were replaced.

As with long-case clocks, the first had an ebony veneer, and this was followed by marquetry, walnut, rosewood, lacquer and mahogany, though ebony and simulated ebony were revived for the Victorian clocks. Sometimes the cases are surmounted by ornate finials, but in the early nineteenth century bracket clocks became more refined with plain uncluttered surfaces and severe black and white dials.

When clocks became more common and the one clock in the household did not need to be carried around from place to place, no doubt Georgian gentlefolk looked around them for a good place to put a permanent clock. The ideal place was on the new-fangled mantelpiece. The full potential of this feature was not appreciated by British makers, but in the hands of the French the mantel clock became a work of art.

The French demanded ornate elaborate art objects rather than mere clocks, and buhl (tortoiseshell inlaid with metal), ormolu, porcelain, bronze and marble were all used to make dazzling timepieces. Chariots and horses, Napoleons, classical figures, lions, eagles, cherubs, all were presented with dash and abandon. Often it was difficult to tell the time. The dial was sometimes dispensed with, replaced by a rotating sphere with the hours marked on an encircling band.

The most characteristic French mantel clock was the lyre clock, in which the superstructure above the dial is in the form of a lyre, occasionally topped by a sun-burst motif, but there was no end to the variations possible. These ornate clocks were made throughout the last part of the eighteenth and right through the nineteenth century with no end to invention. The culmination was the garniture, a clock with two accompanying pieces in the same style, one on either side, known in common parlance as a clock set.

As the nineteenth century got under way cheap copies flooded the market. Instead of bronze, spelter (zinc) was used, with slate instead of black marble. Twenty years ago these slate mantel clocks were bought for 5s (25p) each and were smashed up just for the sake of the very good French movements. The spelter figures which can be found in most antique shops at £40 and upwards were often part of a clock garniture. The average French movement was circular and about 4in (10cm) in diameter, and could thus be fitted to cases of wildly different design without modification.

Wall clocks carried on an independent existence, only marginally influenced by furniture styles. They were easier to design as they could have an extended pendulum. Many were public clocks, brought into being by legislation. In 1797 William Pitt began to levy an annual tax of between 2s 6d and 10s on all clocks and watches, and to help their customers innkeepers put up large circular clocks 2ft 6in (75cm) or so in diameter. These were called Act of Parliament clocks, and the name stuck though the tax was repealed within a year. Dial clocks were, and are, one of the most popular types of clock, sound, almost indestructible, and easy to see from a distance.

Octagonal dial clocks were popular, often inlaid with brass and mother-of-pearl, and a few were made of black papier mâché, a design enthusiastically copied by American manufacturers. Early dials were made of wood, and later ones of painted iron, though up-market examples had silvered brass. Steel replaced brass as the metal used for the hands, which could be plain or ornate.

Of course there are wall clocks and wall clocks. Those at the upper end of the market are named cartel clocks, and the French used their expertise in ornate and elaborate mantel clocks to devise wall clocks a world away from the English dial clocks, using brass, ormolu, porcelain, and gilt bronze in all their diversity. The English cartel clocks are restrained, often in gilt wood with modest formal decoration of the kind used in looking-glass surrounds, and these carry a price tag of up to £3,000. Those at the bottom of the market were imported from America and Germany.

The American clock was always a factory clock rather than a workshop clock. The industry began in 1807, and the principle was the mass-production of interchangeable parts. One of the most common types was what is known as the Ogee, a weight-driven striking clock with an oblong case. On the lower half there was a picture on the glass, either a painting or a print, and pasted on the back of the case, behind the picture, was advertising

George III bracket clock, in mahogany with brass columns and inlay.

The Rolls-Royce of watches, A Breguet.

Interior of the Breguet watch, showing the superb movement.

material promoting the maker, with instructional details.

There were about forty parts in the shelf-clock as it was called and they could be assembled by hand (it is claimed) in a matter of minutes. As many clocks were sold to remote frontier towns by the burgeoning mail-order business, do-it-yourself clockmaking was often essential. The cases were usually made in softwood, the jointing crude with glue and nails mainly used.

Although they were intended as standing clocks most were used as wall clocks, and there were improvements in design, usually of a Gothic nature. One of the most charming of these is the Round Gothic or Beehive, unusual for American clocks in that the movement was reached by the back, but more popular, and produced by the million, was the Sharp Gothic with its pointed top flanked by two prominent finials. It was a favourite design for alarm clocks, and was made well into the 1940s and after. The Cottage design was a return to the early Ogee clock, only squatter.

American clocks were in direct competition in the British market with those from the Black Forest area of Germany, where clocks had been made with mostly wooden parts from the late seventeenth century. It was first of all a cottage industry, with the simplest of mechanisms and a weight furnished by a stone from the stream, but as the eighteenth century got under way the farmers who had made these clocks for their own use restructured themselves and became clockmakers – of a kind. Although the pendulum had been in existence since 1657 the Black Forest clockmakers did not use it until 1740, and then they placed it in front of the dial.

The first Black Forest clocks only ran for twelve hours before needing rewinding, and did not keep time very well, gaining or losing about twenty minutes a day, though this did not matter as the possession of a clock was mainly regarded as a sign of status. The first striking clocks appeared in about 1730, about the same time as the most important event in German clockmaking history – the introduction of the cuckoo. The longer pendulum was introduced with the more reliable anchor escapement, and the labour force was reorganised, with specialisation, one man making the frame, another the dial and another painting the dial. The bits were either assembled on the spot or packed separately and assembled when they reached their destination.

Early dials were of wood, then designs were painted on paper and stuck on the dial. The next step, unusual in clockmaking, was to raise the circular part of the dial from its background. Brass wheels replaced those made from wood and bronze bells replaced the glass ones, and by the beginning of the nineteenth century Black Forest clocks had assumed their classic form, just in time for them to be swamped by the American interlopers.

In the 1840s the Black Forest makers produced the picture clock, in which the movement is set in the middle of a painting, placed in an ornate frame. The effect is spoiled by the weights and the pendulum hanging down below the lower edge of the frame as though forgotten.

With the competition from America strangling the export trade from the Black Forest something had to be done, and in 1861 factory production on the American model was begun with straight copying of the most successful models. American motifs such as the eagle were also used. Sometimes it is difficult to tell which are German clocks and which are American, but the Germans stained and polished their cases. The painted pictures on the German version of the Ogee clock have a distinct Teutonic air.

These copy-clocks are known as Amerikaners, but other nations' clocks were also copied, in particular the spectacular hanging clock known as the Vienna Regulator. This is a large handsome Gothic clock with ornate carving, and was, and is, a far superior clock to the Amerikaner, very desirable and still available in quantity at very reasonable prices. But beware. They are being reproduced.

However, unquestionably the best seller was the cuckoo clock, put into its classic form in 1870 with its surround of carved leaves. But at the same time as the cuckoo clock and the Amerikaners were in mass production the German makers were venturing into superior clocks, known as Massivs, and these are often taken as quality English clocks.

None of these clocks, the English bracket, the French free-standing clocks, or the American or German timepieces, could be called truly portable. They could be carried from room to room but could not be stuffed in a bag or a pocket. This was the role of the carriage clock – the travelling clock, the *pendule de voyage*. Portable clocks, many of them round and looking like outsize watches, had been made from the sixteenth century, but in about 1770 a small square clock in brass or gilt metal was devised for the use of military officers. It survived almost unchanged until 1910, when there was a break until it became worth reproducing, thus providing prizes for television quiz shows. The carriage clock has a rectangular face, three glass sides, and a prominent carrying handle. The dial is neat and easy to read, and sometimes there are subsidiary dials. Its main feature is a shock-proof movement.

The miniature carriage clocks up to 4in (10cm) in height are the most desirable, and clocks which have striking or alarm mechanisms are more highly regarded than those without. As the basic design altered so little, modern carriage clocks may be taken for period ones. Fortunately most of the moderns do not pretend to be fakes.

Until about 1820 most carriage clocks were made in France, but then almost everyone entered the market including the British, the Austrians and the Americans. One of the reasons for their success was their neatness, which made them ideal for ladies' bedrooms and boudoirs.

The skeleton clock was a nineteenth-century freak in which the framework was made up of metal struts, the wheels were pierced, and everything that happened was on view. It was very popular during the Gothic Revival in England, and the framework was often made to emulate a cathedral or other building. Because it was a dust trap it was placed under a glass dome. These clocks are being made today by dedicated amateur clockmakers as a test of skill.

Throughout the ages, clocks have been governed by the technol-

Models in motion

Amongst the best-known of old cast-metal toys are the money-boxes and mechanical banks, made especially in America, Sambo being the most popular. A coin is placed on the hand, which is then deposited in the open mouth.

This model and its numerous variations dating from the 1870s and 1880s are set in motion by the weight of the coin, and by ingenious gearing various actions could be performed.

Early in the twentieth century it was realised that it was difficult to achieve a high degree of realism using tin-plate, and casting became popular for models. The most famous British manufacturer of die-cast toys was Dinky, founded in the 1930s, followed since by Triang and Corgi, and no boy was without his collection of sturdy Dinky cars, ships and aeroplanes. This is a rising market, but condition is all-important and the models should be in their original boxes. Most die-cast toys are fully trademarked and titled.

In 1987 a group of seven 1950s racing cars in mint condition in their original boxes sold for £280, and four American saloons of the same period sold for £220. It is a fluctuating market and even auctioneers can be caught out in this novel category of collectables. Three Watney beer-barrel lorries of about 1952 were expected to fetch £60-£100. In the event they achieved £420.

Dinky toys, though accurate, do not come into the exclusive category of scale models, which are often marvels of precision engineering. The most common are the miniature working steam-engines. In 1987 a scale model of a ploughing engine made in the 1960s 91cm by 1.75m (3ft by 5ft 9in) sold for £6,500. A model of a Morris two-seater car made £700.

Not guilty

At one time most police forces issued lists of stolen property to antique dealers, though many have now thrown up their hands in despair. The typist of Scotland Yard's Art Squad was clearly not acquainted with the terminology of antiques. In her list of stolen property the following curious items appeared: 'a guilt faced carriage clock' and 'a parcel guilt angel'. Yes, some gilt-faced carriage clocks do have a suspicious look to them.

Time on my hands

A private customer had just bought a long-case clock. Not one of the best – this one had a painted face and oak case, and was country-made. But £200 changed hands, and feeling pleased with himself the dealer gave the customer a cup of tea. As he sat down, the dealer saw to his horror the hands of the clock going backwards. What should he do? In the end he said, 'I'm sorry, the hands are going the wrong way.' 'I know,' said the customer, 'that's why I bought it. It's a present for my wife. I know she'll be amused.'

ogy available at the time. Clockmakers knew what they wanted, but they were not always able to achieve it. Sometimes it was the lack of certain materials, sometimes there were no suitable tools available, sometimes promising avenues were blocked because the basic technology had not arrived. The possibilities of the electric clock were seen as early as the 1840s, but the first commercial battery-run clock was not produced for another sixty years. One of the earliest was marketed by the Ever Ready Battery Company in 1902, and an odd feature was that the pendulum swung from back to front instead of from side to side, and as the case had a mirrored back the effect was hypnotic. Most electric clocks were in a glass case or were covered by a glass dome. The early ones were produced in small quantities and are highly sought after, but in 1922 the Bulle battery clock appeared and lasted until 1939. Three-quarters of a million were made and there were at least a hundred different case designs. It is a fairly new field of collecting, but they were very good movements and they are still functional, if it is remembered that they run on a 1½ volt battery (if it still does not work, reverse the terminals).

Modern battery clocks are, of course, very accurate. In the past complete accuracy was not often demanded, and even the good-quality dial clocks of the railway systems lost or gained the odd minute. But sometimes accuracy was necessary, for example, at sea, where time is the basis of navigation. In 1714 a prize of £20,000 was offered to anyone who could make a thoroughly reliable timepiece. John Harrison won it in 1772. In an effort to reduce friction he used wheels of wood with bushings of lignum vitae, a naturally oily wood. He also developed an escapement called the grasshopper to avoid friction. Chronometers are not particularly exciting to look at, because they were work tools. They resemble alarm clocks lying flat on their backs in a square box, and most are inscribed with the maker's name and are numbered. Their movements represent the final triumph of clockwork.

Everybody knows about watches; almost everyone has one. Many of them will do anything except jump about and sing songs. It is easy to overlook what masterpieces of compression they are. The first watches, in the sixteenth century, were spherical, then they became oval, and in about 1630 they began to take on their present form, though the cases were created in a variety of unusual shapes, such as stars, skulls, crucifixes and sea-shells. Watches of the more conventional shape were provided with multiple cases, one within the other. Cases were engraved, enamelled, decorated with gold filagree or made of tortoiseshell, the enamelled ones being the most valuable. Some were set with diamonds and precious stones so they can be regarded as jewellery rather than timepieces.

The application of the hair-spring (more correctly called the balance-spring) in 1675 greatly improved the accuracy but not the appearance of the watch. It was now worth putting a minute hand on, and minute divisions (usually every five) were added to the dial. In about 1725 the cylinder escapement was invented, enabling the watch to be slimmer. Gradually watches became plainer and simpler, and increasingly efficient escapements were

Georgian lacquered long-case clock.

used. Discoveries made during research into the manufacture of chronometers led to precision watches. There did not seem any further avenues of progress, except to make the watches miniscule. Automatic winding had been introduced in the eighteenth century but was not widely adopted.

The main contribution of the nineteenth century was in mass-production, a process begun in Switzerland in 1865 but greatly developed by the Waterbury Company of America from 1880. Many watches were fitted out with musical movements and miniature automata often of an erotic nature in which the tick-tock action can prove embarrassing to the innocent viewer.

Many watches that appear on the market, however, are plain honest examples. Millions were made, and if not working are worth no more than the scrap value of the silver. If the watch has a gold case it may have a superior movement and be worth restoring. The top flight of watches are immensely collectable. In 1964 a recorded price of £27,500 ($48,125) was reached for a watch. In 1974 the average price for a plain 1650s watch was between £2,000 ($3,500) and £2,500 ($4,375). Recently gold hunter-cased (i.e. with a hinged lid) keyless watches have been fetching between £2,000 ($3,500) and £2,600 ($4,550), sometimes to the surprise of the auctioneers who are giving estimates of £600 ($1,050) to £900 ($1,575). Early nineteenth-century gold Swiss watches with musical movements also fall in the £2,000–£2,600 ($3,500–$4,550) group.

Watches are very much a booming market. This includes wrist-watches, which were known as wristlets when they were introduced to the world in the 1880s. The wristlet was not a success, and was derided by both the trade and the public. The trade felt that dust, humidity and rapid arm movements would damage the movement, and the public considered that it was worthy of music-hall jokes and not much else. As for men wearing them, this was effeminate and not respectable. World War I altered that, and in some arms of the services the wearing of a wrist-watch was mandatory. For safety's sake the glass was fitted with a pierced shield, or replaced by celluloid, until unbreakable glass was discovered. Luminous dials were introduced in about 1915. Trench watches had various trade names such as 'Astral', 'Radiolite' and 'Peerless'.

The most important name in wrist-watches is Rolex, formed as Wilsdorf & Davies, which began production in 1905 in England. The name Rolex was established in 1925 after a good deal of opposition (the importers and retailers wanted their names on the dials, not that of the manufacturer). Perhaps in pique, Rolex moved to Geneva, and in 1926 the Rolex 'Oyster', dust-proof and weatherproof, was invented. The 'Perpetual' self-winding watch was introduced in 1931, though a patent had been taken out by John Harwood in 1924.

Ingersoll began business in England in about 1905, and produced the 'Midget' ladies' watch, converted into a wrist-watch by the application of a leather strap with a cup to hold the watch. The idea of soldering wire loops to the watch to hold the strap is attributed to a London saddler in 1906. Wrist-watches of this period have the winding button adjacent to number twelve instead of number three. The first alarm wrist-watch was introduced in

A Preiss bronze and ivory figural art-deco clock of great quality. The rather heavy dial is set in green onyx, a favourite material of the time for all kinds of objects.

1947, named the 'Cricket'.

As with all clocks, as soon as the technology had been fully mastered all manner of things were done to adorn the case, and the wrist-watch was often transmuted into jewellery, and jewellery of the most exquisite and costly nature. Wrist-watches only a few years old regularly turn up at auction. It is still quite a new collecting category, and a show of wrist-watches lends itself to display. There is certainly a huge variety, including novelty watches of the Mickey Mouse type. A collection of wrist-watches could be allied with the collection of novelty clocks and pocket watches, the poor man's automata. Many hundreds of these were produced for children, and still are, but it is probably sensible to restrict such a collection to spring-driven clocks. Angular geometric clocks were produced in the 1930s but they often had cheap mass-produced movements, the case being the most important feature, as it was in the nineteenth century where poor movements were placed in gaudy pottery surrounds.

Probably the most prolific clock of all time was the oak mantel clock produced in vast quantities in this century, usually with Westminster chimes. These, despite their cheapness (£10 and upwards), have surprisingly good movements, and they are still bought for use rather than investment as they carry a notable nostalgic potential. This is true also of perhaps the most characteristic clock of the 1930s, the 'sun-ray' design in which a circular dial is surrounded by a spiky star-like cluster, mainly made of plaster and gilded. Another typical design of the period is the clock with stepped sides, influenced by the fashion for Aztec motifs. Naturally expensive clocks were made in precious metals, often allied with coloured plastics, onyx, rock crystal and other favourite materials of the period. These often had square dials and square numerals, or the numerals were replaced by rectangles or triangular shapes.

There are not many accessories associated with clocks and watches with the exception of the watch stand, which converts a pocket watch into a miniature clock. They date from the seventeenth century, and were produced in a variety of materials including wood, porcelain, pottery, glass, silver and brass, and they were made until about 1920 when the wrist-watch began to oust the pocket watch. Stands in fine porcelain were made from the eighteenth century until about 1860, but the most common types were constructed of wood. The simplest is a pillar on a base topped by a recessed circular disc, which could be plain, inlaid with ivory or bone, or made of Tunbridge ware (tiny squares of different woods arranged to form a pattern or picture). The 'Wellhead' type consists of twin pillars surmounted by an arch from which the watch was suspended. Pull-out holders were hinged, and popular as holiday souvenirs, and novelty watch stands imitated gongs, chairs, and almost anything which would cause amusement. Probably the most attractive were the box holders, which were made in various designs; when the box was opened the watch stand popped up on a spring. These are all insignificant trifles compared with the watch itself, but can add an extra dimension to a watch collection, though to collect them by themselves is rather like playing Hamlet without the Prince.

A stylish art-deco clock, the square dial flanked by stylised baboons.

A gift at the price

'You call that an antique? Why, I've thrown *dozens* of those away!'

'That, madam, is why I'm able to sell that at the price I'm asking!'

COLLECTORS

'Good morning,' she says, 'Are you a collector?' This is one particular lady dealer's sales pitch. It is interesting to see the reactions. Some people positively bristle; others say 'Of course not!' or are non-committal.

To some, collecting can seem out of touch with modern life, somehow reprehensible; buying for use on the other hand, perfectly acceptable, and buying for profit is well understood too.

Fortunately collecting is alive and well, more widespread through all the echelons of society than ever before, whether it be buying compact discs, acquiring weird and wonderful household aids by mail order, or building up a display of objects and artefacts from the past, the past of yesterday or the past of two hundred years ago (the latter being labelled antiques).

Collecting can open a window on the past. Take a mug of 1837 with the picture of the young Queen Victoria on it. How different from the old lady in black whom we see on old newsreels, riding in her carriage with her Indian out-riders! And here is a plain wooden pipe-stopper with a silver top, with the legend that it is part of the oak-tree in which King Charles I hid after his defeat in battle. And here is a tobacco-box

An early nineteenth-century painting, featuring a family and a barouche.

The barouche, recently sold by the descendants of the family.

made from the teak of a battleship that was sunk during World War I (cost – less than £10). And the humble pewter-framed mirror from about 1905 – who knows what it has seen? The voluminously draped Edwardian lady enjoying the sunset years of the British Empire, the young men later to be the cannon-fodder of World War I, the young child who may conceivably be still alive?

Or take the pleasant but amateurish watercolour on the wall, perhaps of some Indian landscape. The signature is difficult to read, and anyway it would not signify much. Was it painted by some English miss a long way from home? Or by some bored diplomat idling his time away and waiting for his retirement to a little Cotswold village? Or maybe the artist was a British officer in the Indian Army waiting for orders to sort out the natives on the North-West Frontier.

There are some objects that we can pin down, for they come with what is known as a provenance. Perhaps it is known that a particular chair was owned by Charles Dickens, and it came directly from the writer's descendants. A picture may be able to be tracked down over half a dozen auctions – painted in 1854, selling for £5,000, reselling twenty years later for half this amount, coming up again at the turn of the century when the artist was dead and famous and realising £6,000, then going out of circulation for forty years until the chaos and upheaval of World War II whereupon it turned up at a London auction room, the windows of which were criss-crossed with brown adhesive tape to prevent splintering in an air-raid, and made a couple of hundred pounds. This is the story of a fictional picture, but it is not an unlikely one.

Such is the romance of collecting. Behind every old object lies a story, mostly unknown. It was owned, used and cherished by men and women just like us. They did not have television, if they wanted to go anywhere they went by horse,

bus, tram, bicycle or train, and if they wanted a hot bath they had to fill it by carrying bowls of water. They had several advantages; if they walked out at night they were not likely to be mugged, and their food was not labelled with E-numbers. They had an eye for beauty, and as the past gets further and further away it becomes clear that what they thought constituted beauty and what we do are not very far apart.

There are all kinds of collectors, as different as chalk and cheese. There are theme collectors, who collect items related to a particular activity such as sewing or writing, or items relating to a calling or profession – the Post Office, surveying, medicine or the law. There are the collectors who buy for use (furniture, drinking glasses, smoking accessories, etc) and there are those who diligently pursue specific items – the collector of Sherlock Holmes material, the philatelist who concentrates on Penny Blacks, the Elvis Presley enthusiast. And there are those who collect the best of a kind – microscopes by the best makers, Bow

During World War II, the pastille burner was the favourite memento to US servicemen; thus their consequent rarity.

Profit by tender

Sales by tender are quite rare in the antique trade. In 1973 'The Battle of Trafalgar', attributed to P. J. de Loutherbourg, was offered by the owner, Roger Walter. This picture, depicting the scene at 1.45 pm on the day of the battle, had been exhibited in 1936 at the Park Gallery, Albemarle Street, London. It had sold for £500 and had been presented to the Conservative Club in St James's Street, where it had hung in the first-floor smoking-room. When the club moved to smaller premises the picture was taken down and placed amongst surplus furnishings and equipment. It was sold to Mr Walter for £23.

There was one point about this picture that made it special. It was *huge* – 134in (3.4m) by 85½in (2.2m). It is the kind of item which has umbrellas pushed through it in the saleroom.

By definition, sales by tender are secret. The hopeful purchasers put in their bid, and the vendor takes his or her pick. Certainly Mr Walter must have made a good profit, for the 1973 valuation put on the picture was around £15,000.

figures, English Delft, Rembrandt etchings, silver snuff boxes.

Of course there are collectors who are persuaded by the media to accumulate mass-produced objects in the belief that one day they will have value, even if a hundred thousand identical artefacts have been turned out (maybe millions as in the case of first-day covers promoted by the Post Office) – medallions, topical bits of china, prints, miniatures of all descriptions, all illustrated in first-rate colour in the advertising handouts. One of the saddest spectacles at markets, jumble sales and car-boot sales is the stamp-album, selling at £3 or £4 crammed with mint blocks of new issues, worth no more than their face value.

There are people who frequent junk shops, jumble sales and other basic sources of rubbish who will always buy little ornaments if they are cheap. It does not matter whether they like them; the price is the thing. These bits of nonsense are often well made; in terms of china technology, they are superior to nineteenth-century German fairings (porcelain miniatures typically depicting indelicate or comic subjects). It may be that these miniatures, rich in permanent non-flaking colour, are the fairings of tomorrow if 99 per cent of them can be made to disappear. Of course, on the law of averages these indiscriminate buyers are bound to buy something worth while.

On a recent 'call-out' a dealer visited a council house to look at a 1930s oak table. He went without great enthusiasm, bought the grimy table which bore traces of jam, cereals and something unspeakable, and glanced around through the massive battalions of bunny rabbits made in Taiwan, egg-shell china Japanese cups of extraordinary garishness, blank-faced bisque girls made in imitation of nineteenth-century German figures which were themselves imitations of Dresden, and the ten-penny acquisitions of a decade. Among them was something that

did not fit in, and he examined it. It was a rare Staffordshire figure. The going rate for any of these pieces was £1, so £1 he paid for it, well pleased with his morning's work.

Specialist collectors are usually more knowledgeable about their subject than general dealers, and often believe that they know more than dealers in their own field, which is not often true, especially with regard to prices. The collector may think that price-guide values or auction prices are what they seem, whereas these can be misleading. Price guides usually take their tone from auction figures, but dealers can manipulate auctions for their own ends. One way to do this is to put specialist items in an auction and then make certain that the collectors of these get to hear about it; the dealer will then get someone to bid the prices up, way above their sensible level, too high for the collector who wonders bemusedly what is going on.

What is happening of course is that the dealer is buying the pieces in; if he has put a ridiculously high reserve on his goods it costs him nothing. But it often happens that the reserves are known to buyers. So the dealer who is willing to speculate to accumulate may place modest reserves on his items, and let the bidding go way past them. If the auction house charges a buyer's premium, then the dealer happily pays this, knowing that the new rate for the collectable item has been registered, either in the trade papers, or in the mind of the collecting fraternity – not just the particular buyers at this auction.

The going rate for an object is therefore subject to a number of imponderables. Two determined collectors after one piece in a sale room can send prices crazy. Often it is a question of status, of putting the under-bidder in his or her place. This happens at country-house sales where the locals are obliged to establish their superiority not only over their neighbours but over interlopers from outside the parish.

How should a collector buy? In one word, shrewdly. If it is known that he or she will buy a certain thing at any price, the dealer will take advantage of this. At auctions, a frenzied flapping of catalogues will be noted not only by the auctioneer, who may take the opportunity to take bids 'off the wall', i.e. from non-existent persons, but also perhaps by the dealer him- or herself or his or her associates, who will be happy to boost the price. It must always be remembered that at auctions the auctioneer is on the side of the vendor not the purchaser.

Most of the avenues for buying open to a dealer are open to the collector. In an auction he or she can outbid the trade because there is no need to make a profit. If known as a good buyer a collector will get the best trade price when it comes to buying at a fair or shop.

Not all buyers are what they seem. The pursuit of a bargain can result in absurdity. At an auction in 1972 a disc musical box was put up for sale; a young dealer who wanted to specialise in mechanical music sent his wife to bid for it with a stake of £300 ($525). It soon became apparent that this was not enough, and it was knocked down to a woman who had the mien of a dealer for £575. The disenchanted wife was about to leave when there was a commotion at the auctioneer's rostrum. The musical box was coming up for sale again; there had been a 'mistake' – the woman had thought that she had bought the machine for £5.75!

This sort of thing happens not infrequently but rarely so spectacularly in public. Dealers are accustomed to give their prices in a verbal shorthand: 'six-forty' is £640. But so often has this been taken as £6.40 that some are now at pains to announce the price in full. It is too often assumed that most people know about antique prices, but it is clear that this is not true; it is also readily assumed that most people are gripped by such television programmes as 'The Antiques Road-Show'. Viewing figures show that it is a minority programme.

The kind of collecting a person does is determined by the kind of money available. It is fruitless for a collector with £200 to specialise in eighteenth-century china, though a fully representative collection of jelly moulds, shaving-mugs or teapots could be built up for this amount. It is also important for a collector to work out what he or she really likes and what he or she quite likes; if a particular collecting field causes uncertainty, it is perhaps the wrong one.

No collector should be worried about making mistakes; a collector who cannot afford to make mistakes in a particular category should pick a less expensive field.

An ideal collector's item combining cricket and advertising, and an excellent cartoon.

DOMESTIC AND PERSONAL ANTIQUES

Many outdoor items have been impressed for service as decorative pieces, such as these two garden urns.

What makes an antique? It is a matter of chance. It may seem to depend on the material from which it is made, but this is not so. The early plastic Bakelite was not just a cheap substitute, but a widely welcomed novel material, as was its Victorian predecessor, vulcanite.

Look at the outside of an ordinary town house, a terrace house. What is of antique interest? Victorian and older houses may still retain their cast-iron railings. They were not merely decorative, but served a useful purpose, for with the development of towns and cities houses became taller. To conserve space basements or semi-basements were supplied. These needed an area outside the basement windows to provide light and air. To stop passers-by falling into this area from the pavement, railings were erected.

So antiques are an avenue into history, the history of everyday things, such as railings, seen but not often observed. There were dozens of different railing-heads in cast iron and the rails themselves were often very ornate. This was also true of balconies, such a feature of Georgian and Regency houses. Eighteenth century urban development was in the form of terraces, and although green spaces were provided by squares and parks there was no room for front gardens. So the main purpose of balconies was to provide somewhere to put flowers or shrubs.

Although brass could be used for railings and balconies it was expensive; iron was ideal, and as its potential was realised the variety of objects in this metal increased. If we look at the outside of a house we will see some of these.

The door-knocker was utilitarian, and its use prevented callers from barking their knuckles by rapping on the wood. These came in a multitude of shapes and sizes, as did the doorknob, which naturally also came in brass. Prior to the introduction of the Penny Post in 1840 the postage charge was paid by the recipient and not the sender, so a letter-box was not necessary. When postage was paid by the sender a hole to receive the letter was essential, and this was framed by a brass or iron plate with a rectangular aperture and sometimes a flap or a simple spring. Letter-boxes came in a range of styles and sizes, many with 'LETTERS' engraved upon them.

Because of the filthy conditions of the roads and streets, a foot-scraper often stood just to the side of the front door. It would be a difficult and unrewarding task to form a collection of representative foot-scrapers, for what else could they be used for, and how could they be displayed to good effect? Balconies and railings have long been incorporated into interior decorating schemes, also being used for more orthodox outdoor purposes.

The personal seal had a large part to play in the ceremony of sending a letter. This magnificent early eighteenth century specimen is of ivory and cut steel, with thirteen different matrices in case the owner got bored with the one in current use.

Other objects likely to be seen outside a house are devices associated with lighting – iron holders for the flaming torches of the eighteenth century are an example. But exterior lighting was a problem until the invention of the electric light bulb.

We pass into the reception rooms, and to the focal point of traditional living rooms, the fireplace. The implements connected with fire in the home are numerous. The earliest is the fire-back, a thick panel of cast iron placed at the back of the hearth to protect the wall from the fire and reflect the heat into the room, made since the sixteenth century and decorated in relief with coats-of-arms, and mythological and purely decorative subjects. The substitution of coal for wood brought in the fire-grate. This could be plain and functional or enormously elaborate, and many furniture motifs were incorporated into the design. The surround of the fireplace became increasingly important; it was ideal for the siting of tiles.

The fronts of grates were made with bars to stop the coal falling out, but this did not prevent ash from spreading or small pieces of coal from spitting out. Ash screens and fenders, with or without a sheet metal bottom, provided protection against this. The term 'curb' usually refers to a fender without this bottom. Fenders could be plain with perhaps a restrained pierced design, or they could be massive florid affairs. The Georgians preferred bright-steel fenders; the Victorians fancied brass, or brass combined

A lesson for all

In 1973 the parish church of Bognor Regis was demolished and a local stamp-dealer who also happened to be churchwarden sold the lectern for £5. The purchaser was the local barber and gift-shop owner who saw the lectern amidst the rubble and thought that it would make a nice plant stand. It was High Victorian, made in brass, adorned with semi-precious stones, and weighed a hundredweight. The new owner put a provisional value on it of £1,000.

3-D in Paris

Although New York and London are commonly regarded as the places to obtain high prices at auction, and sales there obtain the most publicity, Paris must not be forgotten. In 1987 a pair of eighteenth-century bronze groups on mythological themes was sold for more than 13 million francs, the equivalent of £1.36m, the highest price ever for a three-dimensional object in a Paris auction room.

with other metals, and worked every kind of ornament into their fenders, including designs of hounds and deer, and story-telling. Art-nouveau metal-workers found the fender an ideal medium for their ideas – their lily motifs, their writhing leaf forms and their asymmetry.

These living-room fires were not made just to emit heat, but to cook on as well. Cast-iron trivets were hooked on to the fire bars to support a kettle; these trivets, as with much cast iron, were very cheap, retailing at 11s (55p) a dozen. The trivet had started life in the kitchen on three sturdy legs, but with the arrival of tea-drinking it made a dignified entrance into the drawing room.

Before the introduction of the grate the hearth was fitted out with andirons. These were metal stands, of both simple and elaborate forms, on which logs were placed to keep them above the hearth. There was a vertical post at the front, often ornately decorated. These were made in a variety of metals. Smaller andirons are called firedogs, and the grander households used the firedogs to put the wood on, and andirons for show.

Fire irons had always been used, kept on the slant in front of the fire, resting on the decorative andirons, but with the arrival of the grate a new place had to be found for them, either in a fire-iron rest incorporated in the grate or dangling from a stand, which could be disguised as something else. The best fire-irons are bright steel with brass finials of acorn or urn shape; the eighteenth-century irons are longer because of the bigger hearths.

In front of the hearth would be the coal scuttle, made in two basic shapes, the 'helmet' and the 'shovel', these names describing them perfectly; they were usually in copper or brass, the former being the more valuable. These altered very little over the years, and are difficult to date as by the nature of things they tend to get battered. Buyers tempted by these, either for keeping coal in or for use as flower containers, should always pay close attention to the bottoms as they tended to get very thin and were often replaced by sheet copper or tin, cut to shape and left to rest on the edges of the damaged base. A degree of repair and renewal to old scuttles, including an amount of soldering, is acceptable.

In Victorian and Edwardian times there was a fashion for placing the coal container, now rectangular, in a wooden box, usually made of oak. These boxes could be quite elaborate and had fittings of brass.

Bellows could hang by the side of the fire, being both decorative and useful, and a certain amount of wear on the leather bellows is a plus as it shows that they are old – bellows are still made in much the same way for the weekend-cottage trade.

The drawing-room fireplace could also count amongst its furniture toasting-forks for muffins, or chestnut-roasters, but much of the traditional fireplace equipment was for 'working' fireplaces in cottages and kitchens. Hanging kettle-tilters were to prevent burning the hands when pouring out boiling water, pot-hooks were for keeping food warm away from the flames, and chimney cranes were for lifting and lowering food to be cooked.

When going to country-house sales it is a good idea to head for the kitchen to see what is there. The contents are often lotted together in batches by auctioneers who have had a long day and

A stereoscopic viewer of a type introduced soon after the invention of stereoscopic cameras in the 1850s.

do not want to plod through dozens of plain white plates, and have given cupboards the most cursory of glances. The most desirable items to find in a kitchen are objects such as copper kettles and copper jelly moulds, as well as once utilitarian pieces such as pottery foot-baths.

The kitchen was, as today, the power-house of a home. In earlier days bread was made, coffee was ground, and butter and cheese were produced, all needing specialist equipment. Some items were patented novelties which supposedly aided the cook – the curry pan divided into two compartments in which rice and meat were cooked separately, a broiler which was a frying-pan with two close-fitting pans hinged together, or the digester, a stock-pot of iron with a valve to let the steam escape. The good kitchen needed a multitude of pots and pans in various metals, some general-purpose, some specific such as the fish kettle, the sugar boiler, or the sauté pan.

Amongst the most interesting of objects found in an old kitchen were pastry moulds, doubling as marzipan and gingerbread moulds. Are such domestic objects *really* antiques? Most certainly, for many moulds are pre-1837 and are thus antiques even to the purist.

Gingerbread moulds made their appearance long before the reign of Elizabeth I. The variety of designs of moulds was enormous, coats-of-arms, birds, animals, famous people such as Nelson and the current monarchs, highwaymen, pistols and, for children, gingerbread imprinted with the alphabet. Subjects were executed to order by the mould-maker, and birthdays and sporting exploits were commemorated in this manner.

The favourite wood for these moulds was pearwood, which is well suited to such carving, but unfortunately it is a wood particularly susceptible to woodworm. However, there are many existing examples of moulds in boxwood, beech, apple, cherry and walnut. The majority are oblong in shape, but there are also square and round ones. Heart-shaped moulds cut for lovers and named and dated were used for betrothal feasts.

Other wooden objects of great charm that were used in the kitchen were the various boxes for spices and powders of all kinds; spices were much used because there was always a good chance that, without refrigerating facilities, the meat was going off.

Every kitchen, modest or grand, had its pestle and mortar. The favourite wood was lignum vitae, hard enough to stand up to continuous pounding, and the mortars could be up to 1ft (30cm) in height. They were also made of bronze, iron, brass, marble and stone, and a kitchen of any size at all had at least three, one for meat, one for garlic and onions, and one for spices. Smaller mortars and pestles are made from laburnum wood or walnut, turned on lathes, but home-made ones are often found, carved out of the solid. Mortars are often found without their pestles, and those in stone and marble make ideal garden ornaments.

Bread-boards and chopping-boards were made from various woods such as oak and sycamore, the best being made from walnut. In grand establishments the boards may have crests or other armorial devices carved at the top.

The kind of old photograph of almost no value, though interesting as it depicts current fashions in dress.

Everything has a price

It might be supposed that people going into an antique shop are looking for antiques, but this is not always so. On one occasion a customer wanted to buy a carton of dog-food which the dealer had just purchased for her own pets. The same dealer was astonished when a customer came in, rummaged through the greengrocery she had just bought, and asked how much the lettuce was. On one occasion the author was looking after his wife's shop. His wife was a specialist dealer in antique lace and linen. A customer came in and wanted to buy a bra.

Amateur needlewomen had a wide variety of luxury accessories, perhaps kept in enamel étuis (a French word for case or sheath).

At a Date-Line Fair

Outside the Mayfair hotel are men in neat dark suits with walkie-talkies, controlling the traffic. A small Fiat with a sun-roof appears, with a chrome dress-rail poking out of the top. The organiser prowls, seeing that the stall-holders are not intruding on other people's space. Carefully, treasures, sometimes worth thousands of pounds, are stripped of their bubble wrapping, spotlights are arranged, and there is a subdued buzz of conversation. This is not a social gathering; the stall-holders can pay over £100, sometimes considerably more, for a space in a prestige antique fair, and presentation is more important than chat.

'Get that out of the way!' raps the organiser as packing-paper protrudes from beneath the cover of one of the tables. He looks around him.

'Ladies and gentlemen', he says, 'twenty minutes until opening. The best of luck everybody!' A latecomer from the provinces arrives, flustered, carrying a large cardboard box exuding frayed newspaper. Pointedly the organiser looks at his watch.

'Got caught up in the traffic', says the new arrival, peering from beneath her straggling hair.

'Haven't you got someone to help you unpack?'

'He's around somewhere, probably parking the car.'

The dealer on the next stall helps the woman unpack.

'He won't like that', the helpful neighbour whispers as the organiser moves away, 'nor that . . . it's a date-line fair, dear, did you know?'

'Oh yes. It is Regency, isn't it? Regency's all right, isn't it?'

'I think it's Vicky, dear.' ▶

Amongst the most attractive items of kitchen ware were the coopered (i.e. ringed by iron bands) barrels, washing-up bowls, buckets and pails. The reason for coopering was not decorative; it was to hold the staves in position when the wood became swollen through being wet through. Sometimes brass was used for superior articles. Coopered articles have long been used in the garden for plants and shrubs; now, waxed and polished, and the iron Berlin-blacked, they have entered the drawing room. The simple wicker baskets, as well as the Sussex trugs, have also been re-evaluated and are perfect for flower arrangements.

When possible, wood was used in the kitchen, especially the farmhouse kitchen. Metal was often regarded with suspicion, because it was known that certain metals were dangerous, but there were certain duties that wood could not perform, especially those involved with breaking and cutting sugar and other moderately hard substances.

Items of copper and brass other than kettles were to be found in the kitchen, such as skillets and saucepans. The skillet was a saucepan on three short legs, related to the cauldron, and it was intended for use on a plain flat hearth without a grate. The eighteenth-century copper saucepans had rounded sides, but the straight-sided saucepan of the nineteenth century was more functional and has hardly altered from that day to this. Saucepans in grand households had the owner's crest or initials stamped or engraved on the surface.

Skimmers are slightly bowed discs with a handle, usually perforated, and they were made to skim cream from milk and fat from gravy. They were usually made from brass. A flit is a skimmer with a ring instead of a handle, and was made expressly for skimming cream from milk. Warming-pans were probably kept in the kitchen too, and were made in brass and copper. They consist of a circular pan with a hinged lid affixed to a long handle; the latter was first of iron and later of wood. The pan was filled with glowing embers and perforations in the lid kept the embers alight. The warming-pan was then pushed into a bed in the hope of warming it and not setting it alight, but a more sensible solution was discovered in the nineteenth century in which a copper container with a screw cap was filled with hot water. Eventually this was superseded by the earthenware hot-water bottle with a screw cap.

All this domestic copper and brass has been taken up for decorating cottages, and naturally the more picturesque items such as kettles and warming pans have been reproduced, so a feel for age is an asset when buying these items. Sometimes deliberate fakes have been 'distressed' by knocking them about, and it is important to look for genuine signs of wear, at hinges or at riveting, where an amount of looseness is a good sign. Beware of miniatures, as they are almost always modern. If there are elements fixed together by screws, these are a good indication of age; hand-made screws have uneven threads, and are flat bottomed.

Of course, no two kitchens were the same. Some had facilities for brewing beer, many for baking bread, and the old-fashioned brick ovens are still used for this purpose. In humbler households the laundry was done in the kitchen, but in houses with more than a couple of servants there was a laundry room, and here was found the most common of domestic antiques, the flat iron. There is a surprising variety of irons. They were evolved in the sixteenth century, probably in Holland, where brass was used. There were two kinds, the ordinary flat iron called a solid or sad iron, and the box iron, in which a preheated iron slug was placed. The brass irons were often ornately engraved and embossed, but these gave way to the more functional and cheaper versions in steel and iron. The first box iron in Britain was patented in 1738

▶ 'I was told it was Regency', says the newcomer miserably.

'Give it a try, anyway. He mightn't notice.'

But he did. He came back.

'Sorry,' he says, 'but that's got to go. And that. And that ...'

'But she won't have any stock left!' complains the stall-holder's husband who has just arrived, flustered, with his tie awry.

'As it's your first time here, I'll let those two things in. But not that. Can't have that . . . .' He checks his watch again.

'Five minutes, ladies and gentlemen', he calls out. He checks what is going on outside on his walkie-talkie.

'Anybody with car D111 EHV?'

A face pops up from below stall level. It is a guilty face, for the owner has just had a surreptitious bite out of a sandwich, and food and drink are not allowed in the selling area.

'Sorry, dear', says the organiser, 'but a traffic warden's just given you a ticket. . .'

'But it's Sunday!' comes the protest.

'Double yellow. Come on, everybody...'

And the show is open. In they drift, and there is a waft of Chanel Number Five, the glitter of diamonds on a wrinkled hand and the unveiling of cheque-books bearing the names of exotic banks (nobody has the impudence to ask for a banker's card). Minions, some with a chauffeur's peaked hat, come in and bear the goods away. The organiser relaxes. It looks like being a good fair. One of his regulars has already taken £20,000 and the newcomer has sold her ghastly Victorian work-box.

A marvellous group of small boxes, made in enamel in South Staffordshire about 1760. These are bonbonnières *for holding sweetmeats, or bon-bons.*

No-nonsense chairs

When is a country chair not a country chair? This might be asked when confronted with the ladder-back chair, which was made in a multitude of varieties, especially in Lancashire and Yorkshire, from the eighteenth century. There is the clue. These were important centres for industrial development, and people who had worked in agriculture moved into the new towns, creating a demand for no-nonsense furniture, including chairs. In Lancashire there were 20 known workshops in 1790; by 1816 this number had risen to 41. The chair-makers could not go to the nearest stream to get their rushes for the seats; they did not have to go out and cut their own timber; and they had the services of one of the wonders of the age – the belt-driven lathe.

and was produced until fairly recently; an off-shoot was the iron in which hot embers or charcoal were placed, with an air hole to allow the fumes to escape. Especially in America there were a number of inventions to increase the efficiency of the iron including the incorporation of small bellows, and it was amenable to reshaping in the form of a railway engine or a swan. The sad iron patented in America in 1870 had two pointed ends, and a detachable handle so that only the iron itself was subject to heat. This was being made as recently as 1953.

As with pastry moulds it is amazing how much variety there is in a single modest item, but those who are thinking about collecting irons need to ask themselves one or two questions. Pleasant as it is to know that these objects have been used if hardly cherished, do they make an interesting display? The pleasure in collecting irons lies mostly in the chase.

Amongst the most appealing of domestic antiques are those which can be used for exactly the same purpose as they were originally intended, such as the toasting-fork. There is nothing more redolent of times past than toasting a muffin in front of an open fire. Long-handled forks with two or three prongs have been produced since the sixteenth century, made of bronze, brass, iron or steel; some had wooden handles; some were telescopic; some were straightforward and functional, whereas others had decorative piercing. Those with heads in the form of yachts or dogs are fairly modern.

Other domestic items still used for their original purpose are the crocks, usually in brown and cream, the earthenware butter coolers, the tin watering-cans, the earthenware jugs (perfect for cold drinks) and, of course, the jelly moulds, especially those which produce animal shapes, the rabbit being the most popular. Jelly moulds are a common starter for budding collectors before they go on to something more demanding. The most interesting pottery ones are probably the advertising examples produced by, among others, Brown & Polson in the nineteenth century.

If we retrace our steps from the kitchen and make our way upstairs and into the bathroom we will find a range of interesting

A charming box with ivory inlay, probably turn of the century but almost impossible to date precisely.

objects, but few of them antique.

The man of the house may have shaved in the bathroom, or he may have had his own dressing room. Until the 1880s the cut-throat, sharpened on a leather strop, was universal, and many men, even those of humble means, went to the barber rather than risk cutting their throat. A guard along the blade was patented in about 1850, and a 'Hypenetome' or beard plane was produced in 1851 'on the principle of a carpenter's plane'. The American Home Safety Razor of 1891 claimed that it was impossible to cut the face. In 1903 a throw-away blade was developed by William Gillette, and the modern safety-razor superseded the cut-throat – for some. In 1931 the Schick Electric Razor was invented. Associated with the razor was the shaving-mug, often ornate and decorated with floral patterns, marketed in quantity by seaside souvenir shops. Metal shaving-stands, often incorporating holders for candles, could be very elaborate, with spaces for the mugs and brushes; some were made to fix on the backs of chairs with a clamp. Very attractive blue-and-white pottery containers were made for soaps, with provision for toothbrushes, which had bristles set in ivory or bone, sometimes with a silver handle. An electric toothbrush was invented in about 1885 but was too far ahead of its time to be a success.

Men did not go in for cosmetics, deodorants and beautification except for the dyeing of moustaches and the use of pomades and Macassar oil for their hair. Women had a modest range of cosmetics, the most important of which were powder and rouge, the latter of which came in powder or paint form. Some beauty aids were dangerous, such as ceruse which contained white lead. These cosmetics were kept in wooden, glass or ceramic containers.

Face-powder, often made from rice powder, was in a restricted range until the present century – white, pink and a colour called Rachel. By 1925 Coty was producing nine different shades in twenty-one perfumes. The powder-compact became a minor art form, enamelled, inlaid with mother-of-pearl, made of contrasting metals, including precious ones; and for those on a small budget the collection of powder-compacts is well worth considering.

There was a distinction between portable and static aids. The set of brush, mirror and comb, usually silver-backed, often with engraving or repoussé (the pattern pushed up from underneath) decoration, was a necessary dressing-table requisite, together with a ring stand (often in the form of a human hand, made from metal or ceramic), the hat-pin stand (sometimes in silver), and scent bottles (sometimes double-ended, one side often containing smelling-salts). Many of these were made of glass, finely faceted, in blues, greens and reds. Other items to be found on or around the dressing table were glove stretchers, made from bone, ivory or wood, a popular though limited starter for new collectors, and button-hooks.

Although many dressing-table items were traditional, crazes often had an effect. One of the most widespread of Victorian fashions was tartan-ware, which came in in 1852 when Queen Victoria bought Balmoral Castle. Besides putting her children into tartans that had no relevance amongst the clans, she sparked off an enthusiasm for all things Scottish. Glassware, ceramics,

An unusual enamel snuff box, not as might be supposed Bilston and eighteenth century but late nineteenth century and a forgery by Samson, a notorious faker whose work is now highly collected.

Jewels and baubles

The clear-cut division between precious stones (diamonds, rubies, emeralds and sapphires) and semi-precious stones is of fairly recent origin. The aristocratic matrons of the eighteenth century did not regard garnets as the common person's ruby, nor did they scorn the new alternatives to precious stones, such as cut steel, often confused with marcasite because they share the same designs.

Marcasite jewellery is made of tiny particles of iron pyrites set in claws or pans. Cut steel consists of small faceted heads of steel on a thin back plate, or is made into a chain to be worn as a necklace. When the cut steel trade started in the late sixteenth century the raw material was old horse shoe nails. Cut steel was first produced on a commercial scale by Matthew Boulton at his Soho Factory in Birmingham from 1762 onwards.

A group of papier-mâché items for personal use, a tray, stationery box, a snuff-dish, and a collapsible wool tray. The snuff-dish was not to do with the practice of taking snuff; a snuff is the sooty knob on the wick, either of a candle or an oil-lamp. The wool tray was widely used in Berlin woolwork, for taking the different coloured wools from room to room without getting them mixed up.

Queen Victoria and the jet set

Much of the jewellery seen today in antique shops, fairs and markets is Victorian. Queen Victoria was fond of jewellery and sponsored various trends. As for much of her long life she was in mourning for someone, she made jet fashionable. By 1873 there were two hundred workshops in the Whitby area processing jet. Jet is a form of coal, mainly found near Whitby, though Spanish jet, softer and used mainly for beads, was imported. French jet is black glass, and can be recognised by its weight.

Queen Victoria also made snake bracelets fashionable, as well as Scottish pebble jewellery, set in silver, and towards the end of her life Indian and Indian-style jewellery.

and textiles were gaily patterned in tartan, sometimes with charming effect. Tartan-decorated articles also included dressing-cases, spectacle cases, work-boxes, scent bottles and pebble jewellery, all demanding space on the dressing table. Tortoiseshell was a longer-lasting fad, used for the backs of mirrors, brushes and combs, and imitation tortoiseshell continued to be very popular for dressing-table items well into the 1930s.

The demand for pins by Victorian ladies was endless. These were kept in pin trays, made from metal, wood, china, pottery and papier mâché. Or they were prodded into pin-cushions, immensely varied in shape, custom- and home-made, sometimes from velvet scraps decorated with bead-work, sometimes stuffed into silver-plated or brass wheelbarrows, carriages, crowns and indeed anything hollow, or mounted on china ornaments. One of the most common types of pin-cushion was a heart-shaped base into which the pins were pushed so that the heads formed a pattern or spelled out a message, often with a date affixed.

Prominent among the items that were both useful and decorative were candle-extinguishers, made in many fanciful shapes in metal and china; a favourite type was the form of a famous personage, often waist up, and many well-known potteries such as Worcester produced novelty items. Candlesticks of all kinds were all over the house, silver, china and wood, with basic chamber candlesticks of enamelled tin (with a large pan for safety) for the servants; but as the oil-lamp and gas-lighting came in their numbers decreased. Oil-lamps, often with splendid cranberry-glass shades, have been collected for many years and reproduced for the same period; sometimes, unfortunately, they have been converted for electricity.

Some of the objects associated with the lady's dressing table belonged to the categories known as objets d'art and objets de vertu. They can be purely ornamental, or they can have a real (if marginal) use; they may once have been made for a general need. One such need may have been for little boxes, made in every conceivable medium, gold, silver, wood (plain or decorated), china, papier mâché, tin (for the plain person without airs or graces) or, perhaps the most interesting, enamel.

Small enamel boxes can be among the most exquisite of small antiques. Enamel is powdered glass, fused in an oven on a metal base; metallic oxides provide the colours. If a medium is added, enamel can be applied with a brush, on an enamel undercoating. After each colour the work in progress has to be fired. It is thus a time-consuming operation. The great days for enamel were between 1750 and 1780, after which there was a slow decline

Ladies had to look after their complexions, and there was nothing worse than the ruddy glow produced by heat from a fire. There was a choice between standing and portable screens, such as these made from papier-mâché. When bored the users could look at the splendid hand-painted views of Venice and Caen.

Chess was a widely popular game, and furniture was specifically made for it, as illustrated by the Regency games table with chequer top. The set is of ivory, though the better players preferred the Staunton pattern in wood.

A charming piece of drawing-room sculpture by W. D. Keyworth and dated 1881, sold for a modest £520 in 1978. Since then marble sculptures have much increased in value.

until about 1840. The two major names in enamels are Bilston and Battersea, and objects are often labelled as such without any great confidence. Battersea only operated between 1753 and 1756 before going bankrupt. The painting was done freehand or over a transfer-printed outline.

Battersea boxes are distinguished by rich deep colour, and could be circular, rectangular or oval, and were used for snuff, patches, cachous and bonbons, or cosmetics. Those with additional designs on the sides and base, and inside the lid, carry a premium, but all Battersea boxes are rare and expensive, and far more boxes were produced in the Midlands, including fancifully shaped ones in the form of birds and dogs' heads.

As travel became easier as a result of the improvement in the roads and the network provided by stage-coaches, there was an increasing demand for souvenirs of places visited. The enamel box missed the impetus given by the coming of rail travel, unlike other souvenirs such as Mauchline ware – transfer views on wood, often sycamore, which began in about 1823, reached a peak in about 1860, and slowly declined, though a form of the ware persisted until 1939. Early products were hand-done with pen and ink; the early designs were followed by essentially Scottish motifs and the scenes. Photographs were also used. Most of the work was high quality, with crisp detail, and designs altered little. It is difficult to distinguish between Mauchline ware made in the nineteenth century and that made in the 1920s. All kinds of objects were made – boxes, rulers, letter-openers, darning eggs, needle-cases, pin-cushions, napkin rings (perhaps the most common object today), tape-measure holders, and money-boxes. An interesting line was fern ware, where the ferns were applied to wood and then varnished; to cut down cost, fern-pattern paper was later used – not exactly an art object, except to the people who bought them.

Ladies often used their bedrooms to write their letters or fill in their diaries. Some used a writing table; some a desk; some a portable writing slope (often misinterpreted as a Bible box) with a lift-up lid and compartments for ink, paper, pens and envelopes. The quill-pen was rendered obsolete by the metal nib set in a penholder, though some people did continue to use it as it was more flexible than the early nibs. The quill-pen was cut to shape with a 'pen-knife', (the term eventually came to be applied to any small folding knife). Writing with a quill or with a steel nib was always messy, and penwipers were a necessity; they were sometimes made of felt, cut into shapes and stitched together. More elaborate ones on the lines of pin-cushions were sold commercially, with short bristles packed into novelties of silver or another metal.

While women were writing, embroidering or simply looking decorative, men were smoking or taking snuff. Smoking was regarded as manly, disgusting, immoral or just plain dirty, but rarely as dangerous, and in some houses the men were excluded from the drawing room and dining room while smoking and were obliged to indulge their vice in their studies or in special smoking rooms, often attired in smoking-jackets of velvet trimmed with braid and wearing caps, sometimes made by the ladies.

Smoking began in the sixteenth century. Tobacco was introduced from America along with the potato, and was smoked in clay pipes, the earliest of which had flat bases so that they could stand upright on a table when not in use. During the reign of Queen Anne long-stemmed pipes known as aldermen were smoked, and in about 1780 spurs were applied to the bowls. Long curved pipes known as churchwardens became popular in the nineteenth century. Wooden pipes did not make an appearance until the nineteenth century as no wood which was hard enough not to catch fire had made an appearance, and the only alternatives were the mineral meerschaum and porcelain, both expensive. In 1859 a root from an unpromising shrub called *bruyère* in French was discovered to be ideal; hence 'briar'. In about 1750 porcelain pipes by some of the famous German makers began to appear, the bowls beautifully moulded and decorated. It was found that porcelain was not the best material for pipes; the oils from the tobacco drained easily to the bottom of the bowl, making it foul, so a separate reservoir in the form of a Y was provided, made from china, wood, metal, bone or horn. The stems of the pipe could be of any suitable material, but the mouthpiece was usually of horn, connected to the stem by tubing covered with a woven material.

The range of subjects depicted on bowls was enormous – famous people, tiny reproductions of paintings, murderers, mythological and legendary figures, verses, scenes of the chase, military topics, and blatant souvenir subjects. In some pipes there is a lot of braid and meaningless ribbon, and putting one of these pipes together is like trying to assemble a deck-chair. Because of their obvious decorative features, porcelain pipes are still being made for tourists, with cheap transfer decoration.

Meerschaum was first used for pipe-bowls in the 1770s; they were often splendidly carved and were very expensive, retailing in Germany in the 1790s for the equivalent of £20. After use they assumed a desirable colour and lustre, and at auctions were described as 'beautifully smoked'. Much of the meerschaum was imported from Turkey and made into pipe-bowls and cigar-holders in Germany and Austria. Up to the 1850s bowls were large, and stems were long tubes of wood or ivory, but from the middle of the century bowls became smaller. The pipes were kept in shaped leather cases. At the peak of meerschaum-making Vienna alone had more than fifty master-carvers, each with up to fifteen assistants. Modern meerschaums are imported from Turkey and Africa, no doubt suitably aged by volunteer pipe-smokers.

Tobacco was kept in pottery jars or boxes made of lead, brass, pewter or wood, in various shapes and sizes. Wooden containers were often lined with lead; many, beautifully turned, took the form of urns, while others were inlaid. Tobacco boxes may be mistaken for tea-caddies and vice versa. One of the most important ceremonies connected with pipe-smoking was poking down the tobacco in the bowl while it was still alight, and tobacco-stoppers were made in every conceivable substance – wood, bone, ivory, brass, glass, china, pottery, silver, pewter, iron, steel – not to mention inconceivable substances. The stoppers cover a wide range of subjects. One of the favourites was a slender female leg.

An opportunity missed

A novice dealer had recently taken a stall at a weekly antique market in the West Country, and as her stall was near the door she was regarded by customers as an advice bureau, a function she performed admirably. An elderly lady went up to her and from her handbag brought out a small silver object. It was clear she wanted to sell it, but had no idea of its value. Nor did the dealer, who did not have anything to do with silver, so she took it to a more experienced dealer in the market, who assumed that this was the dealer's property and that she wanted an estimate of its value. 'Eighty', he grunted, not too pleased at being interrupted in reading the morning paper. So the dealer went back.

'Eighty,' she said.

'Pence?' asked the elderly woman.

'Of course not', said the dealer, feeling confused, 'you'd better go and take it to that man over there.'

She never found out if the other dealer had bought the Georgian vinaigrette, or what he had paid for it. The actual retail value was probably £100–£120.

Feeling foolish she later told the story to a more friendly dealer, who thought she was mad.

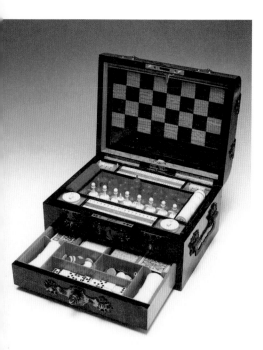

A truly comprehensive Victorian games compendium in walnut, satinwood, and coromandel with brass fittings, sold in January 1987 for £1,550, including at least four packs of cards, a chess set, a draughts set, dice, shakers, bezique scorer and other scorers, tiddlywinks, dice and dominoes.

Quality varies from the crude and home-made to exquisite carving in ivory and bone, often depicting favourite dogs or famous personages.

Pipes had to be lit, and in the smoking room there were often gadgets to provide a light at all times, frequently using gas. For outside, before the arrival of the lighter, there were matches and not much else. The first match was invented in 1827 by a Stockton-on-Tees chemist; this was called the Congreve and cost a shilling a box, and each purchaser was supplied with a piece of folded glasspaper through which the match was drawn. The Promethean followed in 1830. The phosphorus friction-match we know today originated in 1833. Vestas are friction-matches in which the wooden stalks are replaced by wax tapers. They are not to be confused with fusees or Vesuvians, which glowed but did not burst into flame. But it was the vesta (named after Vesta, the Roman goddess of the hearth and its fire) which attained immortality by giving its name to the boxes in which matches were kept. These wax matches or vestas (a term used as late as World War I) were highly combustible and it was necessary to keep them in an air-tight container, the vesta box, one of the most highly collected categories of antiques, irrespective of the materials they were made of – silver, plate, ivory, wood, vulcanite, mother-of-pearl, gold, pottery, porcelain, copper, brass. Vesta boxes are so desirable that objects that are basically more valuable have been adapted by giving them a striker. These include vinaigrettes and snuff-boxes; if of silver they can bear hallmarks predat-

Snuff-taking could be an elaborate ceremony, and the accessories were far more valuable than those used in smoking. The working man kept his snuff in a tin; those marginally better-off used these splendid silver-mounted snuff mulls and boxes, within the date range 1730-1825.

ing the introduction of the wax match.

Up to about 1875 vesta boxes followed the small-box pattern, with engraving the main form of adornment, but the corners were more rounded so that they would not tear the owner's pocket. Then for forty years novelty boxes flooded the market, made in the shape of pigs and other animals, sentry boxes, horseshoes, corks, boots, crowns, hampers, oysters, mussels, heads of famous people, legs, birds, violins, cameras – the list is endless or at least appears endless. A very popular shape was a book, sometimes in vulcanite, with the striker on the 'pages' end. Many boxes had rings fitted so that they could be hung on a watch-chain.

Vesta boxes sometimes had extra compartments for sovereigns, stamps or snuff, or were associated with penknives, pencils and other objects. There were even some with trick or secret opening devices, the reason for which is not readily apparent. With the arrival of the safety match the function of the vesta box was problematical, but its novelty features made it an ideal present for smokers. During World War I it was rendered obsolete by the petrol lighter.

The petrol lighter is one of the new collectables, and as such is admirable, so long as it is not taken too seriously. Early lighters were basic, consisting of a compartment containing cotton wool,

---

Rubbish

In 1972 William Green, a cleaner at Horsham Museum, Sussex, saw a box of loose tissues with an empty cigarette packet and a torn catalogue on top. They were all thrown out and duly crushed in a local-council refuse lorry. The box contained a collection of Wedgwood plaques worth £8,000. The new museum curator was philosophical: 'I am afraid all we are likely to see of them now is a light blue tinge on Itchingfield rubbish dump after a heavy rain.'

In the same museum the Toy Room was closed because it was 3ft (90cm) deep in refuse, and the corridors were impassable. One of the exhibits that was on display was a piece of wood with a nail through it. It was labelled 'A piece of the Chain Pier, Brighton'.

Perpetuated error

A curious example of how an error can be perpetuated is furnished by a small Staffordshire figure entitled 'Buy a Broom' depicting the singer and impresario Madam Vestris (1797–1856) singing the popular ballad of that name. As this figure was intended for the mass market the task of inscribing the message was entrusted to anyone who happened to be around, even if only passably literate. So an example turned out to be labelled 'BY A BROOM'. Eventually when such trifles were taken up by collectors this specimen found its way to a London saleroom, where the cataloguer described it as 'Inscribed, By A Broom'. This made its way into a book and a discussion on potters as yet unknown, including A. Broom. This was picked up by the author of an encyclopaedia of English pottery and porcelain, and under the letter B appeared the full story: 'BROOM, A. Figure maker: mark A. Broom recorded.'

a wick, a cogged wheel, and a flint, but in the 1920s they began to be presented as decorative objects, as powder-compacts were, made in many materials, a favourite being mother-of-pearl for ladies' lighters. It was no longer 'fast' for women to smoke, and long cigarette-holders of the Noel Coward type were delightful dress accessories. Heavy-based table-lighters were made, often disguised as something else, such as a miniature bar in chrome and black plastic or a tennis ball. Probably the most expensive were the lighter-watches made by Dunhill in the late 1920s in gold and silver, in which a small watch is set into the side of the lighter. These have a value today of £800–£1,000. Ordinary lighters of the 1920s and 1930s are to be had for very little money, though one or two makes are more desirable than others. One of these is the 'Zippo' of 1932, a very basic chunky lighter, and so popular amongst collectors that it has been reproduced by the original makers.

From the 1870s match-holders were popular for use in the home, the hotel, the public house and other places where smokers congregate. The basic shape was a flattened sphere, made of pottery, glass, porcelain and occasionally metal. The glass types were usually ribbed to provide a striking surface, and the matches were stored in a circular container in the top. The surfaces of the sphere were often decorated, usually transfer-printed with topical subjects, and some had silver rims and were made by well-known potters such as Doulton. Bases for used matches could be added. There was also a wide variety of novelty match-holders in the form of cupids, rabbits, frogs, puppies, and winsome children, often made in porcelain in Germany.

Hanging match-holders were made from porcelain, papier mâché, wood and metal, and can be taken for spill-containers as sometimes the striking surface is not very evident. These are inclined to be gimmicky and lack the quality of some of the free-standing types. Breweries found match-holders an excellent vehicle for advertising, along with king-size ashtrays, the more recent medium. Advertising ashtrays form a good collecting starter, for there is an immense variety available at almost no cost at all and good potteries did not disdain their manufacture. And they do not have to be used as ashtrays. Among the most collectable are the pewter art-nouveau ashtrays.

The refined member of the tobacco family is snuff, and snuff-boxes are amongst the most collectable of small boxes. Although snuff was taken from the seventeenth century, nothing exists from this time, but in the eighteenth century snuff-boxes began to be made in a great variety of materials including gold, silver, brass and pewter, often inset with mother-of-pearl, tortoiseshell and other materials. Enamelled snuff-boxes are probably the most attractive. The snuff-box did not change much over the years, but until about 1740 the hinge obtruded at the back; after that it was set inside. Snuff-taking was common throughout Europe, and many of the great makers of porcelain such as Meissen and Sèvres produced little masterpieces for top-of-the-market sniffers.

Every man, smoker and non-smoker, drinker and teetotaller, had his collection of walking sticks, kept in a hall-stand inside the front door or in a tall pot, probably sharing space with the miscellaneous umbrellas and parasols. Walking sticks and canes derive from the cudgels and stout staves carried by travellers in olden days, and only gradually did they emerge from functional articles for defence into dress accessories, first of all simply topped with silver or ivory, later fitted with a ferrule of silver or another metal to cut down wear. Elaborate carved heads sometimes unscrewed to disclose an aperture for snuff, and porcelain and enamels were used for handles. There was always a distinction between the elaborate stick and the neat snappy cane with a simple gold or silver band to hide the joint. During the eighteenth century 'dandy' sticks became popular, sometimes 6ft (1.8m) in length, often with a spiral twist.

The most interesting sticks are the novelty ones, the most common being the sword-stick, first used in about 1780, while others incorporated compasses, drink flasks and bottles, telescopes, sovereign-cases, watches, fishing-gear and even 'detective' cameras. Some sticks extended into ladders, others converted to music-stands, lecterns and artist's easels. It was easy to include a baton, or a hook at the end of a rope, but turning a walking stick into a firearm was more demanding. The 'poacher's gun' was a walking stick which doubled as a shotgun, and other sticks turned into airguns, or javelins telescoping out to 9ft (2.7m), and there were nasty little daggers which flicked out from innocent canes (some designed for women) – ingenuity rampant, leading to today's offering, a walking stick incorporating a transistor radio. The most startling is the stick which doubles as a machine gun, the most surprising the canes which incorporated pornographic automata, the most indicative of an age of repression the voyeur's cane, in which there was a mirror above the ferrule. The object? To peer under ladies' long skirts!

Though used for centuries and fashionable since the sixteenth century, the umbrella and the sunshade or parasol did not acquire distinct identities until about 1800. The use of a waterproof umbrella as protection against rain dates from the last part of the seventeenth century, when only women used them, as it was considered effeminate for a man to dodge the spots. Paper parasols from China were first recorded in 1644. The ceremonial umbrella dates at least to the Egypt of the twelfth century BC and was and is widely used as a status symbol in many places in the world, though rarely in Europe.

The first man in England to risk scorn and possibly a brick on the back of his head by carrying an umbrella was Jonas Hanway (who died in 1786). During the last quarter of the eighteenth century the *boursiers*, the makers of gloves and girdles who had been granted a monopoly of the manufacture of umbrellas and parasols in France, improved the design of umbrellas, making them lighter and less cumbersome, introducing the system of folding hinged ribs and the telescopic stick. The French ways spread to Britain largely through the medium of the fashion plate. The parasol became for women an essential accessory like the fan, though the umbrella remained vulgar for men. Only towards the end of the nineteenth century did the scorned 'gamp' acquire some respectability, though it was not quite the city gent's constant companion, yet.

A George III ivory tea caddy banded in tortoiseshell, studded with iron decorations, and inset with a miniature.

Sleepy town

In 1973 an enterprising Birmingham auctioneer offered a prize of £10 for 'the best brass bed in Brum'. No doubt there were a lot of entries, for by the 1870s six thousand brass beds a year were being produced in Birmingham.

AUCTIONS

The most recent phase of the antique trade began in 1958 when a sale of Impressionist and Post-Impressionist paintings at Sotheby's created unprecedented interest amongst the general public. In this sale seven pictures realised £781,000 ($1,367,000) and the media found a new area of interest. To oblige them Sotheby's appointed a firm of public-relations officers to keep the firm's name before the public in the press and on television.

Until that date, the mass of the public was unaware of the great auction houses of the West End, indeed of most art and antiques. As time went by the interiors of Sotheby's, Christie's and the up-and-coming Phillips became as familiar as the sets of soap operas, and the interest led to television programmes such as 'Going for a Song', London Weekend's short-lived 'Collecting on a Shoestring' and, later, 'The Antiques Road-Show', as if antiques was a branch of show business. The trade was wary if not actually hostile; the auction houses were venturing into what had been the traditional territory of the trade and no-one knew what was going to happen. Now they know, and the developments have not been unalloyed good news.

Television and newspaper coverage of the goings-on at the salerooms has always catered for a minority, but a significant minority, those who had a print of Van Gogh's 'Sunflowers' and thought they knew all about art, and it brought to the portals of the salerooms, clutching a masterpiece, the man or woman in the street. It also brought instant knowledge, articles in the tabloid press, and a plethora of antique magazines, many of which stuttered and died as soon as the first flush of enthusiasm was over.

The old days were gone for good. A piece of porcelain with a mark on it even remotely resembling an anchor was Chelsea worth hundreds; a crossed-swords mark was the equivalent of eight draws on a football coupon. How different from days gone by when antique shops were called curio shops, when Jacobean chairs were four to a pound and eighteen old pewter dishes and plates made 35s (£1.75), when auction rooms were sacred to the dealers, the very rich and their agents, and dealers' rings proliferated without let or hindrance.

Today, although the affluence and Fortnum & Mason air of the West End salerooms tend to keep out the ordinary public, provincial auctions and house sales are quite a different matter. The auction room has become not only a place of business but a free show, with the auctioneer judged not so much on the speed with which he or she gets through the lots but on his or her ability to ad lib and make amusing comments.

Selling goods by auction was popular amongst the Romans, but only became important in Britain in the seventeenth century. Sales were held 'by the candle', a ceremony in which a length of candle was allowed to burn down, the successful purchaser being the last bidder before the flame went out. One bidder was very good at this, timing his intervention to the microsecond before microseconds were invented. How? He had observed

the physiology of the lighted candle; immediately before the flame died, the smoke from it went down instead of up.

Auctioneers make their money by charging commission on the selling price, usually between 10 and 15 per cent. Many of them now also charge a buyer's premium of, usually, 10 per cent, a move roundly condemned by the trade, which, however, can do nothing about it. The dealers need auctions to obtain stock; the salerooms do not always necessarily need the trade.

From an early date groups of dealers decided that they did not want to bid against each other in the saleroom. Why should they cost each other money and put their cash in the hands of the person who placed the item into auction (a person who rightfully should have brought it to the dealer)?. Their solution was to band together for saleroom bidding, with one person bidding on behalf of the group, which would then re-auction the goods within itself. Such agreements were deemed unfair, and auction etiquette was set down in the Auctions (Bidding Agreements) Act of 1927. Anyone who disobeyed the rules was liable to six months in prison or a fine of £100. If three people banded together, they could be sent to prison, but if two people bought something between them it was perfectly legal.

The operation of the dealers' ring is simple. One member who is established and financially important will be nominated chairman and a local dealer will act as spokesman. The spokesman will have a catalogue with the choice items 'ringed'. His or her aim is to buy the lots so marked at the

Sometimes at auctions when items sell for hundreds of pounds, it is easy to forget that many of these were throwaway items, or at best sold for a few pence, as we can see from old advertisements such as this one from The Bystander *of 1906.*

Auk-tion

In September 1977 there was great excitement amongst collectors when a great auk was auctioned at Sotheby's Belgravia. The last one had appeared in 1971 and had made £9,000. The 1977 auk had been presented to Dublin University in 1834 by a Rev. Thomas Gisbourne, who had bought it in 1830 for £5. There are twelve great auks in existence – dead, of course. It was finally exterminated in Iceland in 1844.

lowest possible price without dealers of equivalent status battling it out with him or her. But the ring's representative can be out-bid by a private buyer or by a rogue dealer.

After the sale the members of the ring gather in a room in a pub or in the car-park for the 'knock out', and the goods are re-auctioned. Bidding starts at the saleroom price. Suppose this is £200 and in the knock-out the item makes £350; the difference of £150 is divided among the non-buyers, and everyone goes away happy, especially the low-grade dealers and knockers (dealers who go from door to door offering to buy antiques) who have managed to get into the ring without any intention of buying anything. If they are refused entry they can run the prices up and defeat the object of the exercise. So, not surprisingly, for valuable goods there is a ring within a ring that excludes knockers and similar undesirables.

Uncovering dealers' rings makes news, and in 1964 the *Sunday Times* exposed a ring which had bought a Chippendale commode in Leamington Spa for £750, about a tenth of its true value. The reporters also found that some provincial auctioneers connived with the rings to the extent of hiding items away, omitting lots from catalogues, and knocking them out in a back room.

The most spectacular instance of a ring in action occurred in about 1850, proof that ringmanship is not a recent fad. In about 1835 a Welsh gentleman with a taste for collecting found a job lot of eighteen queerly shaped bits of vividly coloured enamelled copper in an auction room in London. He liked the look of them and bought them for a few shillings, taking them back to his remote homestead. In due course he died and his odds and ends were put into a local saleroom. These included the copper bits. The Welshman had listed his collection and the auctioneer's description 'Limoges enamels' was taken from the list, the auctioneer having no knowledge of antiques

(though probably good on sheep). He put them in a brown paper parcel.

Copies of the catalogue reached London, where there was rather more knowledge – but not a great deal more – and a group of dealers travelled in a posse to the wilds of Wales. Eventually the enamels came up at the sale. 'Now gentlemen – what shall I say?' asked the auctioneer, 'A shilling apiece?' No answer. At last one of the London dealers spoke up and said that he 'wouldn't mind giving ninepence apiece for the lot'.

The auctioneer thanked him effusively, but there were dark glances from the Welsh farmers who neither collectively nor individually liked bits of coloured copper very much, but liked the English even less. So they ran the ring up until the enamels went to the dealers for £25. The knock-out took place in the village inn, and the enamels were bid up to £450. The buyer sold them in London for £600, and later the South Kensington Museum (later known as the Victoria & Albert) bought them for £800.

The full story came to light in 1913, when the eighteen Limoges enamels were recognised for what they were, masterpieces worth several thousand pounds each, even then. It is an engaging story. Nobody was hurt. It was reckoned brave even to go to Welsh Wales where it was widely believed that the best place for an Englishman's head was on a pole.

Although a ring can be thwarted by putting a realistic reserve on goods placed in auction, the naive can sometimes suffer by stupid or malicious advice from so-called experts at certain auction houses. In the mid-1950s a lady travelled from Devon to London with a painting on copper by Bassano (1510-92). A demand for rates had caught her unprepared, and family treasures had to go. She was advised by the 'expert' not to put a reserve on the painting, and not knowing anything about auctions she did not demur. The £20 she got for the picture did not seem much, but she had no idea of its value. Only later did she learn that the painting had changed hands in the saleroom for not far short of £1,000.

It may seem that the dealers' ring is fire-proof, but it can come unstuck with amusing consequences. One day at a London saleroom a dealer saw a little picture he fancied; he was not a picture dealer but he stayed on to see what sort of money it would make. The bidding started breezily at £50, went on to £120, and then faltered. Thinking it ridiculous, he put in a bid, and got it. Only then did the truth emerge. The members of the ring thought that he was their spokesman. It cost them £2,000 to buy the painting from him. On another occasion the ring tried to rope in a couple of stray dealers who turned out to be plain-clothes policemen.

An ordinary buyer at a sale will have no idea that the ring is in operation, even if he or she is bid against. Some buyers are known as 'followers'; they may be private or they may be small-time dealers, and they keep an eye on a known dealer who is bidding. If this dealer stops, the follower makes one more bid, reasoning that the item is still a good buy at £10 or £20 more than the dealer is willing to give. The danger in this is that the original bidder gets to know what is happening, and carries on for a while, leaving the follower paying far more than the object is worth.

One of the least intrusive and more important members of the auctioneer's staff is the porter, who, for a small gratuity, will bid, advise and whisper reserves, though these kinds of services are not allowed in the London premier salerooms. Porters will also be able to say what interest there is in a certain lot.

It is often believed by newcomers to salerooms that if they twitch, scratch their ears or look expectant, something they do not want will be knocked down to them. This is quite untrue. The aim of

auctioneers is to get through the sale at a minimum of ninety lots an hour without interruption, and the last thing they want is to have to put up a lot twice because they have mistakenly put a lot down to the wrong person.

Auctions come in all shapes and sizes; all will be covered by the antique-trade professionals looking for the 'standards'. Regulars (professional and non-professional) are known, and they do most of the buying; after buying one or two lots casuals will be recognised, and remembered. Some salerooms operate as they did fifty years ago with smudgy catalogues run off on antiquated duplicators. Others are smooth-running machines, persuading private vendors to put their goods in, opening their doors for people to obtain free valuations from their experts, and relying on an experienced press officer to project their image. Salerooms operate from a position of strength. They are consolidating a position won from the dealers more than twenty years ago, and they can weather the periodic down trends. When the dollar weakens, the shippers are left with large stocks; their buyers therefore cannot move their stock on, and they are either stuck with it or have to sell it off at a loss; and the lower echelons of the trade wonder what is going on. Only the private buyer seems to have any money to spend. The top salerooms are aloof from the turmoil. Expertise and international connections ensure the best market for high-quality goods.

'Non-trade' items such as the more obscure collectables are often cheaper to buy at auction, as the dealers who specialise in off-beat items sometimes have an inflated idea of their stock.

It has become traditional for dealers to rail at auction houses, accusing them of unfair competition, of having their cake and eating it (the selling and buying premiums), of not having to carry the burden of VAT. Probably street traders did the same when the very first shops opened.

Auctioneer at Phillips.

15th Century porcelain

In 1973 a private vendor brought into Phillips's saleroom, London, a group of porcelain items for which he expected between £100 and £200 for the lot. One of the items, a fifteenth-century Chinese blue-and-white vase 13½in (34cm) tall, was sufficiently interesting for the auctioneers to call in the British Museum for their expert opinion. If only more auctioneers did the same thing! It was put up for sale and made £135,000, the highest price obtained by Phillips for a single item in their long history.

POTTERY AND PORCELAIN

There are two kinds of porcelain, hard-paste and soft-paste. Hard-paste was first made in China in the seventh or eighth century; it was first made in Europe in 1709 at Meissen, and thence spread all over Europe despite Meissen's attempt to keep the secret.

Usually porcelain was glazed, but if unglazed was called biscuit or bisque. Porcelain could be painted before being glazed, or after, in which case it was fired again. Soft-paste porcelain was a version invented before the secret of 'real' porcelain was discovered. As losses in the kiln were heavy, soft-paste porcelain was not made on a very large scale, so it is much rarer.

Hard-paste and soft-paste are descriptions of the process. Soft-paste porcelain is not likely to be scratched with the finger-nail; it will not disintegrate in water. The best way to get to know the difference is to buy two badly damaged pieces from a reputable dealer, one soft-paste, the other hard-paste, feel them, get to know the texture, and work out the difference.

Learning about porcelain can be fun, or it can be hard work. Museums can be very correct and efficient, but to newcomers the labels on the pottery and porcelain exhibits can be incomprehensible jargon. Get to know a few good dealers in porcelain; ask questions; take one or two pieces in your hands; if the mood takes you, buy something, but you do not have to. Gradually the world of that classic antique, eighteenth-century English porcelain, will come alive.

There is no need for mystification. British manufacturers were trying to do what the Chinese had been doing effortlessly for centuries; some succeeded and some made a botch of it. The qualities they were trying to achieve were whiteness, thinness of body, and translucency. The results of this enterprise were compared, often cynically, with the genuine porcelain article from China.

In the middle of the seventeenth century China began producing porcelain to suit the needs of overseas buyers. The blue-and-white 'Canton' ware was shipped in bulk as ballast for the ships carrying tea and silks, and was not highly regarded by the Chinese themselves though it seemed miraculous to the recipients. The first of the coloured ware to make an impact on Britain was *famille verte*, with a range of brilliant enamel colours – copper-green, red, purple, yellow and blue – but this was replaced in public estimation by *famille rose*, soft pastel colours dominated by a rosy pink. Designs, including armorials in precise detail, were made to order. With the immense demand particularly from England and, from 1784, America, quality suffered.

Derby winner

In the 1970s the prices of china fairings rose dramatically and in 1973 the £1,000 barrier was passed for 'To the Derby'. It depicted a man, woman and dog on a velocipede (boneshaker bicycle). The original cost was perhaps sixpence (2½p).

Enterprising as were the British nineteenth-century potteries, they were always aware that on the Continent there was a standard of excellence they could rarely exceed, as in this superb Meissen model of the Empress of Russia's favourite dog.

A rare and unusual piece of blue and white, an English Delft lady's shoe of about 1718, sold in December 1986 for £1,700.

There was so much prestige associated with china from China that English factories used Chinese forms of decoration, causing a good deal of confusion at the time, and the Chinese reciprocated, using ill-understood western motifs, though they could reproduce mythological and religious subjects (themes which were particularly popular in 1740-60) with a good deal of accuracy from prints. The finest pieces of Chinese export porcelain get prices commensurate with their worth. A punch bowl with golfing scenes (one of the very earliest of golf collectables, and indeed bought by a sporting specialist) recently made £20,000 ($35,000) and another punch bowl described by the auctioneers as 'one of the finest pieces of Chinese export porcelain' and depicting marvellous views of the City of London was bid up to £24,000 ($42,000). A Ming-period blue-and-white pilgrim flask made not for the all-important English market but for the Spanish achieved £70,000 ($122,500).

All this must be borne in mind when contemplating British porcelain of the eighteenth century. It is a case of the schoolteacher and the pupil.

Some British eighteenth-century porcelain is marked, some unmarked. Sometimes it might be a factory mark, sometimes a workman's mark, and the factory marks change and fluctuate, so a good book on marks is essential to any serious collector or even the person who just wants one good item to set in a place of honour. But a book of marks is not a pattern book; two marks are rarely the same unless impressed.

Of all the factories, the most celebrated at the time was Chelsea (1745-70), noted for its luxury products. There were many influences on Chelsea porcelain, reflected in the wide variety of goods the factory made. Bow (1749-76) was a very large factory for its time, and it concentrated on domestic china. The survival rate of Bow china is not high. The delicate and unostentatious ware was regarded as ordinary and unspectacular in the high-spending years of the nineteenth century, was relegated to the servants' quarters and, when chipped, ended up in the dustbin. Much Bow porcelain was not marked in any way, so budding connoisseurs would not have much to go on. Bow probably had the largest output of blue-and-white china in England, and much of

On the left a Bristol tea-bowl and saucer, in the centre a Lowestoft creamboat and sauceboat, and on the right a Worcester teacup and saucer of about 1770, all classic pieces from the great age of British porcelain.

the early painting is smudgy and out of focus, qualities which would not have guaranteed a place in the exclusive china cabinet.

Worcester was the largest factory, and despite the fact that it produced an enormous amount of goods – and that these were inclined to survive better because they were more thinly potted than the rivals and thus withstood hot water – it is one of the most expensive names. It was also the longest-lived. Worcester took over the stock and secrets of a Bristol firm, and began production in 1751. Worcester pioneered, in 1757, the use of transfer printing, which was so much a feature of commercial blue-and-white in the succeeding years.

Longton Hall was the first factory in Staffordshire to produce porcelain. It was a small factory, did not produce a great quantity and lasted about ten years, some of its workers moving over to the Derby works and precipitating the closure of Longton Hall in 1760. Derby began by predominantly making figures, though of course it manufactured the standard eighteenth-century ware as well. The factory prospered and in 1770 took over Chelsea.

Liverpool porcelain is a generic name covering several factories, the most important being Chaffers, which produced wares reckoned to be akin to those made by Worcester but inferior. Lowestoft was a small and unpretentious factory, and very few of its products come onto the market; if they do they are very expensive. Caughley is another small factory, its products often confused with those from Worcester. Plymouth was the first factory in England to make hard-paste porcelain, and was only in existence for two years before the owner moved to Bristol. The New Hall factory of Staffordshire was small and produced mainly tea and coffee services.

These are the main providers of eighteenth-century porcelain in England. These are the names heard echoing through the aisles

Diamonds

The only gem-stone that is of any practical use is the diamond. Until the fifteenth century it was found difficult to cut; it is immeasurably harder than any other stone, and the only cut possible was the cabochon giving a curved shape without facets.

The Romans tried to make imitation diamonds, now known as paste. Paste is nothing more nor less than glass. Another imitation is the zircon, prized as a gem-stone in its own right, and although much softer than the diamond it can be rendered colourless by heat-treatment and with its natural fire and brilliance it can be confused with diamond.

Until the eighteenth century India and Borneo were the most important sources of diamonds. In 1867 the price of diamonds fell dramatically after their discovery in South Africa – South Africa provides 97 per cent of the world's diamonds.

Throughout the ups and downs of fashion diamonds have continued to hold sway, unlike most other precious or semi-precious stones.

The wearing of stones has always been the subject of conventions. In the eighteenth century garnets, opals and topazes were for daytime, diamonds for the evening. By that time the brilliant fifty-eight facet cut had arrived.

of antique fairs. If we survey the china made by all these factories we see not only the differences but the resemblances, the general refinement of taste even when the techniques are haphazard, the manner in which overseas mannerisms in design are assimilated, and the sense that all the ware was aimed at the same type of consumer. Except for the slavish copies of continental models, the tone is simple, even naive, the choice of subjects limited to flowers, birds, Chinese topics. It was all very humble, unlike the grandiose creations of such continental factories as Meissen and Sèvres, with the exception of the figures.

Is the best of eighteenth-century porcelain beautiful? Why does it occupy such an important place in the antique hierarchy? Is it simply rarity? These are questions which much have been asked a thousand times. If it is beautiful, why is it beautiful? Is it because the forms are just right, that the jugs, teapots and tea bowls are perfectly in tune with their function? That certainly is part of it. It must be remembered that this was the age of reason, the age of Dr Johnson, when conversation and debate were elevated to an art form to the accompanying tinkling of coffee-cups and tea-bowls.

It might be wondered why blue-and-white was so prevalent. Blue was technically the most suitable colour. Initially there were serious difficulties, for cobalt blue was imported from Germany and its processing was not fully understood. By trial and error transfer printing did progress, but there remained a degree of smudginess for some time.

To many the glory of eighteenth-century porcelain is not the table ware but the figures, produced by most of the factories until about 1760 heavily under the influence of the sophisticated and technically adroit Meissen models. Many were made in sets and pairs.

Derby concentrated on figures more than the other factories, and more Derby pieces have survived than those of all the other manufacturers added together. On the other hand, Worcester figures are very rare, as are those from Lowestoft.

It need hardly be added that all these figures are very expensive and often faked. Bow figures, simple and unpretentious especially if compared with the products of Chelsea, were fetching £1,000 or more a pair twenty years ago, as compared with a mug of the same period from the same factory at £80 or so. An average Worcester mug of that time, then worth about £40, would be rated today at about £400, an appreciation in line with traditional antiques. The least expensive of all the lines is the coffee-cup, made by nearly all the factories, though Chelsea, Longton Hall and Plymouth examples are not common. The blue-and-white is cheaper than the all-colour. The coffee-cup is ideal to collect as a collection takes up little room and is easy and rewarding to display, and cups have not been subject to spiralling prices as more exotic vessels have. They therefore have not had the fakers' full attentions, and in the past they have not been worth repairing.

All porcelain, whether period or not, should be closely examined to see if it has been repaired. An amateur job is easily spotted; if there is any doubt go over the surface of the object with a pin, tapping lightly. A repaired area will often be tacky

A Minton Majolica stick-stand with a refreshingly modest colour range, 103 cms tall, fully dated for 1885, and selling at auction in April 1987 for £2,000 and unquestionably a bargain considering the demand for this form of pottery.

A rare Longton Hall polychrome china mug with characteristic floral decoration, sold in October 1987 for £1,950.

A luxury item, a Minton vase with a fine painting by Louis Jahn (employed by Minton 1862-72). Such vases have a value of well in excess of £1,000.

in texture and under pressure the pin will sink instead of glancing off. A light tapping with the teeth can distinguish between a repaired area and the hard coldness of the original surface, though this action should be carried out guardedly as it may be misconstrued.

Old restorations often lose their whiteness and have a yellowish colour. An ultraviolet light is often supposed to detect repairs, but modern china repairers are so skilled that this method sometimes does not work. Especially vulnerable are handles and spouts, and it is often easy to overlook a chip under the rim. In eighteenth-century figures, especially if there is a deal of bocage (trees, bushes, shrubs and plant life), a degree of damage is acceptable, and a piece in less-than-perfect condition is more valuable than one that has been botched up. Haircracks affect values to an extent, and a chip is often easier to repair than a crack; dirt in a crack makes an object look worse than it is, and a cleaning with a toothbrush can work wonders.

Much unnecessary damage has been caused to plates and other hangable objects by the use of plate-hangers, especially the old type ones which were not plastic-coated. It is worse when the plate-hanger is too small for the job, and the wire or spring is stretched, applying constant pressure which can extend incipient cracks.

The eighteenth century was a golden age for British porcelain, but technical developments were imminent, typified by the introduction by Josiah Spode of bone china, made by adding bone ash to the other ingredients. With improvements in pottery technology the once rigid divisions between porcelain and pottery were becoming blurred. It is time to turn to pottery, once the poor relation.

All types of ware made from baked clay are termed pottery, and pottery has been made since the beginning of recorded time. A lump of clay could be shaped with the fingers; sausages of clay could be built up into a pot and then smoothed down; clay could be shaped by spinning it round on a wheel and letting centrifugal force do its work; or it could be put in a mould. The product, when dried by natural or artificial heat to a 'leather-hard' condition, could be scraped, cut, or turned on a lathe. It was then fired in a kiln. It could then be glazed, and fired again if required. It could be decorated or left plain.

It is a simple process with thousands of variations. Throwing salt onto the contents of the kiln produced salt-glazed vessels, with an agreeable pitted surface not unlike the texture of orange-peel. Delft ware used a tin glaze, which made the vessel white in imitation of Chinese models. Any decoration or adornment had to be applied rapidly as the glaze was absorbent, and no second thoughts or corrections were possible. After the decoration had been applied the vessel was fired again so that both glaze and decoration melted into a glossy surface. In Italy tin-glazed ware was called maiolica, in most of the rest of Europe faience, and in Holland, not surprisingly, delft.

Stoneware, patented in England in 1626 though long known elsewhere, was the result of clay fired at very high temperatures which rendered the vessel strong, resilient and waterproof – in fact, like stone. Redware was unglazed pottery, with and without decoration. Creamware was lead-glazed with a cream-coloured body containing flint; it was invented some time between 1720 and 1740, and refined by Wedgwood, and it established itself as the best earthenware product for a century or more.

Stoneware was amenable to coloured glazes, and tortoiseshell was emulated. Semi-transparent glazes gave a very pleasing effect, as did mixing white and coloured clays and giving the results fancy names such as 'agate', 'marbled', 'porphyry', 'mocha', 'blue pebble', and 'variegated pebble'. By adding manganese and iron to the clay the potter obtained earthenware which was black. Wedgwood called his black pottery basalt, and he was unquestionably the leading manufacturer of this ware even though many others were busy in this field, for it was easy to do, cheap and did not need decoration.

The success of basalt encouraged Wedgwood to experiment with other colours by adding other ingredients to the clay, and he came up with jasper, originally intended for cameos but soon seen as a multi-purpose medium. And jasper provided the most famous of eighteenth-century ceramics – Wedgwood blue. Originally jasper was tinted all through, but a short-cut was found by using a surface layer of jasper. Pearlware was another Wedgwood development, this time a whiter version of creamware, and cane-ware was a buff unglazed earthenware which, when modelled in narrow cylinders, was called bamboo.

By the end of the eighteenth century many manufacturers were busy experimenting, catering for the growing fickleness of public taste as the restless nineteenth century approached. Prattware was earthenware enriched with multi-coloured moulded decoration, and only later was to be associated with Pratt's most famous product, pot lids. Castleford ware is white stoneware with a moulded design in relief and often ornamented with blue borders, and though it carries the name of a pottery this is for convenience as many potters were involved in this charming but relatively unimportant field.

From left to right, a Derby jardinière, a pierced Minton plate of 1879, and a Minton 'Pilgrim' vase (because of its shape) of 1873.

Wedgwood revived terracotta, an unglazed red earthenware; he was followed by minor potteries, and terracotta was taken up again at the close of the nineteenth century, but unquestionably the most important development since the evolution of stoneware was 'stone china'. The first thing that needs to be said about this is that, despite what is inscribed on the bottom of plates and other articles, it is *not* china but the latest and best attempt to imitate it. The first factory in this field, marketing the new product under various titles such as 'stone china', 'new stone' or 'semi-porcelain', was Spode, from about 1805, but in 1813 Charles Mason patented his 'ironstone china'. It was a brilliant description implying great strength, which indeed it had. It was much used for table ware, sometimes in vast sets, and was much in demand for what were known as vestibule vases, 5ft (1.5m) high. Mason made ironstone exclusively at his Staffordshire factory until 1827, and it was then taken up by other British and American manufacturers who were in the process of building up their huge potteries to provide practical wares for the rapidly expanding population.

There were two avenues for nineteenth-century pottery, the practical and the pretty, and when they were combined the result was not always a success. Established continental forms were taken up. Majolica, introduced in 1850, was a re-hash at first hesitant, later extrovert and dashing, of early Italian maiolica (notice the 'i' instead of the 'j'); it was given a launch at the Great Exhibition of 1851. Making majolica involved covering with a rich opaque white glaze and then painting on top. Minton recruited the best of the pottery artists, and examples of old Italian maiolica were lent to the firm by the Duke of Sutherland for copying. Minton majolica has rocketed in price over the past few years, and especially desirable are the big pieces, the plant holders

Stone china is not porcelain; neither is ironstone. Not that it matters. The word porcelain no longer carries prestige. In December 1987 a massive Spode dinner and dessert service of about 1820 and comprising 113 pieces achieved £5,800 at auction (approximately £50 a piece).

and the garden furniture, which are highly coloured without being gaudy, and enormously strong, well fitted to remain outdoors through a century of English winters, which a good deal of Minton garden-ware has done before coming up at auction. Chunky majolica is a perfect example of combining practicality and visual attractiveness.

Now that almost everything that could be done to clay had been done, the manufacturers had to rely on new forms of decoration for novelty, and one of the most charming is lustre – silver lustre from platinum and copper lustre from gold, applied in the thinnest of washes so that the colour is partly determined by the underlying pottery, gold on a dark surface resulting in copper, gold on white producing purple. Successive washes could be added as required. In a way it was watercolour painting applied to ceramics.

The name of Sunderland is associated with lustre, especially with 'splash' lustre in which globules of oil are dropped onto the copper lustre in a random fashion. A good deal of lustreware was adorned with engravings of fashionable subjects, bridges being exceptionally popular or lines of doggerel.

Although blue-and-white pottery has been collected for years, both for display and for everyday use, it is an area in which the new collector with not much money to spend can operate in freedom simply because such a vast amount was made and, because of its charm, is still being made. The most famous design is of course Willow Pattern, but there are others which are about in quantity such as Asiatic Pheasant and Italian. Although old designs are still used, it would be laughable to suggest that modern-day manufacturers are in any way indulging in something disreputable.

Is there any safe and sure way of determining what was made a hundred and fifty years ago and what was made yesterday? It

A magnificent pair of ice-pails by Flight Barr and Barr of a quality that stands comparison with the best of Sèvres.

Treasure trove

Many antiquities come onto the market through the activities of marine archaeologists, who number more than 20,000. In 1972 they plundered the wreck of Charles II's yacht, the *Mary*, lying off Anglesey. The matter was alarming enough for it to be raised in Parliament by Tam Dalyell (Labour member for West Lothian).

A group of Staffordshire figures. The two dwarfs on the right are modelled on china originals made in Derby.

is mainly a question of using commonsense. Modern pottery is white and perfect; there is no sign of yellowing, no age 'crackling', and no signs of wear. Modern manufacturers also use a fairly narrow range of subjects. If an item is marked 'England' or 'Made in England' it is certainly less than a hundred years old and therefore cannot belong to the great blue-and-white tradition that ended in the mid-nineteenth century, but that scarcely matters. Although prices have increased for quite ordinary blue-and-white, there is no point in investing in blue-and-white pottery for profit – blue-and-white porcelain is another matter altogether.

Blue-and-white pottery was made to be used. It was robust and functional. It was not meant to be put on plate-hangers or placed on a dresser. The usages of fancy pottery, such as lustre wear, must ever remain in doubt. Certainly a lustre jug could function perfectly well, but would it actually be used for such a mundane purpose as pouring out milk? Certainly the more exotic products of the later part of the nineteenth century, even if cast in everyday costume, would never have seen the inside of a kitchen. However, there is no doubt about the traditional pottery figures, the best known of which was the Staffordshire dog which traditionally stared goggle-eyed down from the cottage mantel-piece at visitors.

Staffordshire pottery figures – which, to confuse matters, were also made in Scotland, Wales, Liverpool, Yorkshire and elsewhere – can be divided into two periods: 1750 to 1837, when Queen Victoria came to the throne, and from then to about 1870, when they began to slip into the oblivion brought about by disapproval. Most of the potters were male artisans producing folk art, helped by women and children; there were probably nearly a thousand potters in Staffordshire making figures, which divided into two major groups, classical and rural. The potters interpreted the themes as they wished.

These early figures are rare and expensive, and are naturally faked, but specialists maintain that the originals have a unique colouring and glazing that defies even the most cunning faker. Long may this continue.

Somewhat apart from the usual run of Staffordshire figures was the toby jug, named after Toby Fillpot, the nickname of

Henry Elwes, a Yorkshire inebriate who died swollen and distended in 1761. The true toby wears fashionable clothes and sports a three-cornered detachable hat, supposedly used as a cup. Later variations include a squire, a thin man, a convict, a man on a barrel, a night-watchman, and a variety of other tradesmen and traditional comic characters. The toby jug did not exclude women, including Drunken Sal, in torn black dress and pink hat, with pipe and glass, and the celebrated Martha Gunn, who ran a bathing-machine at Brighton and was an intimate of the Prince of Wales. The straightforward toby is probably the most reproduced piece of genre pottery, both full size (8-12in [20-30cm]) and miniature (1in [.2.5cm] upwards), though original miniatures rather than reproductions were also made in the nineteenth century.

The jug is especially interesting as it anticipates the taste of the Regency and early Victorian periods, and was aimed at a raffish and bucolic market which was not interested in Minervas or ambiguous characters representing the four seasons. The potters were learning to cater for a real demand, and they did this by producing figures of real people or tableaux illustrating real events. One of these, a well-known pottery group known as Polito's menagerie, sold in October 1987 for £7,000 ($12,250) (plus the buyer's 10 per cent premium), even though it lacked two figures – and a parrot! But this is an exceptional figure. The piece is known, attributed to a well-known potter, Obadiah Sherrat, and is an absolute must for a dedicated collector.

Who was suitable for immortalisation in the form of a pottery figure? Who was not? Politicians, sportsmen, criminals, all were fashioned by the potters, who took as their models the engravings in the weekly illustrated papers (which were sometimes less like the originals than the figures themselves, which is something of a feat). To avoid confusion, the figures had an inscription at the foot, sometimes impressed, sometimes embossed, sometimes painted.

The Staffordshire potters were pioneers in giving the ordinary people what they wanted instead of what their betters thought they ought to have. An early example was a piece modelled in 1793 depicting the murder of the French revolutionary Jean Marat in his bath in that same year, but the potter had a sense of decorum and Marat was shown fully clothed. A rare and sought-after piece reflects the interest in the gory case of Maria Marten and the murder in the Red Barn, perhaps the most celebrated murder case in Victorian times and commemorated on stage until the close of the century.

For the more respectable working classes there were portrait figures, especially of those who seemed to be on their side such as Cobden and Peel, though strangely enough Napoleon I seems to have been the most popular of them all. So great was the appeal of Staffordshire figures that during World War I a set was made of eleven war leaders. There was great excitement in 1973 when a figure of Sir Robert Peel on a horse fetched £1,680 ($2,940) at auction, then the world record for a Staffordshire figure.

There are four main strands in nineteenth-century pottery and porcelain – naive folk art, utilitarian table-ware which could be

---

Anything goes

In Victorian times the oddest things could be turned into jewellery – fluorspar from Derbyshire, ammonites (tiny fossils looking like coiled snakes), human hair, lava, bog oak, as well as the cogged wheels of watches, tiny metal locomotives, coal-scuttles, and ladders used as earrings. There was a fashion for imitation insects which crawled over bonnets, parasols and veils, and appeared as brooches and on rings or bracelets. But there were also huge clusters of gems and pearls for those who wanted to impress with their wealth.

A Liverpool creamware jug with one of the strange mottoes that appear on provincial ware.

Doll's Houses

There are doll's houses in museums dating back to about 1600; for many years they were known as baby houses. The most familiar have a façade consisting of a hinged door which swings away to reveal the boxes that form the rooms, either visualised as leading to other parts of the house with doors, staircases and windows, or merely containers. The most expensive were custom-built, modelled on the owner's full-size house, and fitted out with miniatures of the real furniture. Exquisite treasures were cannibalised to provide doll's house accessories; lids of enamel boxes served as pictures.

The best furniture was made from walnut, rosewood or mahogany, jointed and not glued. A good piece of doll's house furniture can fetch more than £500. Small items such as teapots were made in silver. Contemporary wallpaper was made in miniature, a useful guide to dating. Doll's houses for the mass market were made of cardboard with paper printed with bricks, tiles and slates pasted on the exterior. For the American buyer, sand was sprinkled onto a gummed surface to give the illusion of brownstone.

In the seventeenth century tiny kitchens were made in Nuremberg in Germany, with splendid miniature metal-work, meat carved from wood or moulded in plaster, and minute glass and pottery vessels.

In America the toy grocer's shop was used as a medium for advertising, with branded goods produced in small packs, tins and bottles. Toy grocers, butchers and *modistes* (made mainly in France) led on to toy banks, post offices, railway booking offices, and garages, each with their train of accessories such as paper money, coins, stamps, tickets and stationery.

cheap or expensive, up-market decorative items, and oddities made for those who did not go with the crowd and were looking for something stimulating.

Nineteenth-century ceramics are one of the most rewarding spheres for collectors, offering scope for everyone. By 1815 manufacturing processes, modelling, designing and painting had reached a peak, exemplified in the rarified products of the Worcester factory then under the aegis of Robert Chamberlain. The prestige porcelain of that period was extremely expensive; in 1813 the Prince Regent was charged £105 for three pieces painted with figure subjects. Flower-encrusted china from Coalport (often termed Coalbrookdale), ornate painted vases from Davenport equalling the best French models, superb-quality figures and groups from Derby, exquisite flower-painted ware from Nantgarw in Wales, multi-hued decorative objects from Minton, and lavish vases from Spode, all dazzle the sight, so much so that it must have appeared at the time that nothing further could be done and that perfection had been achieved in the few years preceding the accession of Queen Victoria in 1837.

What could the Victorians do? Could there be any advance on the marvellous productions of the Regency factories? It is no longer the custom to accuse the Victorians of debasing everything they touched, and to imagine that the products of the Great Exhibition of 1851 were typical of overall contemporary taste. They were decidedly not, though they encouraged the new rich to indulge themselves in fripperies that historically had no past and no future. The cultivated classes did not go into hibernation when they heard that they were in a new reign; they and their children continued to buy what they had always bought from the great factories.

Skilled, even manic, in invention, the Victorian manufacturers did their best to come up with something new, and in Parian they triumphantly succeeded. First known as statuary porcelain, Parian was a creamy-white body ideal for figures and ornaments, less impressive in table ware, and is supposed to have been discovered by accident at the Copeland factory in 1842. These figures, some of considerable size, were often impressed with the artist's name and that of the manufacturer, and the better-quality ones were beautifully modelled and are still undervalued. One point about Parian is that repairs are easy to see, and even expert restorers have not acquired the knack of reproducing the exact texture and colour. To some, Parian can be confused with bisque; there is no reason why it should be, for bisque is matt and Parian has a pleasant sheen.

Bisque figures were also produced in quantity, especially in France and Germany for the English market; they were lightly decorated in pastel colours and depicted personages in early nineteenth-century costume, which might cause the unwary to believe that they are from that period instead of the last part of the century. These bisque figures are rather characterless, and are of less consequence than the porcelain figures on similar themes exported to Britain at about the same time. The bisque figures are fairly cheap, which cannot be said of fairings produced for the same market by the Germans, the rarest of which top the

£1,000 ($1,750) mark. Fairings are porcelain miniatures, usually depicting indelicate and risible subjects, and are sometimes known as early-to-beds. Favourite subjects were 'Last in Bed to Put Out the Light' and 'Shall We Sleep First?' Earlier specimens were heavier, have recessed bases and are sometimes marked; later ones are cruder in colour with a good deal of gilt embellishment. The Japanese copied the German fairings for the British market. Contrary to popular opinion they were never made in Staffordshire. The legend 'made in germany' indicates a date later than 1890.

With the popular demand for these trifles, short-cuts were found to eliminate the hand-painter. The 'glue bats' method was used on unglazed china; a greasy pattern was pressed onto the surface, and then dusted over with the required colour. Only the greasy portion took the colour.

The worst of Victorian pottery and porcelain is that which seeks to emulate fine quality in a cheap and slipshod way, typified by the pairs of pottery vases with a transferred colour picture. These, surprisingly, are collected, though they have not even the merit of being honestly naive. The best, on the other hand, is pottery and porcelain produced by a designer or painter left to his or her own devices despite commercial pressures.

Amongst the more characteristic nineteenth-century ceramics were china cottages and castles, sometimes called pastille-burners because that was their original role in Holland in the eighteenth century. These were made in vast quantities in the first part of the nineteenth century, but most of them mysteriously disappeared during World War II. Why? Because it was the favourite memento for US forces to take home with them. Lace figures, which evolved in about 1840, are sometimes taken to be continental figures, but they were originally made in Vauxhall. They were made using a particularly ingenious method. The lace dresses these figures wear were made from real lace dipped in china 'slip' before firing. The heat of the kiln burned the lace away leaving the china. Lace figures were often placed under glass domes to avoid damage.

Noddies were porcelain figures with detachable heads perched

Thoroughly English, a Staffordhsire saltglaze bear-baiting jug and cover, which recently sold for an impressive £4,800.

Three eighteenth-century Delft dishes, one blue and white, two polychrome.

on elongated necks. When pushed, the heads nodded. These were another import from Germany, and were copied by the Japanese for the British market. Sometimes they were in blue-and-white and were attributed to Staffordshire. In the 1840s patents were taken out for transferring coloured prints to china, and the makers of containers for hair-grease, ointments and other substances realised that by decorating their pot lids they could couple visual appeal with advertising. These pot lids are much collected, and faked, though the crazing on the originals is difficult to reproduce convincingly (though the fakers try). Pot lids without pictorial content are not valued very highly, though the lettering and lay-out can be very attractive. All ceramic containers displaying advertising material are well worth a second look.

It is very interesting to see how various fashions led to new designs or variations on existing objects. The Crimean War (1854-6) brought in the vogue for moustaches, worn without beards, but it was found that men with heavy moustaches were at a disadvantage when drinking from a cup. So the moustache cup was invented, with a perforated ledge beneath the inner rim. As men began to shave themselves instead of going to the barber there was a demand for shaving mugs, or so the manufacturers led the public to believe. They were a popular gift for men from wives and sweethearts, sometimes inscribed with loving messages. When emblazoned with a printed view of a seaside town or a coat-of-arms they added to the stock of objects destined for the souvenir market.

The souvenir, meaning remembrance, was first used in its customary form in 1782, but it was not until the railways had brought travel to the seaside within reach of all that the makers realised that the provision of mementoes was a profitable business. Presents from this or that place, on mugs, wooden knick-knacks, plates, cups and plaques, could be good, bad or indifferent. Many were made and printed in Germany, a role that was taken over by Czechoslovakia after World War I. But by and large souvenirs are a pleasant undemanding collecting field. The most famous examples are the Goss armorial miniatures, emulated by other firms such as Arcadian, whose products are almost identical except that they are much less collectable.

The last twenty years of the nineteenth century saw other manufacturers exploiting the tourist industry, and typical of these were the Devon factories of Aller Vale, Watcombe and later Longpark, which produced motto-ware. Red earthenware was coated with a rich creamy slip and the motto was hand-written, usually in brown and often in a 'hoots mon' Scottish style. Again, as with Staffordshire figures, the market was responding to a demand, with a similar type of buyer in mind.

However, there were certain developments in Victorian ceramics which do not seem to have been related to any other trend. In theory salt-glazed stoneware was an anachronism, but it was revived with great success by Doulton in fine vases, figures, groups and plaques, and one of Doulton's artists, Hannah Barlow, found fame with her incised animal and bird studies. Doulton was one of the more adventourous in this new field of art pottery and was very ready in inventing new names for its products –

Minton pate sur pate vase and cover by Marc Louis Salon made in 1903. It could take months to make such a vase, and the wastage rate was high. Thus the high prices paid them – and today (£2,000-3,000).

A pair of bisque figures of about 1895 of exceptional quality, and not trying to copy Meissen. Because of the delicate floral extras these were usually enclosed in glass domes.

Impasto, Silicon, Carrara, Marqueterie and Chine (in which the ware was impressed with various fabrics to give an interesting texture and pattern).

Salt-glazed ware was an interesting echo of the earlier so-called gin-flasks, made by Doulton when the firm was Doulton & Watts, as well as by other manufacturers, between about 1820 and 1856. These were portrait flasks, sometimes a full figure, sometimes just a head, usually with the personages named and often marked with the name of the manufacturer and of wine and spirit merchants. They have a surrealist air, and bear an uncanny resemblance to the salt-glaze stoneware produced by the Martin Brothers who worked from 1873 to 1914 and may well be considered the first of the studio potters.

The Martin Brothers produced oddities – monstrous birds with detachable heads, ungainly vases, vessels painted with designs that are half nightmare and half memories of Japan. Compared with them the other art potteries are refined to the point of insipidness.

Whereas Martinware looks as though it has been made on the spur of the moment in response to some peculiar whim – though of course it was not – *pâte-sur-pâte* looks expensive, and was expensive. Cameo-type designs were built up layer by layer by applications of creamy slip on Parian, and when enough had been applied the cameo was carved before firing. If all had gone well the decoration on the Parian was semi-transparent. Some of the more spectacular pieces could take months to complete, and there was a high wastage rate. The process was brought to England by Marc Louis Solon in about 1870, and he trained others in the technique, introducing them to refinements characteristic of the best French ceramics.

Throughout the eighteenth and nineteenth centuries the best continental ceramics influenced the British potters. Sèvres, Meissen and Capodimonte had royal patronage, giving them advantages over the English factories, and giving them a ready market for the best and most expensive objects that could be made regardless of expense. Sèvres started in 1756, a good deal later than other major manufacturers such as Meissen, and although between 1720 and 1750 Meissen was the dominating force in European porcelain gradually Sèvres took over, influencing styles all over Europe. Many of the prized products of the great English factories such as Worcester are interpretations of the Sèvres *grandes machines*. The influence continued throughout the nineteenth century on lesser makers, the result being neither one thing nor the other, a bastardised Frenchification.

There was one area where Britain was to make a particularly important contribution – art pottery.

The volatility of antiques, near-antiques and collectables, is something that makes collecting – and dealing – endlessly fascinating and sometimes mind-boggling. It is almost inconceivable that a mass-produced novelty such as a fairing should in the early 1970s fetch over £1,000 at auction and yet a marvellous piece of studio pottery obtain only a fraction of this. In 1971 a large Moorcroft vase of c1893 sold for £42 ($73); a Bretby jardinière sold in March 1971 for £48 ($84); a large Ruskin vase sold for £24 ($42) in the same year.

A group of saltglaze flasks of a surprisingly wide period, from Lord John Russell on the left (c.1832) through the Edwardian prime minister Asquith, a solid piece 'Who are you?' Lord Brongham, Prince Albert, and an early Victorian comic figure. Many patterns were involved in this trade, the most famous being Doulton.

In the 1920s and 1930s there was a big demand for unpretentious country-style pottery that was cheap and matched the chintz curtains.

There are a handful of major names in art pottery, and they each produced something distinctive – so distinctive that it has taken more than sixty years for their qualities to be fully appreciated. When so many fields of collecting are limited for those of modest means because of rocketing prices, named art pottery offers immense scope, one of the reasons being is that it is not always recognised for what it is.

One of the least-known but most important is Linthorpe, named after a village near Middlesbrough. One of the founders was Christopher Dresser, who is at present regarded as the most important designer of the period and whose creations in all mediums fetch high prices. The firm started in 1879, and almost all pieces are fully marked, and in pottery, using an original streaky glaze in a range of somewhat dull blues, browns and greens. Some vessels were innovative, and some splendid; some went wrong. Linthorpe ceased production in 1889, and was briefly revived in the following year, but the last recorded serial number, 4,196, indicates that somewhere about, unobserved and sleeping, is a lot of Linthorpe pottery.

Linthorpe influenced other potteries, especially Ault and Bretby. Bretby began in 1883 and was joined by exiles from Linthorpe. The designers were greatly influenced by art-nouveau pewter, even to the extent of glazing on medallions to imitate the enamelling that decorated the pewter. The founders of Bretby broke up and one of them, William Ault, started the firm that bears his name in 1887. Two of the important Linthorpe designers left to join the new firm of Burmantoft, which specialised in a kind of heavy glazed majolica and whose jardinières were particularly successful. Moorcroft has recently been taken up. Started a good deal later than the others, in 1913, this firm was especially good with fruit and flowers in rich lustrous colours against a dark ground.

The products of these factories, all decorative and rarely functional, bear a family resemblance, not surprisingly as the founders and designers were playing musical chairs much of the time.

A flood of arks

Farms and farm animals have always held a special place in the affections of children. Probably pre-dating them were Noah's arks, in use from at least the sixteenth century. These arks were crude, but the animals were often delicately carved in wood or, from 1740, made of *brotteig*, a mixture of flour and glue-water moulded over a wire structure. In 1815 kaolin was introduced into the mixture to stop the models being eaten by insects (and probably small children as well). At about this time moulding began to compete with carving. By the middle of the nineteenth century twenty-four firms in one area of Germany made nothing but arks, some with four hundred individual creatures including Noah, Mrs Noah, Ham, Shem, and Japhet, traditionally skittle-shaped. Some arks were seaworthy.

A large number of arks were made by wounded soldiers and Belgian refugees in World War I. The refugees were recruited, irrespective of talent, to give them 'remunerative employment without competing with British labour'. These arks can be identified by their Union Jacks and Belgian flags, crossed. And their do-it-yourself air…

There are three other art potteries that are a world apart, Ruskin, Pilkington and de Morgan. Ruskin was founded in 1898 by W. Howson Taylor who managed to produce by a secret process an eggshell-like pottery, which he adorned with pitted granular glazes of the most exquisite subtle colours. Pilkington's Royal Lancastrian pottery was established near Manchester in 1892, first of all producing tiles and then, from 1897, decorative wares, mainly vases, lavishly adorned with Greek-style boats, fish, animals and sinuous plant forms, but rarely anything unpictorial. Pilkington had the services of one of the greatest designers of the time, Walter Crane, perhaps best known for his book illustrations.

William de Morgan began in 1872 in Cheyne Row, Chelsea, decorating tiles, vases and dishes bought in the white from Staffordshire. These early wares sometimes bear the name of the potter who supplied the raw material for de Morgan's artistry, based on Greek designs with echoes from the East and Middle East. De Morgan experimented with lustre painting on very large dishes; the result was powerful and original. In about 1881 he decided to establish a factory at Merton, and his range and scope increased as he moved into enamel colours strongly suggesting Islamic sources. In 1907 at the age of sixty-eight de Morgan gave up pottery and began a successful career writing novels. He is probably today better known as a writer than as a master-potter.

Many of these art potteries continued well into the present century, maybe in a lower key as a result of the disappearance of the founding fathers. Some changed their names or were amalgamated with commercial potteries; Pilkington for example was taken over by Poole Pottery. Bretby was very prolific in the art-deco period with bright-coloured wares with matt or semi-matt glazes.

Naturally there were many other potters, and most of the large manufacturers had art-pottery divisions. Amongst them were Howell & James (renowned for naturalistic floral work), Maw & Co. (for which Walter Crane also designed), Craven Dunnill & Co., Della Robbia Pottery (very luscious with bold designs), C. H. Brannam, and Edmund Elton (very chunky with bold raised floral designs). Some potters, such as Bernard Moore and the Upchurch Pottery, preferred simple unadorned forms.

It must be emphasised that this is decidedly a field for adventurous collectors, and these largely unknown names should be kept in mind. Most art pottery is marked. It was a time when the back-to-nature movement was in full swing, and home pottery was regarded as a rewarding pastime. So there can be hideous pieces of art pottery as well, and the worst of the potters were the most anxious to inscribe their names or initials on their creations, though at least their work could be as interesting as Edwardian commercial pottery, which was bland and unexciting.

Occasionally the spotlight picks out, for no apparent reason, a hitherto obscure pottery, and the attention of the world focusses on it. This has happened to the Scottish Wemyss (pronounced 'weems') ware produced by the Fife Pottery from the early 1880s until 1930. This firm produced a range of products, fluent realistic flowers on a cream base, and marbled 'ox-blood' vases, but almost all interest is centred on what is regarded as the speciality of the house – rounded animals in cream decorated with flowers, thistles and other motifs, sometimes with a motto. The most popular is the Wemyss pig; Franklin D. Roosevelt was a famous collector of Wemyss pigs.

Naturally Continental manufacturers and potters were producing work that echoed that produced in Britain, though there was nothing quite like Bretby or Burmantoft, which were provincial in the best sense of the word. No turn-of-the-century French potter enjoys the acclaim of the French glass-maker Gallé.

Pottery and porcelain between the wars can seem an uncharted area, with a few chosen potters and manufacturers standing as beacons. To collectors, the three major names are Charlotte Rhead, Susie Cooper and, the most famous of them all, Clarice Cliff. Their products are, at best, lively and inventive, but they can be no more than off-the-peg deco.

A good deal of art-deco pottery was anonymous, typified by rectangular vases, sometimes bound together in groups, cubist teapots with inset handle and spout, jugs with zigzag handles, angular and distorted animal forms, wall plaques in the form of women's heads or circular landscape plaques of a curiously unpleasant texture, the surface of which flakes off as soon as it is looked at. The 'fun' pieces are too numerous to mention, though many have a certain off-beat charm. Certain of the factories, such as Shelley, have been pushed into the limelight but their products are no better than those of a lesser-known firm such as Midwinter. Many of the firms made objects which are not quite decorative nor utilitarian. There are toast-racks which would never hold toast, teapots which would scald the user, dinner-services so angular that they would drive a hostess mad.

Art-deco at its most stylish can be found in figure and animal work, but the figures of the period most sought after today have nothing at all to do with contemporary trends and fashions. These are the Royal Doulton figures, which began shortly before World War I and have continued in a mellifluous sequence ever since until they now number about two thousand. These are so much a part of the antique scene today, with auctions devoted just to them and Doulton 'character jugs', that it is easy to forget how superbly modelled and coloured they are; often they are dressed in antique garb but they are in no way pastiches.

It can be very confusing surveying the vast field of between-the-wars ceramics, but it does give collectors the opportunity to explore the unknown at no great cost, to determine without being brainwashed beforehand what is quality and what is not, even to discover for themselves minor factories that have not been exploited and are still just names, even to the non-specialist trade. It can be very satisfying too.

For those with a sure taste contemporary art pottery can be a stimulating area to explore, especially that which is concerned with 'truth to material', in which the glory is in the textures, the shapes and the glazes – returning to the preoccupations of the ancient Chinese masters, who were making objects that can now realise £300,000 while the western world was turning out dismal objects that look as though they were made at a night-school on a bad evening.

A magnificent Charles Toft candlestick of 1885-6, valued at £600-800.

FAIRS AND MARKETS

All winter the winds lash down. In the summer the stall-holders are fried. This is the traditional open market, where the sellers of odds and ends, even real antiques, rub shoulders with the vendors of fruit and veg. One step up are the antique markets of Portobello Road and Bermondsey. Then there are the fairs where a three-day event can cost £200 or £300.

All are carrying on a tradition dating back many centuries, for there was a time before the shop when this was the only form of trading. The latest form is the car-boot sale, where the vendors supposedly sell from the boots of their cars, though few do, preferring the far more sensible trestle table.

The open-air antique markets of London have a long history. The Bermondsey market, open every Friday from the early hours, is still known to the old hands as the Caledonian because it was originally in the Caledonian Road in the no-man's land between Islington and King's Cross in north London. The Caledonian market was intended as a meat market to replace Smithfield, and until the 1960s the original market buildings were still there, impressive Italianate towers surrounded by a wasteland. Grandly named the Metropolitan Cattle Market, it never really became established, and was soon given over to junk, second-hand goods and what are now antiques. It was in the wrong part of London, however, and eventually the traders moved to Bermondsey.

For many years, Bermondsey market was little known and the buyers were mostly trade, but in the 1960s, with widespread interest in antiques, the public began to arrive in force, and surrounding buildings were taken over for indoor stalls. It was a rough and ready market, working on the first-come-first-served principle, lorries parked on pavements, little old ladies from the East End with a suitcase containing an alarm clock and assorted cutlery, and occasional visits from the police because traders were not only parking illegally but selling illegally – Bermondsey was a good place to dispose of stolen property for cash, no questions asked. Traders were also obliged to watch out for the inspectors of markets who had the

A glimpse of Camden Passage market, Islington, soon after it opened in the 1960s.

90

power to 'black' a trader. The earliest arrivals at Bermondsey came in the small hours; these were the middle and lower orders of the trade; they did not have stalls. Many of them had driven two hundred miles or more, and as soon as they arrived they were met by torch-carrying hordes, the 'snatchers', who swarmed around and into vans and lorries seeking the magic item that would make their fortunes.

The veteran traders pack their vehicles with the expertise born of experience, hinting at hidden wonders. In the darkness a cabriole-legged something can be espied; on this promise there is a cry of 'Put that down to me' and £50 changes hands. It is a gamble; it could be nothing; it could even be an odd leg. But, perhaps surprisingly, such deals are usually honoured. A buyer who welshes will not have a second chance with any of the regulars.

This is grass-roots dealing, a world away from the antique boutiques or the grand date-line fairs where there is nothing under 150 years old. Those dealers who are reluctant to open up are besieged; hopeful buyers hammer on the sides of their vans with the handles of the heavy-duty torches, especially if the owner of the van looks new to the game.

The enemy of all-night trade is the rain, and dealers have to assess the value of pieces of furniture from which the veneer is dripping off. On one night in autumn 1971 there was a Georgian or Regency serpentine-front dressing-table which had lost every bit of veneer it ever had, but even as a carcase it was recognised for what it was in the dim light and in the pouring rain by unshaven ruffians. It sold for £28, and probably changed hands half a dozen times in the next half-hour.

With dawn the stall-holders arrive, the collectors and the specialist dealers make their appearance, and the lorries and vans have all gone. What furniture is left is woe-begone and undistinguished.

The chaotic anything-goes open markets that proliferated throughout London in the 1950s and 1960s are less common today. One of the best was off Whitechapel Road, where the East End knockers and totters held sway and where urchins straight from Dickens sold their treasures and the smallest of silver coins would buy something. Development spelled the end of a lively market a few hundred yards north of Warren Street Underground station, and antique supermarkets and warehouses prospered as the street markets declined in numbers and interest. The street markets relied on the sense of community of old London. As entire sections of the map were redrawn, as the Victorian terraces were swept away, as even the streets disappeared, these markets could no longer operate, and were no longer a primary source of goods for the trade.

For many years Portobello Road was London's main open-air antiques market, though it was always more of a peepshow and tourist attraction than Bermondsey. In the 1830s Notting Hill was nothing but a small cluster of cottages, and a lane ran to Portobello Farm. The lane became a road, and as North Kensington was built up as a residential suburb Portobello Road was extended and in the fullness of time became a centre for antiques and second-hand goods, with hundreds of stalls straggling down it. Some of its importance has since been lost, rival markets having opened in Islington and Camden Town.

At one time it seemed as if London could support any number of antique communities, whether they were open markets, antique hypermarkets or whatever, but this has turned out not to be the case. There *are* fewer goods about, more than twenty years of intensive exporting *has* denuded overall stock, and, with a strong pound, the continental tourists are no longer such a buying force.

Surely, it may be argued, goods come on the market with the same

A gold, ruby, and diamond brooch. Because of the size of the ruby it is not surprising that it sold for £2,800 at auction.

The kind of modest rush-seated chair that can be seen in quantity. But this design is by Ernest Gimson, and if the product carried a good provenance it would certainly be more than the few pounds of its humble contemporary.

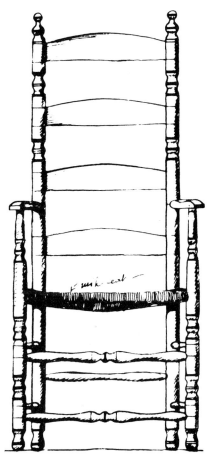

frequency as they did in the past. Affluence must mean replacement of goods no longer wanted with others that are. Yes, but what sort of objects? Not those of interest to collectors. At one time, working people inherited furniture and odds and ends, using them, not knowing what they were, putting them in the spare room if they were not wanted, and periodically clearing them out by way of the rag-and-bone man and the junk dealer. The old houses and slums contained anything and everything, from proudly displayed oleographs which the owners thought were hand-painted oil paintings to Victorian monstrosities worth £5 to the junk dealer and £500 to the furniture dealer. Somewhere someone had something to get rid of. Space was needed for a nylon-fur three-piece suite, and an old settee with a funny sort of legs and a curved back and not very comfortable either had to go, and someone would take it.

There are no spare rooms in high-rise apartments; there is no place to store the superfluous. And the totters and junk men who did the rounds also live in high-rise flats. They have nowhere to store their acquisitions. So a basic supply has dried up. Of course, rubbish vastly outnumbered antique-type goods, but there was an enormous amount of everything going the rounds. The picture is not all black, however. Street markets in the provinces have not altered so much, and they continue to supply the same range of goods as they always did.

Antique markets are often no more than street markets taken indoors, lacking only the fruit and veg stalls and dealers selling second-hand clothes and domestic appliances. They should rightly be called flea markets. The best of the antique markets contain custom-built stalls and are open just one day a week, which enables dabblers to attend. A market made up of highly professional dealers means that there is a certain predictable level of prices except for the more obscure collectables, and there is less chance of a buyer scooping up a bargain – which is what buyers want to do. Hybrid markets which are not quite antique fairs have been given the name 'collectors' fairs'.

Antique fairs vary enormously, from flea markets to prestige events with an admission charge to buyers of up to £5 and expensive catalogues in full colour, so that they are really high-class exhibitions where, for a consideration, purchases may be made. Some dealers take part in just three or four major fairs – or venues – a year, spending the rest of the time searching, buying and preparing. Date-lines are often applied, and the exhibits vetted by the organiser. Where the exhibits are not considered up to standard – even if they are within the date-line set – a stall-holder can find his or her display denuded. Sometimes, and the embarrassment must be total, a dealer finds that he or she has nothing left and is obliged to slink away.

These top fairs are organised like military operations, with the organisers and their minions equipped with walkie-talkies. There is strict supervision of the behaviour of the stall-holders – no cups of tea on the stall, no untidy boxes, no rustling of tissue-paper before the advertised closing time. It is important for premier dealers to be seen at these fairs and to have on their stalls something that is so expensive that it borders on the unbuyable. Such are the quirks of fate that it is frequently the expensive item that is first to go – and the purchaser makes it known that he or she is the person who bought it. This establishes status.

Descending from the sublime to the ridiculous, from Vesuvius to the smouldering cigarette-end, we pass from the quality fair to the car-boot sale – the logical development of the street market for car-owners. It has taken on some of the tone of street markets, including the less pleasant aspects, the snatchers who encircle newly ar-

Tin plate toys

A few years ago an old tin toy was junk. The early ones were crude toy soldiers, but they were then given motion, either by using the wheels to trigger off various actions by fitting an eccentric axle, or by installing a simple clockwork mechanism. The most collected tin toys are those made by the Brothers Bing of Nuremberg. Founded in the 1860s, by 1908 they were employing four thousand workers. Monkey knife-grinders, acrobats, performing seals, the latest road, rail and sea transport, airships as soon as they were invented – the Brothers Bing made them all, and provided novelty goods to order. Their wares included the warship *Kaiser Wilhelm* for the home market, and the same ship overprinted '*King Edward*' for the lucrative British market.

Amongst the most popular lines were submarines and torpedoes which travelled underwater, and the great ocean liners such as the *Mauretania* made in clockwork form and powered by steam. Motor-cars provided a profitable field, with lights from a small battery. Great pains were taken to ensure accuracy, especially in the train market. ▶

rived cars and grab likely items, even taking things out of the boot before the vendor has a chance to draw breath. The snatchers at Bermondsey had a code; if they took something they bought it. At car-boot sales there are no such fine feelings, and thieving is rampant.

Although car-boot sales are usually advertised as starting at 10 am buyers and sellers get to the supermarket car-parks, the school playgrounds, the public-house forecourts and the fields earlier and earlier, at 7.30 or 8 am perhaps. Three years or so ago when car-boot sales began to get into their stride it was a civilised leisurely operation. Then the lower orders of the trade, the knockers, the general riff-raff and the jumble-sale commandos moved in, jostling and elbowing, taking advantage of bewildered householders who had a few bits to sell and wanted a nice day out. Fortunately the hard core concentrate their efforts on boot sales in or near towns, and the more remote sales potter along blissfully.

Dealers often sell at car-boot sales, and it is a good way to dispose of the rubbish that they are sometimes obliged to buy to get something decent. The dealers do well, because by and large the general standard of goods for sale at car-boot sales is abysmal, and they are swooped on by the snatchers who pay more for the goods than they would have done from the dealer's shop. It is known that there are bargains at car-boot sales – and some remarkable finds have been made – but the discovery of a bargain requires some knowledge on the part of the purchaser.

Some town councils have tried to ban car-boot sales, and one or two prosecutions have resulted from infringement of local laws governing markets, even though most car-boot sales are run for some good cause, even if it is only the local cricket club.

Unquestionably the car-boot sale has provided the only new route for stock to get on to the market. It may be replaced by something else, but alternatives have not become established. The garage sale, in which a householder sells off surplus items from his or her own property, has never caught on, though those who have tried it have been surprised by its success. Perhaps it is the atmosphere of markets that people like, an echo of long-gone days, when the market hall was one of the most imposing buildings in any town or city.

▶ Locomotives, clockwork and steam-powered, were painted in the correct livery with rolling stock that included mail vans containing workers sorting the post, cattle trucks containing animals, and even car transporters. Ticket sets were available, together with uniforms and a booklet, *The Little Railway Engineer*.

To give some idea of values, a tin-plate toy '*La Conquête du Nord*' representing a fur-clad explorer driving a sledge drawn by four dogs realised £1,300 in March 1987. This toy dated from about 1909. A more common toy, 'Hullo Ragtime', a dancing couple dating from World War I (when a show of that name introduced jazz to Britain) made £800. Condition is vitally important in tin-plate toys. A chipped version of the dancing couple made £300.

A selection of miscellaneous cricketana. The mug and the jug are Royal Doulton.

LACE, EMBROIDERY AND TEXTILES

Lace and embroidery are wonderful areas to explore. There is a remarkably wide range from the fineness of Honiton lace to the glaring colours of Berlin woolwork.

Much has survived from early times, even of the most fragile. One of the reasons is that lace and embroidery were always valued, and all classes from royalty downwards were involved in making them. Embroidery was never looked upon as the work of hirelings, and when other articles of antique interest were consigned to the rubbish-dump or the fire, embroideries and lace were cherished.

The word 'lace' comes from an old French word meaning noose, and strictly speaking lace can encompass many kinds of embroidery, crochet and knitting, but lace in its commonly accepted form is of two kinds – needlepoint and bobbin (sometimes called pillow lace).

Bobbin lace is made on a round or oval pillow held on the knees of the lacemaker or placed on a frame. The pattern is drawn on parchment, which is stretched on the pillow, and the design is marked out with pins. Around each pin a thread is looped; then the thread is wound round a bone or wooden bobbin held in position by a groove. A separate bobbin is used for each thread; there can be two hundred of them, and to stop the lacemaker becoming confused each is different, either in its decoration or in the number and colour of the beads which run up its length. These bobbins are thrown and twisted around the pins, building up an airy delicate texture.

Needlepoint uses a single needle and a single thread, and was first employed as a decorative filling for small holes cut in the fabric.

Lace as we know it was probably first made and worn in the sixteenth century, though a similar process was earlier carried out using gold and silver thread. Italy and the Low Countries were the foremost producers and so eagerly sought after were their laces that in most countries there were heavy import duties, resulting in smuggling, with lace wrapped around corpses in coffins, travellers swathed in it, or lace landed in the dead of night on rocky shores in the time-honoured manner. Items made from fine lace were extraordinarily expensive; a cap could cost £1,000 – multiply this figure by at least twenty for a present-day equivalent.

There are about eight important types of needlepoint lace, and the same number of types of bobbin lace. Some lace is delicate with exquisite floral motifs, some is robust and padded (such as *point de Venise*) and some is severely geometrical (such as *reticella*, an Italian needlepoint lace). Needlepoint could be used in conjunction with bobbin, and lace could be used as trimming or edging; for inserts; or as an item in its own right. There is a family resemblance between laces, the same sorts of designs and the same traditions, and this is not surprising as the lace-workers moved from country to country, and few lace industries started from scratch. Many of the lace-makers in England were refugees from European oppression. And of course the smuggled lace was dutifully copied, and the copiers often enjoyed a greater fame than the originators, as was the case with the Honiton lace-makers (Honiton is now a general name for Devon lace, though much was produced at other places such as Beer on the east Devon coast).

In about 1800 a machine was invented which made net, and the most boring part of lace-making – providing a background – was overnight eliminated; applying hand-made motifs to the

A Kashan rug of typical design with characteristic rich colouring, valued at around £1,000.

Soldiers and civilians

Model soldiers range from crude eighteenth-century pressed-tin 'flats' to exquisitely painted scale models. In about 1870 the French began producing three-dimensional soldiery. In 1893 William Britain of England evolved a new process, hollow-casting; his first set was the First Lifeguards, followed by the Royal Horse Guards and the Fifth Dragoon Guards. All Britain's sets were numbered; by the time lead-soldier production came to an end in 1966 he had made nearly ten thousand different sets.

Recently the Tenth Bengal Lancers at the canter in their original box made £750; the Band of the Lifeguards from 1899 made £540, even though two of the musicians were absent without leave.

Hollow-cast soldiers had their civilian and animal contemporaries – Negro jazz musicians, gypsy caravans, stagecoaches, Robin Hood and his Merry Men, Mickey Mouse, Donald Duck, Snow White and the Seven Dwarfs, and soccer teams in correct strip. One of the most popular was Britain's Home Farm series, a cross-section of rural life with gardens, sectional flower-beds, shrubs, bushes, trees, and assorted humans. Non-military lead figures and accessories are a virgin field; a mixed collection of people, animals, buildings, and odds and ends was given an estimate of £120-180 at auction, which looked silly when the lot sold for £1,700. On the other hand, a massive collection of non-military items made £320 (which works out at 37p per item) – decidedly a bargain day for someone.

Nuns designing lace patterns in Ireland in the 1880s.

machine-made background was a pleasant and much easier task. It was not long before a further machine made the actual lace. This machine lace is widely regarded as antique lace simply because it was used in the manufacture of obviously old clothes, such as the flounces tacked on to crinolines and the circular collars known as berthas. It was not long before it was realised that the huge demand for lace could not be met by slow workmanship, the steady plod of highly skilled piece-workers. Lace-making became a sweated industry with the workers glad of sixpence (2½p) a day, and standards suffered, so much so that indignant ladies, aghast at the situation, set up schools of lace-making. Most of these foundered, but in Ireland, where the poor were not merely destitute but starving, lace-making prospered and became a major industry from the middle of the nineteenth century. All kinds of lace and lace-type work were undertaken in Ireland, from simple homely crochet to close copies of the best Europe could offer, and if harps and shamrocks had to be included in the designs, so be it.

Lace can be collected for a number of reasons. It can be worn in conjunction with modern clothes (it can withstand a good deal of hard usage, despite age). Small exquisite pieces of lace, such as butterfly or floral motifs, can be framed, laid on dark velvet. A fashion has arisen in America for mounting and framing christening gowns. The most popular lace accessories are collars, which can often be worn without modification. Lace-edged Victorian and Edwardian nightdresses are also in great demand.

Closely allied to true lace is broderie anglaise. This form of work involves stitching round the edges of round or oval eyelets distributed in a pattern on such articles as tablecloths and underwear.

Just as peasants in Ireland were making lace to stave off starvation, crofters in Scotland were busy on their 'Ayrshire' work, widely used on fine unlined garments such as baby robes and bonnets because it looked equally good on either side.

Crochet is a form of lace that involves the use of a hook instead of bobbin or needle, with a series of chain-stitches looped into one another. It was popularised in the early nineteenth century under the name of 'shepherds' knitting' because from the sixteenth century shepherds had used wool to make garments for themselves using hooks whittled from wood or bone.

One of the most attractive forms of lace is filet or lacis, widely practised from the Middle Ages, in which a pattern or picture is darned into a fine net, sometimes using coloured silks or gold thread. At its most common, filet is represented by circular pieces weighted with beads. These are used as milk or sugar covers, with appropriate designs or texts darned into the net. However, large pictorial pieces can be worked.

Occasionally fragments of fifteenth-century embroidery appear in the salerooms. Floral motifs are predominant in Elizabethan embroidery, with book covers, cushions and draw-string purses (alleged to be sweet-bags) worked in silk, gold and silver thread, onto velvet. The best-known kind of embroidery from this time is 'blackwork', designs worked on linen in black silk. Canvas work involves embroidering with silk, wool, gold and silver threads on linen using tent-stitch, a small diagonal stitch. This could be small-scale, laid on velvet, or large-scale, used as hangings.

Better known is stumpwork, padded and raised from the background, with some elements, such as butterfly wings, left free. Fanciful scenes were created in this manner, and there were additions – mica for castle windows, for example, and coral for rock, and figures could be rigged out with seed-pearl necklaces. Silk was largely used, but so also was wire covered with silks. Contemporary with stumpwork was beadwork, using beads in mass, strung on wires, or sewn on white satin. There was a similar range of naive subjects, some of them influenced by calico hangings and covers brought to Britain from India.

An increasingly sophisticated public wanted more than quaint knobbly articles which were largely useless, and if Britain could not supply them the Continent could and did. France was unquestionably the most important centre, and the French used silks and linens with a flair that was largely unknown in Britain, except amongst the growing expatriate French communities who established a thriving silk industry in Norwich, made ribbons in Coventry, and settled in Spitalfields in London or moved north to the unknown region of Macclesfield. However, whether it be stumpwork, beadwork, or finer embroideries on satin, it is now very expensive. A panel of early seventeenth-century satin worked with a design of floral sprigs and insects recently fetched £18,000 ($31,500); a casket of a slightly later date using stumpwork and seed pearls, and decorated with conventional pop-eyed figures, sold for £25,000 ($43,750); a beadwork basket, a favourite form, can make up to £15,000 ($26,250).

With techniques and equipment established, embroideries reflected the various fashions and trends, such as rococo (a frivolous reaction against classical forms, sensuous, elegant) and chinoiserie (which reflected European images of China). The potential of the new materials brought from India and the Far East, the chintzes and the cottons, was fully exploited, and although there were innovations, such as the use of quilting, usually on satin with two outer layers and padding, there was nothing much more to do except to wait for the arrival of machinery.

Hobby embroidery could be delicate and time-consuming, as

Secondhand treasure

There is always some story of treasures being found in an attic, in a damp basement, or in a garden shed. The odd thing is that many of these stories are true. What about 600 dresses of the 1920s and 1930s discovered in the stables of a manor house in the Lizard, Cornwall? Twenty years ago they would have been given to the local theatrical group to use as costumes. But not today. In June 1988 they were sold at auction by Phillips. The result? £52,000, with one dress making £3,500.

Horses in the nursery

The classic nursery toy is the rocking-horse, dating from the seventeenth century. It could be crudely carved and painted, or lavish, with a realistic head with glass eyes, mane and tail made from horse-hair, a leather seat and accurate trappings. Bodies were made of stuffed hide or wood, usually pine for the body and beech for the legs. Its poor relation was the hobby-horse, a carved head on a pole.

A variation on the rocking-horse was the prancing-horse, liable to tip its young rider out and give him or her a taste of things to come. The swinging-horse was suspended by ropes from the ceiling. Ride-on horses often had a spiral spring concealed in a box beneath the horse. Horses with wheels often had an eccentric axle so that the rider went up and down as the pedals were pushed.

in the creation of pictures made from hair. The art consisted of using separate hairs in the style of pencil lines, using satin as a base. Blonde and brunette hair were acceptable, red hair not. Less demanding were pictures made from wool, especially what is known as Berlin woolwork, embroidery-by-numbers, which eclipsed all other forms of domestic embroidery. Berlin was a centre for brightly coloured wools, and these were marketed in kit form with canvas backing and, most important, a tremendous variety of patterns. The craze began in Britain in 1831, and one firm produced well over 10,000 different patterns, many based on popular paintings of the day, and soon Berlin woolwork was used for every imaginable purpose – slippers, bags, fire-screens, cushions, carpets and chair-coverings.

For many years even the best of these woolwork items, pictures or whatever, have suffered neglect, and have too often been dismissed out of hand, even not recognised for what they are, a charming folk art.

Naturally there were rival forms of embroidery, such as Breton embroidery, popular in Britain in the 1870s and 1880s, based on a supposedly Breton group of designs featuring stylised flower and plant motifs and applied in silks and gold thread. Breton embroidery was used mostly on dress fronts. Church needlework societies such as the Ladies' Ecclesiastical Embroidery Society and the School of Medieval Embroidery proliferated to provide vestments, banners and altar-cloths for churches with aspirations.

Samplers and art needlework have in common the fact that they were worked by amateurs. Samplers were made by young children, sometimes very young children. The word is derived from the Latin *exemplum* meaning example, and a sampler is just that, examples of stitches and patterns worked on a piece of cloth. Although the Peruvians were making them in about 200BC the earliest known samplers in Britain date from the sixteenth century and depict a variety of animals, insects, birds and flowers on long narrow strips of linen which were wound round wooden or ivory sticks, thus forming a portable reference library. During the eighteenth century square samplers were introduced, driving out the strip, bringing in borders so that the sampler could be framed, and introducing new motifs and themes, such as maps with the county borders worked in different colours. Samplers were now teaching subjects other than stitching – religion, spelling, lettering and darning – and were decked out with flowers, animals and insects, and fanciful houses and palaces. There was a good deal of pious verse in the samplers, and a fair measure of gloom.

As the sampler became increasingly an educational tool, there was a decrease in variety and in the abundance of different stitches, until only the cross-stitch was used, known as the 'sampler stitch'. The sampler was introduced to the United States in 1628 by a young woman who took her sampler with her, and the form became extremely popular, taking on a particularly American style. American samplers were more pictorial than their British counterparts and had less of a tendency to platitudinous wording. There are a very large number of samplers in circulation dating from the eighteenth and nineteenth centuries. Some were dated and some were not. Dates were sometimes diligently picked out

Old photographs give an idea of the variety and range of Victorian fabrics and textiles. The wall-hanging is particularly interesting.

by the maker who in her mature years did not want to disclose how old she was.

Ten years ago £30 ($52) was a fair price for a sampler. In June 1987 a pair of early nineteenth-century samplers made £850 ($1,487). This is not an unusual price. Why should samplers have climbed so much in value? One reason is that they are highly valued in America, where the sampler is part of the traditional antique scene.

Patchwork is another area that has appreciated very much over the past few years, and once again there is a strong American interest because, although patchwork had been practised since medieval times, its modern form originated in New England in the late seventeenth century and was introduced to Britain a century later. Patchwork was intended to be functional, mostly to be made into quilts, and it was soon found that the making of patchwork could be a communal activity.

A Victorian first

On 27 November 1987 Rossetti's 'Proserpine', better known as Persephone, became the first Victorian painting to break the million-pound barrier, realising £1.3m at auction. It was signed and dated 1877, and was the sixth painting Rossetti had done of Proserpine. In 1873 a Proserpine had been painted for the Liverpool shipping magnate F. R. Leyland of Speke Hall. It was damaged in transit, and the artist painted a new version, now in the Tate Gallery. The head and hands of the damaged picture were incorporated in yet another version, dated 1877 and bought by the Manchester businessman W. A. Turner. His collection came up for sale in 1888. It reappeared in 1964 and was bought on behalf of the artist L. S. Lowry by the Lefevre Gallery. A beneficiary of the Lowry estate put it in auction again, and it was bought by the London dealer Christopher Gibbs. An interesting footnote: on each occasion, Christie's were the auctioneers.

Pieces of different materials were cut in the same shape using templates of card, ivory, brass, copper and any other convenient substance, and each section of material was backed with paper cut ¼in (6mm) smaller so that a hem could be turned back. Two pieces were then hemmed together on the wrong side, and the patchwork was gradually built up. The paper backing was usually left to add additional warmth, and the patchwork was applied to an inner lining and a backing material, the three layers being quilted together. There were distinctive regional varieties both in Britain and America.

It is sometimes possible to date patchwork quilts by the paper tacked to the shapes, often sections of letters, bills or newspapers, but the material itself can be misleading as the maker might be using fragments a century old or more. What is certain is that patches of printed cotton indicate a date no earlier than about 1825. Sewing-machines began to be used in about the middle of the nineteenth century, though in country districts hand-sewing continued well into the present century. Patchwork was some-

A Paisley shawl, more explicit in an 1862 engraving than a modern photograph, made in Norwich, where many French silk-workers settled when they were expelled from France in the distant past.

100

times made without an inner lining, and was used for cushions or similar items. Although cotton is preferred by collectors, if only because it has survived better, patchworks in velvet and in silk were also popular, especially from the mid-nineteenth century, and these have not lasted well, for the heavy weight of the velvet has pulled the stitches and the silks have shredded.

Weaving can be intensely personal or thoroughly automated, and for a time in the distant past ran parallel with plaiting, as in baskets and rush mats. It reached its artistic culmination in tapestries and carpets. Tapestries are sometimes confused with types of embroidery such as Berlin woolwork, and at a time when many arts were in their infancy, tapestry-making had reached its high point. Tapestries covered the bare walls of medieval castles, were draped over tables and beds, and brought colour into a world that was dangerous, austere and sparse. The nobility travelled extensively from one fortified bastion of civilization to another and their tapestries went with them.

Although the first British manufactory was established in about 1560, most tapestries were imported from Flanders and later France. Early tapestries exist in surprising numbers, and come onto the open market at frequent intervals, but by the end of the eighteenth century the demand for tapestries had dried up and most of the workshops had disappeared.

In modern English usage carpets and rugs differ from each other only in size. What we term rugs were used in the sixteenth and seventeenth century as table-covers. Carpets and rugs are made in several ways: by using a technique akin to tapestry-making; by working material such as rags through the mesh of a coarse canvas (very popular in America); or by the classic method, the knotted pile, a technique widely used in Turkey and across Asia, but not so much in Europe because it was laborious and uneconomical and was most suited to sedentary nomadic tribes.

An example of mid-nineteenth-century lace, overpowering and unsympathetic.

The knotted-pile technique can be briefly described. A warp is stretched vertically between the two beams of a simple upright loom; around the warp threads short lengths of yarn are looped or knotted to form a pile. One, two, three or four threads can be knotted together. The more there are, the coarser the final product. Work proceeds by making a row of knots, using variously coloured yarns as needed by the design. Plain weft threads are then woven through the warp to stabilise the fabric. Then another row of knots is made. And so on, and on, and on.

Some antiques are easy to approach without a great deal of knowledge, but carpets cannot be 'boned up' on by someone with an hour or two to spare. It is often difficult to know what degree of wear is acceptable; in twentieth-century examples it is not much. Eighteenth-century carpets can still be found in very good and sometimes perfect condition. It is agreed that from the middle of the nineteenth century there was some deterioration in quality.

The most easily recognised of carpets is the so-called Turkish prayer rug, not necessarily always used for prayer. These carry what is known as the mihrab design, which is simply a graphic design representing the prayer alcove in a mosque, sometimes interpreted as a rectangle with a triangle stuck on top: or it can resemble the side view of a decanter. All the motifs used in

Turkish rugs have religious connotations, and because the Turks are Muslim they are forbidden to incorporate human or animal forms in their work. There is a strong emphasis on geometrical design and shapes, and often there is a series of borders representing the Seven Heavens of Allah. Colours vary enormously through the country, from pale pastel to vivid hues, and the texture can vary from thin with a silky pile to shaggy.

Turkoman carpets are often known as Bokhara, and are characterised by regular geometrical designs in basic colours, often incorporating a medallion-type motif which has been variously interpreted as a flower or a badge. Afghan carpets are not highly regarded as they were coarsely woven with a shaggy pile, were crudely dyed and were inclined to wear out. Some of the tribes had no sheep and therefore used goat and camel hair.

Adjacent to West Turkestan, where the Turkoman tribes lived, is East Turkestan, the rugs from here being known as Samarkand, simply because the western importers bought them there. Ornamental, rich in colour, often in silk, the rugs from parts of East Turkestan are regarded as more sophisticated than those of the neighbouring land.

Chinese carpets are generally supposed to be thick-piled, luxuriant and thoroughly compatible with high living, which is as it should be for they are recent products made for the European market and a carpet industry was built up in the Peking district just to satisfy this need, particularly to export to France. Such carpets carry the title 'Continental'. Old Chinese carpets are subdued in colour, most in browns, whites, blues and yellows, and

A tapestry screen of familiar type, long neglected, but now being appreciated.

A nineteenth-century commemorative silk handkerchief of Lord's Cricket Ground in 1837, sold at auction for £1,300.

although the area of China was much larger than that of the totality of the carpet-producing countries to its west there was a national style, a central figurative device on a plain or lightly decorated background.

Perhaps the most famous carpet-weaving country in the world is Iran, and although Persian tribal rugs have affinities with those of neighbouring states there were certain weaving centres which provided immensely decorative and sophisticated carpets in both wool and silk. The Persians were very particular about the quality of the wool they used, even importing the best spun wool from Manchester when the home-reared product was reckoned inferior.

Abutting both Persia and Turkey, the Caucasus was a land of independent tribespeople before being swallowed up by the Soviet Union, and it produced a variety of colourful rugs, usually small, and large runners. They could be coarsely woven and very tribal, with stylised almost primitive animal and human motifs, or they could be severely geometric. Being nomadic, the weavers of the entire area of south-west Asia could cross over borders without realising it and it is not surprising that attributions are often provisional, and that 'prayer rugs' produced by non-Muslim weavers merely indicate influence and not religious beliefs. As prior to World War I Turkey controlled a sizeable chunk of south-east Europe it is not surprising either that weaving spread into such countries as Rumania, which introduced its own individual features.

During the seventeenth century India rivalled Persia as a carpet-producing country, differing from Persia in the attention given to animals, humans, flowers and birds in the designs, and a number of these carpets were brought to England by the British East India Company, along with the famous Kashmir shawls and the chintzes. But India was only able to produce poor wool, the climate being unfavourable, and carpet-making became a purely commercial industry, with fulsome but mechanical designs carried out in response to European demand. Perhaps had India been truly tribal and preserved her independence she might have ranked with the best.

From the thirteenth century carpets had been imported into Europe via Venice, and a manufactory was set up in France in 1604 to copy them, and in the same century foreign weavers settled in England to make 'Turkey carpets'. A charter was granted to weavers in Axminster and Wilton in 1710. The difference between the carpets of the East and those of Britain is that from 1735 machinery was used in Britain and machinery could not make knots, at least not until 1906. Knotted-pile carpets were made in England, but it was never a major industry.

Compared with carpets from the East, British pile carpets are fluffier, thicker and more luxuriant, with broad sweeping designs. The three most important categories are Wilton, Axminster and Brussels. These names do not indicate place of origin, but a technique of manufacture. Brussels carpets were made at Kidderminster, and Axminster carpets were never made at Axminster, and the Brussels power-loom was invented in America 1846-8. Tapestry-Brussels is a printed carpet, in which the warp yarn forming the pile and the pattern is dyed in stripes of the approp-

---

'Dollology'

In America dolls have been collected enthusiastically since the early 1900s. By 1950 'dollology', a term coined in 1936, had ten thousand serious adherents.

Dolls with jointed limbs have been found dating back to ancient Greek and Roman times, and until the eighteenth century did not alter much, being made mostly of wood. Papier-mâché dolls were the first alternative; there was some attempt at character. The most basic wooden doll was carved from a peg; at the other end of the scale was the finely painted, exquisitely clothed jointed doll of the late seventeenth century. In March 1987 a doll of about 1690 fetched a record £61,000 at auction, even though it lacked a hand and part of a leg. ▶

riate colour before weaving. The pile of tapestry-carpet, as with all machine-made carpets, is formed of loops. If the loops are cut it is known as tapestry-velvet.

Millions of acres of machine-made carpet were produced in Britain in the nineteenth century, but rather less in Europe which was a generation behind in its use of advanced technology. The French carpet-makers were not subject to the commercial pressures affecting their British contemporaries, and their Aubusson and Savonnerie carpets drew their inspiration not from the East but from ceiling design in the grand manner, with large central oval panels, garlands of flowers, and wonderful frames. The British consumer favoured broad patterned borders, fern-leaf designs, bouquets of flowers, and cabbage roses. There was no reticence in the use of colour, and golds, greens, blues, pinks and blacks were used.

It is still possible to obtain these carpets in reasonable condition, but they have not worn as well as the classic knotted-pile carpets (the more knots the better). So far their collectability is insignificant, unlike the carpets of the Arts and Crafts movement, the manufacture of which was carried out using the hand loom and the knotted-pile technique. At the bottom of the scale are the patterned lengths or pieces of felt and other substantial materials used for stair carpeting and cheap floor covering as an alternative to linoleum.

Carpets and rugs with art-nouveau motifs were produced but they are not common, perhaps because those chiefly interested in buying art-nouveau items favoured folksy plaited work and plain materials, or the reintroduction of oriental designs, but it is an area open to investigation as the motifs of the period lend themselves to carpeting. During the art-deco age rugs and carpets were produced in great quantities reflecting the current interest in Cubism and geometric pattern, and this is a greatly neglected area, as most carpets and rugs were unattributed, with the exception of those designed by the Frenchman who revived the art of tapestry, Jean Lurçat. Splendid art-deco carpets do turn up, often in ordinary household sales, and if they happen to appear in specialised art-deco auctions in London they achieve high prices. It is worth-while looking round household auctions and the warehouses cluttered with household junk for these carpets, especially the huge ones made for cinemas, dance-halls and hotels, which have the potential of being cut down and made something of. It is also worth seeking out art carpets, made using the needle by the leisured classes and paralleling the vogue for Berlin wool-work.

There is no better way to learn about carpets than to handle them or, a second-best, to look at them in museums. Many people own old rugs, handed down through the family, and they are largely disregarded, walked over, spruced up with the vacuum cleaner and accepted as something utilitarian, something that has always been there. Look at them, pick them up, turn them upside down, see how they differ from the wall-to-wall Axminster, poke into them to see how tight the knots are – and if you can count 1,000 knots in the square inch (6.5 cm^2) you know you have something that little bit special.

▶ The best dolls were made in France in the nineteenth century, with heads of porcelain, Parian china and bisque. They were adults in miniature, but in about 1880 dolls ceased to look like elegant young ladies, and took on the attributes of babies and young children. Thus their name, 'bébés'. Although the Germans had entered the doll market in the 1870s, their work is considered inferior to that of the best French makers such as Jumeau and Bru, but as the Germans had the better organisation they produced and exported more.

There was a struggle between idealism and realism. Character dolls modelled on real children made their appearance, as did 'piano babies', who crawl, sit or lie down. They were thought cute, as were the 'kewpies' (a corruption of 'cupids') made in America early this century. Early wax dolls were a British speciality, but the technique spread throughout Europe.

Portrait dolls in wax modelled on famous women had appeared in the nineteenth century, and this was a popular trend in the new materials available in the present century, with Shirley Temple the most copied, in rubber celluloid and plastic, all with a low survival rate.

Among the most charming are the pedlar dolls, with their uniform of dark bonnet and red flannel cape, who come surrounded by their wares in miniature. There are haberdashers, fruiterers and flower-girls, with matching men. Sometimes they have a basket to display their specialities, sometimes a whole stall. The best can make £800, and are much faked, as are the French and German dolls. The original moulds for Jumeau have found their way into unscrupulous hands. In July 1987 a Jumeau doll sold for £6,000, but a reproduction would be worth about £100.

THE ART GAME

There are pictures on the market today which cost less *at face value* than they did fifty or a hundred years ago. There are other pictures that have appreciated more than fifty times in as many years.

Pictures are certainly the most profitable field for the forger and the dishonest dealer, for wherever there are collectors willing to pay the prices there are craftsmen willing to give them what they want, substituting a signature or supplying a provenance.

As the really important works find permanent homes in galleries and the great collections, there is more temptation to create trends and fashions, to make swans out of geese, and painters almost totally unknown even to experts are introduced into the auction rooms.

It often seems that Britain acts as a clearing house for paintings. The aristocracy of the eighteenth century collected them on a massive scale; they remained, often stacked six deep, in the great country houses, and when the agricultural recession of the nineteenth century came, crippling landowners by loss of rents, these pictures were brought out for the benefit of Americans and the new rich. There were wild prices, and there were shocks, for some of the prized paintings, believed to be old and valuable, were merely old, copies of works seen in continental art galleries and painted to order, or daubs, heavily varnished so that it was difficult if not impossible to see what the subject was.

We have a good idea how many paintings were imported into Britain, for at one time the government, never averse to making money, taxed pictures at the rate of 1s (5p) a picture, plus a shilling per square foot up to a maximum of £10. The year 1845 was typical: 14,091 pictures were brought into the country, and these competed with home-made products, such as those from a factory in Fulham which made Canalettos, baked in ovens to achieve a semblance of age. Later in the nineteenth century some European countries prohibited the export of certain works of art, and there was widespread smuggling. In the early 1900s the American millionaire Widener smuggled immensely valuable Van Dyck paintings from Genoa to Nice in a false exhaust pipe attached to his car.

One millionaire with a passion could make prices spiral. The Rothschilds were largely responsible for the fashion in Gainsborough portraits. His 'Duchess of Devonshire' made £50 in 1839; in 1876 the asking price went up to £10,605. In 1901 'Lady Louisa Manners' by Hoppner became the highest-priced British painting to pass through an auction room (in the 1950s Hoppner portraits averaged out at £1,500 apiece). The high point of glamour dealing was probably 1921 when one of the most famous pictures in the world, Gainsborough's 'Blue Boy', sold for £148,000.

The golden age of picture madness was rudely shattered by the slump of 1929-33, which saw prices plummet, and resulted in a completely new evaluation of the market. Victorian paintings crashed; a Landseer painting 'Taking a Buck' which sold for £2,047 in 1888 now made £27 6s (£27.30), and this dramatic fall in value was typical of the slump experienced

An oil painting by Dorothea Sharp, an artist whose pictures are appreciating at a considerable rate.

by a whole range of despised products of the happy times of long ago when if America sneezed no-one caught a cold. Yet as Victorian paintings were consigned to oblivion, modern paintings by the Impressionists and Post-Impressionists were coming on to the market (the Tate Gallery bought an early Picasso for £700 in 1934) and 'Giovanna Tornabuoni', by an Italian Primitive, Ghirlandajo, made £103,300 to the joy of the intelligentsia who espoused the cause of artists who had not yet sorted out the nuts and bolts of perspective.

No wonder that those on the periphery of the art world thought it was all mad. Walter Sickert was one of the great artists of the time; one of his paintings fetched a mere

Drawing-room sculpture, such as this superb greyhound and puppies by Joseph Gott, commissioned in 1825, are only now being re-evaluated after the price madness of the 1920s and consequent years in the doldrums. To give some idea of the demand for Gott, a sculpture group Ino Teaching Bacchus to Dance *recently sold for £209,000.*

The kind of Victorian painting which was sold for a few pounds after the war, and because the artist is little known still undervalued. It is A Roman Bath *by Edwin Douglas, dated 1899.*

£140. But a set of Wheatley's sentimental and perfunctory 'Cries of London' sold for £1,280. And these were *prints*, run off in huge editions. If all this was bizarre, it was nothing compared with the post-war scene, when a masterpiece, Holman Hunt's 'The Awakening Conscience', made a ridiculous £210, in 1946, the same year that saw the highest price paid in a London saleroom since 1928 – £43,050 for Constable's 'The Young Waltonians'. If only those who were aware of the absurdity of prices had jumped in!

In 1949 the author looked in on a small commercial gallery in Cherry Street, Birmingham. On show was a watercolour landscape by Edward Lear, who was then known as a practitioner of the limerick but not much else. It was priced at £20. He did not have £20, otherwise he would have bought it. Today this picture would have been worth well in excess of £2,000. There were bargains to be had, even though the Americans, spurred on by tax incentives, were about in force.

Certain painters, especially the French, were targets. Minor masters such as Boudin, known for his seascapes and gravelly textures, were rediscovered; if they were pioneers of a particular painting technique, so much the better. In

1957 three small crayon studies, executed probably in a few minutes by the pointillist painter Seurat, made £6,200. No sum was too much to pay for a masterpiece – unless it was out of fashion. Victorian painters of the highest calibre were still in the bargain basement; even in 1960, almost within throwing distance, major works by Alma-Tadema and Lord Leighton were in the £100-£200 bracket. But the inflation spiral of the 1970s makes it difficult to make any sense of past prices.

What are we to make of the vogue for action painting in the early 1960s? One artist, Mathieu, was said to be able to cover a 15 ft (4.5 m) canvas in twenty minutes. Was it reasonable to pay £25,000 for such a work (when a very personable house could be bought for £2,000?) There was a good deal of honest indignation afoot; the Tate Gallery was obliged to formally deny that it had paid £25,000 for an action painting by Jackson Pollock (the controversy about the Tate Gallery's bricks came later).

Was the art scene mad? Is it mad? The rules that govern *most*

categories of antiques certainly do not apply in *every* category. But throughout all the fads and fashions there has been continuous quiet dealing in traditional types of painting. One dealer bought any well-painted landscape that included water, whether it was a puddle or a tidal river. Another, even in the dog-days, bought any picture which had a ship in it; and it did not have to be a well-painted ship. He is now reaping the reward. The ship portraits for so long scorned as primitive and child-like are as gold dust. All the artist had to do was to put in plenty of detail and get the flags right.

The provenance of a picture is its detailed background, when it was painted, whether it was recorded amongst the artist's works, when it was exhibited, whether and when it has been illustrated in any book, and when it was sold. Provenances can be drawn up by anyone who has access to a good library and auction room and exhibition catalogues. In a sense it is bluff, because a buyer is inclined to believe any kind of credentials if they look right – and a supply of old paper and scratchy pen-nibs

When is a picture not a picture? When it is a Berlin plaque.

Portrait of an antique dealer after a good day? No, The Miser *by E. Von Blaas.*

helps. A lowly form of provenance is often supplied with old portraits, much sought after by Americans looking for ancestors. Named and known characters are preferred to the anonymous, and these can be culled by the unscrupulous from old copies of *Who's Who* or *Burke's Peerage*.

Modern art is easier to fake than the traditional, because the forger does not have to bother with the right kind of paper, canvases or pigments. Many forgers have come to grief because of lack of knowledge, using artificial ultramarine for pictures alleged to be pre-1826 (real ultramarine, lapis lazuli, is extremely expensive), or pigments derived from coal tar. The black-and-crackle method of ageing forgeries is at least three hundred years old; cracks in paintings can be produced by baking in an oven, by rolling the painting round a roller, by applying glue before the varnish is dry or by applying a sharp instrument to the reverse of the canvas.

In some kinds of old paintings a degree of damage is acceptable. Fakers do not mind doing minor damage but there is a psychological block against damaging an important part of the picture, especially if it has taken a lot of time to do. Unwanted figures have always been taken out of paintings, and pictures which do not have enough happening in them are often supplied with supernumerary figures or animals, a man on a horse making the best of both worlds.

Prints are the orphans of the art world, unless they are early and by the very famous. For twenty years the pundits have prophesied a great future for prints, but this has never arrived. Fine Victorian etchings with their 'plate marks' ensuring that they are what they seem and not photographic copies (the plate mark is the depression seen around the picture where the printing plate has pressed down the paper) are seen around everywhere at ridiculously low prices (£4 and upwards). Mass-produced Victorian colour prints,

on the other hand, are over-priced – but only relatively.

The term 'print' covers a variety of different techniques. An etching involves covering a metal plate with a waxy material and drawing a design in the wax. This plate is placed in acid which eats away the exposed portion; this is done repeatedly, 'biting in' more design and 'stopping out' when required, producing gradations of tone. An etching can be completely altered in the making, and for artists such as Rembrandt the various 'states' are of vital importance to collectors. A woodcut is carved out of a block of polished wood: the raised part prints the design, and the scooped-out parts are left blank – the same technique as is used for lino-cuts. In many kinds of print the reverse applies; the cuts and lines hold the ink. Texture is obtained by close lines, dots and hatching.

There is great scope for print collectors, and the more unpretentious prints are more likely to be originals. There are expensive categories – hunting scenes, naval and military subjects - but there are rewarding byways, as there are in watercolours. There are millions in circulation, good, bad and indifferent. Ignore the signature; look for the quality; go for detail well done rather than splashiness or bravura. Unless a lot of money is involved, buy now and research later – and the research itself can be great fun. But even if the artist is not found in any of the excellent reference books it does not mean that he or she is insignificant. The amateurs always outnumbered the professionals; most amateurs did not exhibit, and so remained unknown, but many were as accomplished as those who made their living from art.

Prints can be found everywhere – mixed up in job lots in auctions, at car-boot sales, antique markets and fairs, and in antique shops. Second-hand bookshops are worth keeping an eye on; watercolours may be intermingled with prints, or stuck in scrap books. Water-

Art works are not necessarily oil paintings or water colours. Many talented artists made their living painting china or, as in this case, making enamel plaques.

colours can sometimes be found hidden behind existing framed pictures, or even used as backing.

It is not always easy to tell prints from watercolours. If there is doubt examine the picture with a magnifying glass; a pattern of tiny dots will establish that it is a print, but it is not always so simple. Look for the tell-tale brush mark, and if there is no glass run the hand gently over the surface of the picture; try to detect any irregularity produced by different paint layers. The best course is to take a small slightly damp soft brush and selecting an unimportant section of the painting see if the brush takes up any paint. This is obviously not a good thing to do in an antique shop, but no reasonable dealer will object to the glass being taken out or the backing removed, to see what is on the reverse of the painting. Although watercolour paper can be smooth (known as hot-pressed), most old paper is slightly rough with a distinct 'tooth', not at all like the paper used for prints.

One of the categories causing confusion is miniatures. 'Hand-painted' miniatures often turn out to be painted photographs – skilfully painted photographs, for this was a major industry in Victorian times. Profiles of famous people were also cut carefully from nineteenth-century magazines, painted with opaque black paint and turned into instant silhouettes. The hand-tinted topographical watercolours so often seen in the higher-class gift-shops in tourist resorts were almost all originally uncoloured. This cannot be called faking, but the practice is mildly unethical.

Pictures are one of the few classes of antiques where a fortune can be made overnight. Any research can be well rewarded. And do not be put off by scepticism on the part of others. If you have bought a picture in which you have confidence, put it in a good auction with a solid reserve on it – and spend £30 or so reframing it. A good frame can transform a good picture into a marvellous one.

SILVER, SILVER PLATE AND PEWTER

The dealer in an antique market often sits like Ruth amid the alien corn, surrounded by a diversity of objects, often munching sandwiches with a vacuum flask of tea or coffee within easy reach. If there is a furniture dealer there he or (less likely) she will be polishing some choice piece, while the jewellery dealer will be presiding over flat glass-topped display cabinets, usually with an air of authority. The silver dealer is somehow slightly aloof from the hurly-burly of the trade, sitting confidently amongst the quiet glitter of the precious metal.

Whereas a general dealer can scrape along for twenty years without knowing much about anything in particular, the dealer in silver has to be an expert, for silver items, made from the most amenable of all metals, may not be what they seem, despite the presence of innumerable marks which are, contrary to first impressions, easy to understand and very sensible.

Really early silver is rare and extremely expensive; it is estimated that less than four hundred silver articles survive from the period prior to 1525. Until the nineteenth century and the advent of the collector, silver was regarded not as a heritage but a commercial asset, to be melted down and made into something new, and it is surprising that so much antique silver has survived.

To talk about silver as a precious metal can be misleading. The scrap value of silver in October 1987 was £4.10 ($7.17) an ounce, much less than when the price zoomed in the late 1960s, so when inflation is considered silver is a relatively cheap metal. Why should silver be valued at all? In its raw state it is useless and it has to be mixed with a small amount of copper to be worked. Silver is regarded as valuable simply by tradition. In bygone days it was rare, and as it was used for coinage it was protected, and a standard of purity (which varied) was rigidly enforced; hence the hallmarking, which was not designed as a help for future collectors but as certification that the item on which the marks were stamped was a fit and proper article to be sent on its way. But of course not all silver was marked.

The virtues of silver are that it is easily hammered into shape, is brilliant when polished, grows old gracefully and does not easily tarnish except when exposed to certain chemicals, salt or egg-yolk. It can be rolled to a microscopic thinness, and an ounce of silver can be drawn out into a mile of wire. It can be ornamented by engraving, by chasing (making marks without taking out any metal) and embossing (raising the surface by using a hammer on the reverse side). It can be gilded; gold is mixed with mercury and spread onto the surface to be gilded, the article is heated, and the mercury is dispersed in poisonous fumes leaving the gold

Crown and Anchor

In 1773 deputations from Sheffield and Birmingham went to London to petition for their own assay offices, so that they could mark their own silver. They stayed at a tavern called the Crown and Anchor. What should their marks be? They tossed a coin. Sheffield had the crown, Birmingham the anchor.

clinging to the silver permanently. Parcel-gilt is partly gilded.

A simple object such as a bowl could be made in one piece by using a sheet of silver which was beaten with a hammer on a wooden shape. Complex articles were made from separate silver shapes soldered together. Solid parts such as knobs and finials were cast from moulds.

Prior to the eighteenth century silver was often chunky and richly ornate, and had a foreign look attributable to the influence of the Germans and Dutch. Towards the end of the seventeenth century silver was used for massive objects such as table-tops, wine-coolers and cisterns almost too heavy to move, but this coincided with the influx of Huguenot silversmiths and a move towards Frenchified taste. English native taste was inclined towards sobriety, good proportions and plain surfaces. In an age of affluence there was room for all tendencies.

The drinking of tea, coffee and chocolate created a demand in western Europe for new types of vessels that would complement the Chinese porcelain, and if possible upstage it, not only teapots, coffee-pots and the more obvious items but also silver salvers. Refined eating habits also brought in tureens, trays, sauceboats, salt-cellars, cake baskets, sugar sifters, and a variety of functional articles, beautifully designed, with ornament that was never intrusive.

These are the classic silver articles made throughout the reigns of Queen Anne and the Georges, articles made for eating and drinking. The novelties and 'fancies' were few. That successive generations would take up these objects, scrutinise them for maker's marks and search them zealously for repairs and renewals, would have struck their first users as something akin to madness.

The vagaries of taste ensured that these silver articles changed in shape throughout the eighteenth and nineteenth centuries and sometimes alterations were made to the basic design for the sake of increased efficiency. As new commodities came onto the market silver vessels were conjured up to contain them. The history of table silver can be seen as running parallel to the story of culinary sophistication.

All eighteenth-century silver plate is expensive, as it was originally, and it is not surprising that so much attention has been paid to the smaller items dating from the end of the eighteenth

A Victorian Scottish silver medal of 1887 engraved on one side with a cricket match being played with a Highland landscape in the background.

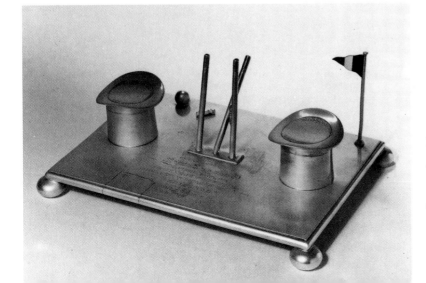

An ideal present for the sporting man who has everything, a silver-plated inkstand with a cricketing interest. The various components are easily identified, though the purpose of the flag in the corner must ever remain mysterious.

113

A selection of antique jewellery and objets de vertu.

century and from the nineteenth, the little knick-knacks, the tiny boxes and novelties, prices for which have begun to tremble as these articles have begun to be over-exposed.

With the emphasis on silver as something to be used there was no objection to restyling practical objects in line with requirements. A plain silver tankard could be given a spout, a simple dish would be given feet and turned into a fruit bowl, and at any time an undecorated item could be engraved, or vice versa (a more difficult operation but not significantly so). Naturally this kind of thing was done also with intent to deceive, often in a haphazard manner. So we have a teapot with Elizabethan marks, despite the fact that the Elizabethans did not have tea. A forger has taken a genuine communion cup of the period, turned it upside-down and added a spout and a handle. Conversion of the bowl of a ladle to a sauceboat by adding a handle and a spout might have been innocent do-it-yourself, but the odds are against it.

It is only since the nineteenth century – and fairly late in the century at that – that silver marks have been understood or even looked at. They have a long history; in 1363 it was decreed that each master goldsmith in London was to have his or her own mark, to be registered at Goldsmiths' Hall. In 1681 all these names became unknown overnight as a fire at the Assay Office destroyed them all. The main mark on sterling silver (silver consisting of legally required proportions of silver and copper) is the lion, certifying that the silver is up to standard. In 1697 it was decided to have a higher standard of purity, and a seated Britannia

Rare breed

The rarest of all silver hallmarks is perhaps that of Gateshead. There are believed to be only two examples. So watch out for a silver mark depicting a goat's head.

114

replaced the lion. She lasted until 1720 when the lion was restored, though occasionally Britannia reappears for no very obvious reason except to proclaim an extra-special piece.

Provincial silver was stamped by regional assay offices, the most important being Birmingham, Chester, Dublin, Edinburgh, Exeter, Glasgow, Newcastle and Sheffield. Birmingham had an anchor, Sheffield a crown, Chester the city arms, and so forth. A small book of silver marks has all the details, and of course the date marks, revealed by a letter in the alphabet. This was changed every year to the next letter, until the alphabet was exhausted or a new cycle was started irrespective of whether twenty-six letters had been used. Distinctions were also made by altering the form of the letters, into italics, into lower-case, into capitals. Or the surround of the letter was changed, from a shield to a shape which is almost identical and, if worn, might just as well be so. There was no synchronisation between the assay offices. For instance in 1700, London (leopard's-head mark) was on E, York was on A, and Dublin was on N. It was all very ad hoc and amateurish.

In 1784 an extra mark was added, the sovereign's head, to show that a duty had been paid by the maker; this lasted until 1890 and is very useful to collectors as a person's head is more easily picked out than anything else. As for maker's marks, these have also been subject to legislation. The law which brought in the Britannia standard in 1697 decreed that the maker's mark should consist of the first two letters of his or her surname. This was rescinded in 1720, when it was ordered that the mark should consist of the initials of his or her Christian name and surname.

Despite the changes in silver styles throughout the eighteenth century – the main one being the revival of classical motifs such as festoons of foliage, ram and lion masks, geometric patterns and laurel leaves, combined with chaste and restrained design – the most significant development was the advent of mass-production in Sheffield and Birmingham. There had been a lot of bad feeling between the London silversmiths and their provincial col-

George III swing-handle cake basket by John Edward Terry, London 1818, 24.3 oz.

George III cream jug by Hester Bateman, London 1788, 87 gms.

At a Market

It is six in the morning in the open market. The early-birds are setting up their trestle-tables, and there is already a smattering of dealers in hooded anoraks watching what comes out. A middle-aged man in a brown corduroy coat dives as something choice emerges from a van. Without examining it he asks 'How much?' 'Forty', says the girl. Her young son aged about eight diligently unwraps a tea-set.

'Thirty-five', says the man; the girl nods, and he counts out the money in fives, a sure indication that he belongs to a modest league and this is something of a venture. Somebody else approaches. 'It's sold', says the girl without looking round. The buyer examines his purchase quickly. It is a tall Regency stool known as a bandsman's stool without very good reason, and is in good condition. He values it at between £80 and £90, but knows that he will let it go at £70, doubling his money. He also knows that if he took the trouble to put it in a London sale it would easily make £200, but country dealers two hundred miles away from 'the Smoke' prefer to take their profit and turn their money over.

He leaves the stool with the girl and goes searching elsewhere, trying to keep an eye on half a dozen stalls as the sellers unpack. There are some stalls that can be ignored – the junk jewellery, the hippies supplementing their dole with odd cups and saucers, the street traders with their transistor radios and unsaleable record-players of 1960 vintage. The carpet man arrives, looking as though he had been wrapped in one overnight – unshaven with a scruffy beard. He hangs his rugs on a strong metal rail. The dealers eye them suspiciously, for who knows about carpets and rugs in this neck of the woods? ▶

leagues. The provincials had accused the Londoners of being shoddy and of using sub-standard materials. They were right. A committee of the House of Commons bought twenty-two pieces of silver in London and found twenty-one of them were below standard. Had this not happened, Birmingham and Sheffield might not have got assay offices.

Mass-production methods meant stamping machines and dies turning out repetitive patterns, and huge rolling mills resulted in thinner quality-controlled silver sheet. The consequence was that ordinary silver became cheaper. There were disadvantages; thin sheet silver meant that candlesticks, for example, needed to be strengthened, sometimes with iron, sometimes in other ways. But it did mean that some classes of people who in the past had not been able to afford it were now able to buy silver goods for the home.

Naturally engraving was a casualty of mass-production, but in the 1790s there came a taste for the unadorned and modest, which in turn gave way to the Regency, with its Egyptian revival, mock-Gothic and Chinese trends. The search for novelty was in full swing. The silver work was often very bold, and led imperceptibly through the 1830s, when there was a new emphasis on naturalistic forms, into the Victorian period.

Silver became a status symbol, and large impressive display pieces bestrode the sideboard, pieces which were once spurned as the epitome of vulgarity even when conceded to be well made. But traditional silverware continued to be made. Perhaps it was more likely to be castellated and had a greater tendency to bumps and nodules, but often it was no more obtrusive and self-conscious than some eighteenth-century silver. Throughout the period there were conscious reversions to old tastes, a revival of Queen Anne silverware so close to the original that only hallmarks tell the story. Some of the refashioning of traditional dining-room table equipment is charming, such as the Gothic mustard-pots, or the salt-cellars in the form of figures.

Silver is the most stolen of commodities, and one of the most anonymous. Some of it is melted down, especially if it has a monogram that looks traceable or has no intrinsic value (a some-what battered silver cigarette case has scrap value and nothing more). It is fenced through dubious dealers or passed through to 'runners', who buy for dealers from other dealers and from auctions and house-calls. Some silver is not what it seems. It may bear a hallmark which belongs to something else, the piece of silver on which the hallmark is stamped having been transposed to something more desirable. It may bear false hallmarks.

Any kind of damage greatly reduces the value of a silver article, and the kind of old repair acceptable in furniture is not in silver. Worn marks detract from the value, and marks ought to be well-nigh perfect if they are in a position where the article is not usually polished, such as the base of a vessel. Constant polishing wears away embossing, and as the silver here is stretched anyway, because it has been hammered out from the inside, small holes may appear. The bottom of flat-ware can be scratched by usage and if it has been polished the metal may be wafer-thin. Hectic polishing can also remove the patina that comes with age.

Unlike with pewter, where anyone is free to add marks intended to deceive, and unlike with furniture where two pieces can be made into one or amended out of all recognition, anyone who meddles with silver can be sought out and penalised, and though today a transgressor is not likely to be pinned by the ears in a pillory he or she can still go to prison. Laws under the old hallmarking acts could theoretically send anyone who owned a suspect piece to prison, but some amelioration was introduced with the Hallmarking Act of 1973. It may send readers into a tizzy to realise that if they knowingly possess silverware with counterfeit or transposed marks struck or transposed after 1854 they are committing an offence; the item should be taken to an assay office for the marks to be obliterated and replaced.

Articles with just a maker's mark can only be sold if pre-1900 and not altered since. Unmarked silver pre-1900 can be sold if the metal is at least 80 per cent pure, fortunate indeed for collectors of Victorian jewellery where the silver content was often unmarked. Of course, the key word is 'knowingly', for why should anyone possess counterfeit silver of any kind unless he or she is a villain? Those who have been taken in by some antique or modern piece of sharp practice can rest easy in their beds.

Although the emphasis has swung away recently from small articles to more substantial items such as tea services or trays, there is still scope if collectables such as vinaigrettes, nutmeg-graters and wine-labels are by-passed. Theme collections are worth considering – items relating to drinking, writing, lighting, needlework, travel, beautification and cosmetics, and so forth. Beautification could include dressing-table equipment such as silver-topped containers, combs, mirrors, and brushes, trinket boxes, hat-pins, etc. Needlework would naturally include the most popular of all silver collectables, thimbles.

Tax on silver was removed in 1890, and thereafter products were mass-produced for the gift market. Silver items such as vesta boxes and card cases were now costing not much more than the same products in other metals, and it was usual to have them engraved with the monogram of the recipient. At about the same time there was a break away from traditional design. On the one hand there were the products of the Arts and Crafts movement, eschewing modern production methods with a vigour not far off hysteria, and on the other there was art nouveau. Elongated maidens in flowing dresses, sinuous plant forms, enwrapping tendrils, all these motifs were ideal for the pliable nature of silver. A novel feature of art nouveau silver was the associated use of enamels in rich colours.

There were certain items more suitable for treatment than others. Clocks, looking-glasses, hand mirrors, bowls, cutlery and photograph frames lent themselves to all sorts of cavalier handling. The best known silver was Cymric, marketed by Liberty's on a large scale, which convinced hesitant buyers that the style was not an aberration despite what the papers said.

Silver was also eminently suitable for the austere designs of people such as Christopher Dresser, which anticipated the fitness-for-function movement of the 1930s. But there is always a danger of regarding novel achievements as the norm. For the more trad-

▶ On one of the stalls appears a model church with an interior bulb lit by a battery. Bits have broken off, and the trellis fence in front of it looks as though a hurricane has recently passed. But anything unusual sells. (It started off at £12 and passed through three pairs of hands within ten minutes. It is now in a shop about ten miles from the market, priced at £80, and looks likely to stay there for some time yet.)

It is still crisp enough for breath to hang around like fog, but it is lightening up, and the tea-waggon has arrived, together with the boys in their walk-in lorries. A set of four chairs is taken from one of the lorries. They are seen from afar. 'How much the chairs?' comes a shout. 'Sixty'. 'All right, put them down to me.' And that is it, a commitment to buy, never retracted amongst real dealers.

Around nine o'clock the private buyers come, pulling their shopping trolleys, looking for the bargains, the cup to make up a set, an enamel saucepan, the paperbacks at 10p each. If they find something they want the odds are that the stall-holder will not be there but sitting in his or her car eating sandwiches. And there are the collectors, looking for something no-one has ever heard of. Some of them try to impart their enthusiasm to anyone who will listen, but this is not really the time or the place.

Edward VII double heart-shaped photograph frame, London 1901, sold in December 1987 for £550.

itional silver was still being made to old designs, and there was an outbreak of trivia such as miniature tea services and children's cutlery with nursery rhyme characters on the handles.

The silver of the 1920s was inclined to be humdrum, but in the 1930s it proved ideal for geometric and functional shaping, though not so suitable as chrome. It was perhaps too refined a material, and except in luxury items such as top-of-the-market powder compacts and other cosmetic items or cigarette-cases, silver was employed for purposes carried out better in cheaper materials. But because of the cachet of silver it had to be used for those determined to have the best money could buy.

Silver of all periods is ideal for display purposes and for contemporary use. The marks on the vast majority of pieces from the mid-nineteenth century will tell exactly when it was made. It is not economically worth-while to fake Victorian pieces. Continental silver is not so explicit, but the figures 925 indicate that it is what it seems to be. But it is likely that the silver substitutes made in Britain will also have an array of marks, including the ubiquitous EPNS (electro-plated nickel silver), which sometimes bear an uncanny resemblance to real silver marks and continue to mislead the unwary.

The first substitute for silver was Sheffield plate, sometimes called Old Sheffield plate to make it more desirable. This arose from the discovery in about 1743 that a sheet of copper and a sheet of silver stretched at almost identical rates, that if small amounts of lead and zinc were added to the copper it was more workable, and that if the sheet copper and sheet silver were hammered together and put in a furnace silver upmost the two would fuse. The metal could later be made into objects hitherto made in silver. There was one disadvantage; Sheffield plate could not be engraved, for otherwise the copper would show through.

But it could be pierced by an ingenious method called fly punching; as the punch cut through the metal it dragged silver with it, covering up the exposed copper.

Although Sheffield plate was made for more than a hundred years (and until about 1900 for buttons), it was never a fully successful medium, because with wear the copper showed through the silver. Improvements were made in the technology; by about 1765 it was possible to make a silver-copper-silver sandwich, but this was an expensive luxury (for the aim of Sheffield plate was to produce a cheap substitute) and objects such as teapots, coffee-pots and urns where the interior was not seen were tinned, to stop the copper poisoning the user.

Perhaps the fact that with wear copper 'bleeds' through the silver is a relief, for even experts find old Sheffield plate a problem to identify if it is in good condition. To confuse matters, the makers deliberately used imitation silver marks, a practice stopped in 1773. From then until 1784 there were to be no marks. In that year a new Act was passed, obliging makers to register a new mark in Sheffield, preferably a symbol together with the manufacturer's name in full; this law was largely ignored.

One of the most vulnerable parts of Sheffield plate was the edge of the article where there was constant wear. This edge could be silvered, but that too would wear away, and so silver wire was soldered on, adding a decorative flourish. Despite being

Group of gold-mounted objets de vertu *including snuff-bottle, vinaigrettes, nécessaire, carnet de bal, and snuff-box.*

a quality product, with or without bleeding, Sheffield plate is still regarded as under-valued.

Old plated objects in which the underlying metal is not copper are not Sheffield plate. Items stamped 'Sheffield plated' are not Sheffield plate, but represent a dodge to outwit the law. On the other hand 'Best Sheffield heavy silver plating' is Sheffield plate. To confuse matters even more the French entered the scene with their version, and to counter them the assay office allowed British manufacturers to impress a crown amongst their marks in the years 1820-1835.

This was wasted effort, however, because Sheffield plate was doomed. Over the years the percentage of silver to copper dropped from one part in ten in 1760 to as low as one part in fifty in 1840. The final indignity occurred in about 1840 when an alloy (of copper, nickel and zinc) known as German silver or nickel silver was substituted for the copper, and being yellowish did not stand out when the silver was wearing.

Sheffield plate was made obsolete overnight by the introduction of electro-plating. To connoisseurs this development was like the invasion of the Goths or the entry of the hounds of hell. The process was patented in 1840 by George Elkington of Birmingham. Silver was placed on a base metal by electrolysis, using a bath of liquid and an electric current. It was not a new process; it had been carried out as early as 1801, but Elkington was the first to see the commercial possibilities, and he had the new unappealing alloy German silver which proved ideal.

Besides making all the range of domestic ware, skilfully and not without taste, Elkington produced massive decorative objects, both in silver plate and solid silver, and he licensed out his patent to various silversmiths not only in Britain but on the Continent as well. There is a confidence about Elkington's work that might well encourage collectors to look around for products bearing his name.

To some, electro-plate was anathema, but to others it was just a medium like any other and Christopher Dresser was not too proud to venture into these waters. With the birth of EPNS (the most common initials, probably, on moveable objects), it was time to look for some other metal or alloy that could be sent up-market by electrolysis. It was found in Britannia metal, the poor person's pewter, an alloy of tin, antimony and copper, also known as white metal. Unlike pewter Britannia metal could be rolled in a sheet, spun into vessels over wooden moulds and sent off into the world without any further preparation. It had been evolved in the mid-eighteenth century by pewterers worried about the new-fangled Sheffield plate, manufactured in quantity from about 1780 and mass-produced from 1804 by James Dixon who exported it in bulk to America from 1816.

Nineteenth-century electro-plate does make an appearance in the auction room. In 1983 a large tray was sold for £1,000 ($1,750), and a soup tureen and cover from the period (1850-5) made £700 ($1,225), with the buyers presumably being fully informed about what they were buying. Ornate electro-plated jugs of the time would be in the £150-£200 range, four-piece tea-sets somewhat more. Nevertheless, because of prejudice, it is an under-rated field, and has not been looked at objectively.

Electro-plating had the same disadvantage as Sheffield plate in that wear would take off the silver surface and reveal the base metal beneath. A gimmick was the Princes plate of Mappin & Webb, marked 'Triple deposit' and 'guaranteed to wear like sterling silver for thirty years'. Electro-plate could never be suitable for deep engraving, though ingenious chasing (pressing the metal into shapes rather than cutting it) gives the impression of engraving.

For the fashionable streamlined ware of the 1930s, electro-plating was ideal, and designers were thinking in the medium rather than regarding it as a cheap substitute, combining it with the new range of plastics in decorative objects such as candlesticks, and even using it in jewellery. With uncluttered lines and an absence of ornament electro-plate ware of the 1930s is ideal for replating, and this is true also of the excellent Scandinavian and Scandinavian-inspired products of the 1950s, a possible collecting area, though there may be an in-built prejudice against electro-plate that will take a long time to allay.

Pewter was the poor person's silver long before the later compromises were devised, and for hundreds of years table ware made in silver was also made in pewter. Pewter is an alloy consisting mainly of tin, the best containing copper and bismuth, the worst containing lead, so that the plates and drinking vessels, bowls, spoons and general household goods used by most people were dangerous. In the sixteenth century a more decorative type of pewter was developed on the Continent, especially in France and Germany, called display pewter, to be shown on dressers and sideboards.

Pewter is cast in moulds of clay, brass or stone, and the decoration was cast with the object. It is easily dented and scratched, and worn or damaged pieces were recycled, sometimes using the original moulds. When new, with a low percentage of lead, pewter could be mistaken for silver, and imitation silver marks were stamped in, to the indignation of the Pewterers' Company which tried to keep a strict control over its members, obliging them to register 'touch-marks'.

The glory of pewter is the broad-rimmer charged, a large plate which can measure up to 27in (68.5cm) in diameter; the best were mostly made in 1650-80 and these were quite common in the early 1970s but are rare today. The most common antique pewter objects are measuring and drinking vessels, the most desirable of these being the lidded tankards dating from the seventeenth century, with their restrained decoration and elaborate thumbpieces; these are now sold at well over £1,000. The lidded tankards were made well into the nineteenth century, and the later ones are now worth about £100 each.

Open-top tankards are worth considerably less, and were used in inns long after pewter had been superseded by pottery and electro-plate and in fact are still used by those who believe that beer tastes better in pewter than in glass. The customers' tankards were kept on hooks at the back of the bar. Measures are often confused with mugs or tankards but can usually be identified by markings indicating capacity. Mugs with a pouring lip were made

▶ And it shows. 'Come on, love, you can do better than that. I'll give you fifty.' 'I can't come down any more. Look, I've got eighty-five on it. I'll do sixty.' A gentle smile. Fifty pounds is peeled off a wad of six or seven hundred. There is no doubt about it.

'All right, Fifty. Thanks.'

The trade comes in, moving quickly between the stalls. Goods are taken off the tables and put to the back, for payment and collection later.

'Trade's thin', says someone.

'There's nobody big.'

The private punters come in, picking and prodding, not knowing what they are looking at but it is cold outside and it is something to do on an autumn Sunday morning. One stall-holder is not selling antiques, but a new brand of silver-cleaner, and as he demonstrates his product the crowds gather around him. This is something they understand, the spiel.

At eleven o'clock the place is dead. There will be a little flutter after lunch, but for many the day is over. But they will have to hang on until four. It is part of the rules. Some have barely covered their stall money of £15. They go to the bar for a drink, and a ploughman's lunch at £1.50.

'How have you done?'

'Not worth coming. I think I'll pack this one in.'

But he will not do it. There may be better times ahead.

as measures. Tankards and mugs are often found with glass bottoms; these are usually no more than a stylistic gimmick. There are various theories as to why they originated, the favourite being that in the days of the press-gang a shilling was dropped in the mug while the drinker's back was turned. As the beer was drunk, the shilling could be seen on the glass, and presumably the drinker would make a bolt for the door. An alternative theory was that the press-gang leader placed the coin on the table, and if perchance the drinker placed his tankard down on it he would see it. Another idea is that a tippler when downing his ale would see a possible enemy through the bottom of the vessel.

Many objects have no maker's mark but do have a verification mark, stamped on tankards and measures to indicate that the capacity had been tested by the authorities. This mark consisted of the reigning sovereign's initials such as 'W.R.', 'G.R.III', 'G.IV.' and 'V.R.'. As these initialled tankards are of relatively little value no point has been found in faking them, unlike the marks on early or imitation-early pewter. Many of the pewter tankards seen today which look as though there is some age to them are modern, and at £5 (an average price charged for them) are not bargains.

Far more interesting are the small pewter items, the table accessories such as salts, sugar sifters and other useful containers, and such items as snuff-boxes, whistles, buckles, buttons and medals. Amongst the most interesting are the chimney ornaments, moulded contemporary figures for putting on a fireplace. During the eighteenth and early nineteenth centuries many medical pieces were made from pewter including bleeding-bowls, pap-boats, syringes and feeding-bottles.

Old pewter grows old gracefully, and even considering the amount that was melted down to make something else it may appear surprising that there is relatively so little about, considering the vast quantity made – millions of items. One noble lord in the sixteenth century ordered 1,200 pewter vessels to last his household a year. One of the reasons was that as early as the first part of the seventeenth century pewter was being shipped by the boatload to America (which set up its own pewter industry in 1635 or maybe even earlier.) Pewter was eminently suitable for pioneer countries and rough travelling, whereas pottery was vulnerable to breakage, and silver to theft. And, when the waggon trains reached their destination, pewter was perfect for display, especially on the ledges of oak dressers where the warm lustrous tones showed up marvellously against the dark wood. Silver is displayed to its best with mahogany, satin-wood and the precious woods, but pewter calls out for oak and the rough-hewed, certainly one of the reasons why it was revived during the art-nouveau period after a time of unpopularity (except for lower-class tavern use).

The new middle classes who supported art nouveau in the suburbs and the garden cities loved plain unvarnished wood, particularly oak and pine, and pewter decorative objects appeared in abundance, sometimes modelled on silver items, sometimes novel, as in embossed pewter mottoes to go over the door or fireplace, looking-glass surrounds, chunky vases set with enamels or roundels of art pottery, and candlesticks which, when used, were inclined to melt in the heat of the candle flame, a disadvantage of pewter candlesticks from the earliest days. The most important pewter of this period is that made by the firm of Liberty and called Tudric; in production from 1902, it sometimes echoed designs in the Liberty Cymric range, and was sometimes new and extremely charming, with crisp modelling, delicate embossed motifs, and the flat surfaces hammer-marked. By and large, Liberty's pewter was more successful than its silver because it could not be engraved and therefore made unnecessarily fussy.

Old pewter was also rediscovered and marvelled at, and as there were old moulds in existence unscrupulous makers (not necessarily pewterers, for the process was a simple one) provided supplies for the market complete with any amount of impressive-looking marks including a genuine one dating back to about 1692, 'Extraordinary ware', topped in about 1750 with 'Better than Extraordinary'. These fakes are now eighty years old, and have begun to acquire the patina of age.

Many books and articles were published in the Edwardian period extolling pewter, and even having a good word to say about Britannia metal, and a collectors' society was formed. Pewter continued to be made, and Liberty kept its best lines going, but there was little further innovation. Pewter was for easy languid times, when the sight of a pewter spoon melting in a cup of hot coffee – an Edwardian horror story in the form of an anecdote – was mildly amusing.

George III two-handled sauce tureen and cover by Paul Storr, London 1802, 25.5 oz.

IN THE SHOP

Outside there is a stiff wind blowing and a hint of rain. Dust swirls outside the door, and fish-and-chip papers from the night before rustle up and down the road. The dealer turns his sign round from 'CLOSED' to 'OPEN', and looks around his stock. It looks stale and unpromising, and as trade has been slow, as it always is in January, he has not been buying any new stuff recently, not since before Christmas which in the provinces is death to antiques.

He settles down in his little cubby-hole at the back, and picks up the morning paper. He anticipates getting through it without interruption. Unlike a sweet shop or tobacconist's there is no constant coming and going in an antique shop, and it is the ideal place to be afflicted with self-doubt. He wonders if he ought to look up the takings for the same period last year and compare it with this, but that might be depressing and he would rather not know.

Of course, he thinks, putting the paper down for an instant, his stock is not all boring. There are a few items which he could put into auction with the sure knowledge that he would get more than he paid for them, but the local saleroom would take three or four weeks to get an item into the sale and ten days to send a cheque. Someone comes in. But it is only the man doing his rounds trying to sell stationery, and today is a no-thanks day.

The next caller twenty minutes later, just before the dealer makes coffee, looks more promising.

'Good morning', says the dealer, 'Bit breezy, eh?'

'You can say that again', says the visitor. The dealer's heart sinks. The man is wearing bicycle clips, and is looking round with an air of assessment, looking at prices.

'I've got one or two things here', he says.

The dealer makes a quick mental calculation. How much cash has he got? If he has to pop over the road to the bank is this the kind of person he can leave in the shop?

The man is not carrying anything.

'Where is it?' the dealer asks.

'Strapped to the bike. I've put it in the alley next to your shop.'

So it could not be a choice piece of Georgian furniture. Nor, God willing, was it likely to be a 1930s three-piece suite. And if it was jewellery or silver the man surely would not leave it strapped to a bicycle? But if he did, it would prove that he did not think it valuable and there might be something worth-while, the chimera pursued by every low- and middle-range dealer since the beginning of time.

Whatever it was was in a canvas bag, wrapped up in scraps of newspaper. The dealer could tell a lot from scraps of paper. He could tell for instance that these items had been wrapped and unwrapped several times. Slowly, as if anxious to keep the dealer in suspense, the man stripped off the scrawny pieces of paper. And there it all was. An old brown beer bottle, one of the Codd's bottles with a marble in it, a blue ink-bottle, and a group of old jars, one with an old Boots-the-chemist lid.

'That's quite a rare one,' said the man.

'Oh yes,' said the dealer, unim-

The 'rough-end' of Portobello Road, longest established of the antique and junk markets. This photograph was taken by the author in the early 1960s. Note the superior Victorian button-back chair in the foreground amongst the rubbish. It would have cost then about £5.

pressed. 'Have you been anywhere else?'

'Oh no,' said the man, 'I came straight to you.'

'How much did you want for the lot?'

'Well, I know that Boots one is a rare item. It's in the book, you know.'

'What book?' asked the dealer. But he did not need to ask. Nor did he need to ask where these things came from. The bicyclist was a treasure-hunter, a prowler around tips. And lots of these objects, cracked, battered, encrusted with limestone and other unspeakable things, were the subject of paper-covered booklets which set out their prices.

'Of course, I wouldn't want book prices', said the man craftily.

I should think not, thought the dealer.

'It's not my kind of thing', he said. 'If I were you I should put them in auction. Or take them to the lady up the road. It's more her kind of thing.'

From the expression on the ven-dor's face he knew that the vendor had already tried them out on her. So the man went away, and the dealer had his coffee, deciding that he would pack up at midday. Eleven o'clock came and went. At half-past a little old lady came in to see if he had any old saucepans. He directed her to the junk shop fifty yards down the road.

At just before twelve a Volvo stopped outside his shop, half-way on the pavement in blissful disregard of double yellow lines. The shop turned dark, for the car had a large sideboard strapped to the roof-rack which obstructed the light – what little there was this gloomy winter morning.

'Morning', said the newcomer, 'How much is the corner cupboard in the window?'

The dealer made a quick calculation.

'A hundred and forty', he said. He was about to add that it was rather expensive, but he had paid a lot for it. He managed to stop himself in time. Other dealers had given him that spiel and he had always wondered why they bothered. If they had paid too much for it it was their bad luck.

The visitor reached in the window and brought it out, skilfully, showing that he had been in shop windows before.

'It's clean', said the dealer.

'One-two-five', said the newcomer. 'And that little water-colour. You've got sixty on it. One-seventy for the two, and I'll give you ten for that vase.'

'It's a Shelley', said the dealer.

'OK?'

'OK.'

Three fifties and three tens changed hands.

'Cheers', said the man, and got in his car and drove off.

So it was not a bad morning after all. Even the coffee tasted better.

Something for everybody at no great cost.

REPAIRS AND RENOVATIONS

During the nineteenth century when everything that stood still was French polished, many marquetry pieces were stripped down and given the treatment. Fortunately this marquetry bureau, probably Dutch, remained untouched.

It is very easy to start repairing something and then to find that the task calls for expertise which is not there. So it is always worthwhile starting with operations that can be reversed if need be. And it is always wise to have a clear idea of what you are doing, rather than following some half-understood instructions, hoping that all will turn out well.

Cleaning is a different matter. If common-sense is used, no damage can possibly occur to an object, no matter how fragile or vulnerable. Soap and water cannot be improved upon for certain tasks, such as cleaning horn, tortoiseshell or amber. Ivory can be sponged with water but should never be soaked. Soap and water is acceptable for white marble, but petrol should be used for coloured marble and also alabaster. Warm water with a splash of ammonia is good for cleaning china and glass.

Brass can also be cleaned with an ammonia solution, followed up with vinegar with salt added. Copper responds well to, of all things, brown sauce, liberally applied, left overnight and then washed off.

Bronze should be treated with caution, for over the years it ac-

quires an attractive greeny sheen called patination, which is sufficiently desirable to be faked.

The softer the material the more vulnerable, and silver should be polished with a chamois leather. Pewter can be cleaned with whiting or silver sand but care must be taken if it is old pewter and there are 'touches' or a maker's identification mark.

Probably the most susceptible metal to the ravages of age is iron, and rust-remover as sold by retailers of car accessories is as good as anything, though the strenuous use of wire-wool and oil may be necessary.

It must not be supposed that water is safe for everything. Plaster of Paris and gesso (as used in picture frames) should never be brought into contact with water.

Grime on furniture can be removed with vinegar and water, but it should be applied on small areas at a time and wiped dry. There are some very good wax polishes on the market, but restorers complain that many are too soft and make their own. There is no substitute for a good rub. There is sometimes a problem with areas of veneer lifting. If it is a large self-contained area it is best to take it out completely and reglue. The way to do this is to cover the area with a cloth, slightly damp, and apply a hot iron. This will melt the original glue, and enable the veneer to be lifted off. If a small area of veneer has bubbled up, try injecting a small quantity of glue with a hypodermic syringe and then applying pressure; or cut the bubble carefully with a sharp blade, insert glue, and press, if convenient using clamps, with the jaws wrapped round with towelling.

If there are areas of veneer beyond redemption it may be necessary to replace them—no major task. Veneer can be obtained from marquetry kits sold by craft shops.

It is often a temptation to try and smarten up old repairs, and where metal braces have been put in to strengthen heavy furniture such as couches and settees the temptation is difficult to resist. But some old repairs are charming and do not detract from the furniture.

Shaky furniture may merely mean that a mortise-and-tenon joint has lost its peg, and rather than messy gluing it is often more appropriate to replace the peg. Round-sectioned wood of all sizes can be bought from a good ironmonger. If glue is used there is much to be said for Scotch glue, for if the repair goes wrong there is time to think again before the glue hardens, and if a further repair is necessary in the future the glue can be melted under heat and replaced.

Sagging furniture may merely mean that the webbing has frayed or broken, and that the spiral springs attached to the webbing have come adrift; this is easily rectified, though the job is a dusty one for Victorian upholstery can contain an inordinate amount of horse-hair and other stuffing.

China and pottery repair is a highly popular leisure activity, but a poor repair can destroy the value of a damaged quality piece. It is often best to leave well alone. A repair can almost always be seen. Repairs done with glue are very often offensive and improper. Keeping a plate together by riveting is much more acceptable. A fine piece of porcelain with extensive damage can be very valuable. Something which is damaged can never be undamaged, and if a good repair is effected there is always the temptation for a dealer to sell it on without revealing the extent of any repairs. As a hobby, of course, china and pottery repairing has a lot to commend it.

Repairs to marble or alabaster are never successful and this applies also, to a lesser extent, to soapstone, though some restorers claim that sealing wax can be used to repair soapstone.

Whatever the object, the final choice will be up to the owner, whether to bring the object up to condition as new, and possibly destroy much of its character, or accept it, warts and all.

The type of furniture almost impossible to repair successfully, and which every deficiency shows. This is an ebonised cabinet on stand, probably Spanish.

Aquatic antiques

Antique dealers of the old school are gradually dying off. One man with a small shop in St Leonards-on-Sea, Sussex, only dealt in furniture. Instead of botching a piece of furniture he bought nondescript items such as wardrobes and chests-of-drawers which nobody wanted, for the sake of the veneer. He took out the panels, and placed them in his bath so that eventually the veneer floated off. This could take several weeks, and until then he was obliged to take his bath surrounded by a navy of floating wood. He never had a car or a van – he could not drive.

GLASS

It is possible to build up a representative collection of certain types of glass for very little outlay. Some types of antique are difficult to display, but glass can be highlighted in cabinets and its transparency exploited to the full. By clever lighting, a collection of Victorian cut-glass wine glasses or Victorian coloured glass, available at small cost, can make a very sparkling show.

The fragility of glass can be over-estimated. It is not so subject to accidental breakage as porcelain, though if glass is broken or chipped there is no way to repair it satisfactorily. So it is always important to ensure that any glass is not damaged in any way. Flaws *in* the glass are another matter. Tiny air bubbles or impurities are acceptable in many categories, and were sometimes deliberately introduced.

Be very careful when you are buying drinking glasses in a hurry. It is easy to overlook a nick under the rim or at the foot. Do not buy a glass which has obviously just been washed. Unscrupulous dealers may put a glass with a crack in it under water; for a time, until the glass has thoroughly dried out, the crack will miraculously disappear.

Glass is made by fusing sand, quartz or flints with soda-ash or potash in a furnace. It can be moulded, or it can be blown, a process discovered in the first century AD in Syria, and by adding different substances the glass can be coloured. Glass can be cased (i.e. made in layers) and it can be decorated with enamels or

Two characteristic Lalique glass items. The one on the left is immediately recognisable by the budgerigar motif, and the naked lady theme was often used by Lalique for his highly valued glass car mascots.

other substances. Most glass techniques were known to the Romans and their contemporaries, and used with various degrees of skill. After the fourth century there was a decline in the quality of glass.

Glass drinking vessels were not highly regarded and were only used by the poor. The rich used cups of precious metals. Up to the fifteenth century glass was brownish or greenish, due to impurities in the mix, but then the Venetians found that they could create crystal-clear glass by adding oxide of manganese. The glass produced was comparable with rock crystal, a kind of quartz found naturally; hence the name *cristallo* for Venetian glass. Today 'crystal' glass simply means good-quality hand-blown glass as opposed to mass-produced electrically blown glass.

The collector is more likely to come across Roman glass than Venetian glass. Early Venetian glass was utilitarian and simple but, influenced by shapes in contemporary silver, it became more elaborate and sophisticated, and was so fragile that it could not be engraved except by the delicate use of a diamond point. It was eagerly sought after all over Europe. With the decline of Venice as a major power the workers migrated, especially to Germany, Bohemia and Holland.

English glass was not highly rated; nor was French glass, though Venetian glass-workers had moved there too. But in 1674 George Ravenscroft introduced lead into his glass. Before then soda glass was used; this was cloudy, broke easily and deteriorated with age. The glory of English glass of the eighteenth century was the drinking glass. This might appear to be a narrow field, but there is immense variety, and the connoisseurs of drinking glasses are connoisseurs indeed. These are not glasses to be put on a shelf and whisked over every so often with a feather-duster. A better place for them is a locked cabinet or a bank.

There are more than a dozen different types of stem, and these are subdivided. The stems can have protuberances known as knops, and these knobs come in various shapes and sizes, and have their own names. Amongst the most delightful of the stem shapes is the air twist, spirals of air enclosed in the stem, made by puncturing the molten glass before the drawing and twisting process. Sometimes opaque white glass was introduced into twist stems, with dazzling effect. Then there are the bowl shapes, each of which has its specialist collectors.

The bowls could be plain or decorated; engraving was done using a copper wheel and an abrasive, or using a diamond point, or by stippling (making a pattern of tiny dots). The engraving could be purely decorative, informative (a glass bowl engraved with an apple meant it was for cider) or political. It could be subversive, as in what are known as Jacobite glasses of the 1720-50 period, made for those who supported the Stuart cause and especially Bonny Prince Charlie. As much of this work was done by amateurs, Jacobite glass is very vulnerable to faking. It might be a genuine glass, with an engraved message added two centuries later. An imperfect set of wine glasses with a Jacobite message made £6,000 ($10,500) in July 1987 at Sotheby's. In the same sale an early glass of about 1700 of undoubted genuineness made £2,600 ($4,550).

An early bottle dated 1755, with the typical seal. Glass was very expensive and not a throwaway item, and were custom-made for the user. Wines and spirits were filled from barrels into the owner's bottles.

Any empties?

Everything is collectable. Jars of rusty nails? Yes. Old milk bottles? Yes – a man in Surbiton has more than 2,500.

It takes a brave person to venture into these waters. Glass does not age like other substances. As with other antiques, there is no substitute to handling genuine glasses to get the feel of them. Is the rim of the bowl too sharp to the touch? Is there something wrong with the proportions? Could this mean that someone has taken a glass with a chip in the rim and ground it down? And could this plain uncluttered glass which looks right be not 280 years old, but maybe 50, and made in Czechoslovakia? Why Czechoslovakia? Because the modern state of Czechoslovakia contains Bohemia, which in the nineteenth century had the biggest glass-works in the world.

Towards the end of the eighteenth century the forms of drinking glasses became heavier, and the light style of cutting gave way to a kind of furrowing, with diamond shapes in high relief. Another fifty years on and these became 'prickly monstrosities'; there was a frenzied desire to cut and slice every glass surface. This became the English speciality, cut glass, so sharp that it reflected every ray of light and could do the careless drinker an injury.

Decanters took the same path. Very simple to start with, with a globe base and a long narrow stem, then adopting polygonal forms with sharp-cut facets and stoppers to match. Decanters were status symbols, because decanting of wine was not widely understood amongst the rising middle-classes who had their newly acquired coats-of-arms on their glasses and engraved labels on their decanters to show that they only had the best. The most unusually shaped decanter was the ship's decanter. These have large bulging bases, the body tapering to an ordinary neck, so that they have the appearance of half-collapsed balloons. Despite their name, they were by no means used exclusively at sea.

Another innovation was the introduction of glass rings – one, two, three or four – round the top of the neck of the decanter. These were not just for decoration. Drinkers, especially if they were not quite sober, found it difficult to hold a full decanter by the neck, as the hand slid up and the vessel crashed to the ground. The rings prevented disaster. Sometimes decanters were made of coloured glass, especially opaque white and blue, and the enamelled decanters are very desirable.

Sometimes decanters have a cloudy stain inside, and there is nothing more difficult to get at than the interior of a decanter. This stain is caused by damp or the dregs of long-drunk wine. The most drastic treatment is using a weak solution of nitric or hydrochloric acid, but this must be treated with respect as careless handling can result in nasty burns. This acid takes off the top layer of the glass. More orthodox is the use of ammonia or vinegar, or the old-fashioned sand-and-water or lead-shot-and-water treatment, which involves shaking the mixture vigorously in the decanter. The aim of this is to wear away the cloudy level of glass, but it can fail, so if a decanter is purchased with this ugly discolouration there is no guarantee of a cure.

The stopper of a decanter should be a good fit. Some unscrupulous dealers maintain that a little play between stopper and neck does not matter, but it does. Never take a stopper on trust; the bottom of a stopper is very vulnerable to damage, though a tiny chip is acceptable. Even in impulse buying always take the stopper out of a decanter. It may look right, but it may be too small and wedged into the neck with a strip of paper. Most dealers keep a stock of decanter stoppers, and if they have decanters with missing stoppers they may find one of the right size but in the wrong style.

Even the right stopper can jam in a decanter, and this can be infuriating. One tried and tested method of removing a jammed stopper is to use a mixture of glycerine, salt and alcohol. Another is to soak the stopper and decanter neck in methylated spirits or cooking oil. A sharp tap with another piece of glass might do the trick, but is risky.

The worst thing that can happen to glass is 'glass sickness' which turns the glass opaque and is seen as a grey or white film on the surface which, when rubbed, flakes away. A terminal case of glass sickness produces an agreeable opalescent sheen. This is most often seen on bottles that have been discovered by treasure hunters on tips or otherwise buried. Damp is the enemy of glass, and it is not advisable to wrap it in tissue and stuff it away in drawers.

Collecting eighteenth-century drinking glasses is top of the range; collecting bottles, fascinating as it can be, is lower down, unless they are really early. The collector is unlikely to come across anything earlier than about 1660 except in a museum. These early bottles are known as 'globe and shaft' (bulbous body, long thin neck) and, to give some idea of their rarity, one was sold in July 1987 for £5,500 ($9,625). Even the auctioneers were surprised; they had put an estimate on it of £1,000–£1,5000 ($1,750–$2,625). But it did have a hitherto unrecorded seal on it.

Why did bottles have seals on them? It might be supposed that a bottle is a throwaway item not worth customising. But from 1623 to 1860 it was illegal to sell wine by the bottle in Britain. Wine was bought by the barrel and poured into the customer's own stock of bottles, which – because of heavy duty on glass, which made bottles expensive to buy – were personalised by the addition of a glass disc or seal, bearing a name, initials or a family crest. Some shady characters did sell wine in unmarked bottles, but this was illegal. Bottles with seals are worth three or four times as much as those without. There are at least a thousand recorded different seals, probably a lot more.

Gradually, for the sake of convenience, bottles took on an onion shape, then a mallet shape, then gradually they became more cylindrical and taller. By the 1760s the diameter was down to 5 ins (13cm). To help keep the bottle upright there was a deep 'kick' in the base, still retained in modern wine bottles. From about 1730 bottles were made in wooden moulds, and if there is a mould mark on the bottle it is sure to be of later date than this, though we are still in the world of high-value items compared with the plethora of Victorian bottles, often believed to be really old because they are in dark green, dark brown or even black glass whereas in fact earlier ones are in a palish green or brown, known, appropriately enough, as 'bottle glass'. These dark bottles were not made to look pretty, but to help sales; they prevented the sediment and cloudiness in the wine from being seen.

Wooden moulds were replaced by metal moulds. These made

A Webb white overlay cameo vase.

A selection of fine French paperweights.

A Stourbridge cameo glass vase with characteristic floral decoration.

it possible for bottles to carry advertising through embossing. The bottle reached its efficient best with the invention of the screw thread (screw tops date from 1872). There are not only wine bottles, but beer bottles, mineral-water bottles, medicinal bottles, household bottles – the list is endless. The mineral-water bottles come in a variety of colours; cobalt blue is the rarest and is sometimes assigned to Bristol for no very clear reason. The most common of the collectables is the Codd bottle, patented by Hiram Codd in 1875, which had a marble in the top to keep in the gas.

An interesting Victorian bottle which may baffle is the Torpedo or Hamilton bottle, which has a pointed bottom. Obviously this was to stop people trying to put it upright on a surface. But why? The story goes back to the 1790s when the first commercial medicinal soda water was bottled by Jacob Schweppe. If the bottle was upright the gas escaped through the cork; if it was on its side, liquid against the cork prevented the gas escaping. This kind of bottle lasted until about 1905 when it was rendered obsolete by the soda-syphon.

There are keen collectors of medicine and poison bottles. There is a surprising variety in poison bottles. In 1847 a law was passed obliging the vendors of poisonous substances to sell them in glass bottles with the word POISON embossed on the surface. Unfortunately no-one thought about people who could not read; nor about people who kept medicines by their bedside and took the occasional dose in the night. There are a large number of cases of people dying from accidental poisoning. In 1859 a patent was taken out by two Bond Street chemists for a bottle of six, eight or more sides with fluting, so that bottles containing dangerous substances could be found in the dark. As if this was not enough, poison bottles were made in the form of coffins, bones, wedges and skulls, and other bottles had hidden openings or were given diamond-sharp projections. So a patient might escape poisoning but could get a nasty cut.

As for patent-medicine bottles and domestic glass bottles there are really only two categories – those with embossing and those with paper labels. Labels have a nostalgic interest, and are a good deal more interesting than the bottles themselves, providing reminders of days that were more innocent than ours and when added flavours had no E-numbers. Ink-bottle collectors have their own magazines and their own societies. Many of these bottles were not throwaway items, but were filled with ink from a stoneware bottle. The basic ink-bottle was squat with a sheered lip so that the cork would grip, but there were some exotic varieties, shaped as tents, umbrellas, cottages, animals, kettles, spinning tops or indeed anything unlikely. Colours ranged from bottle-green through dark green to amber and blue (the most desirable colour).

At the other end of the spectrum is the paperweight. Recipe: take a number of microscopic canes of coloured glass; cut them into tiny lengths; arrange these in a small round copper tray; take a ball of molten glass on the end of a rod, place over the pattern of glass in the tray, picking it off the tray; shape into a dome. The result is the classic *millefiori* ('thousand flowers') paperweight.

Or take a piece of glass with tweezers and shape it under heat into a snake, a butterfly, a flower or almost anything tiny, and incorporate it into a molten ball before shaping the ball into a dome.

The above is a simple process, needing artistry rather than genius. Under the dome the shapes or patterns are magnified. The results can be magnificent, but it is still rather surprising that glass paperweights even of the classic period achieve the prices that they do. The classic period is 1845-50, the three principal glass factories being St Louis, Baccarat and Clichy, the first two in the Vosges region of France, the third near Paris. Paperweights of a fairly crude design evolved in about 1820, were seen at a Vienna trade fair and sent to a shop in Paris. French glass-making was in the doldrums, but the techniques and the expertise were there. And the paperweights were popular from the start, and were immediately copied by the British and the Americans. *Millefiori* was also used for inkwells, small bottles, doorknobs and other suitable (and unsuitable) objects.

As for prices, in the early 1960s a then record price of £720 was paid for a Baccarat piece; in 1972 a paperweight made £6,800 ($11,900); in July 1987 a St Louis paperweight achieved £9,000 ($15,750) and this was not a record but an average acceptable price.

Of course there are paperweights of a different type altogether, made of green bottle-glass or clear glass, with an engraving glued to the bottom. These could be commemorative, decorative or for advertising. Moulded paperweights could also be embossed with advertising material and could also have air bubbles introduced into them to form a pattern.

Paperweights have a rich literature, and prospective collectors should read widely, bearing in mind the difficulty of obtaining first-rate specimens. But what is wrong with collecting the vast variety of *millefiori* made in the French tradition? Such a collection can make a superb display. As can the immense variety of Victorian coloured glass, which is still underrated.

The most popular type of coloured glass is 'cranberry', sometimes known as ruby, especially to the trade, discovered in Potsdam in 1680 by Johann Kunckel when he dropped gold coins into the molten glass. It was thus expensive to make, and although high-quality blue and green glass was produced in the beginning of the eighteenth century cranberry glass had to wait for a cheaper process, which duly came. Cranberry glass came to Britain and America in the early 1850s and was immediately popular. It began to be produced in quantity, especially in the glass-houses of Stourbridge in Worcestershire. Much was made in small backyard 'cribs' set up surreptitiously in the Midlands to avoid excise duty. These were so numerous that the excise officers could not supervise them. The glass was poor, and the colour helped disguise this fact. Novelties such as shoes and boots were produced; in vases the rims were crimped; glass beading was added; the glass was pierced; and the surfaces were often adorned with enamelled or gilded flower decoration. The gold in the cheaper lines destined for the fairs and open markets was applied without heat by 'oil gilding', which meant that the colour was glued. Over the years

Games

Board games, jigsaws and card games have one thing in common – bits go missing. Nevertheless they all offer scope to collectors. Some board games are very early; the Game of the Goose originated in the eighteenth century, and later ones were often topical (Officers and Sepoys was invented after the Indian Mutiny). Some games turned out to be classics, such as Ludo, and the Victorian game Moneta was eventually to develop into Monopoly. Snakes and Ladders spawned many imitations, and the Victorian word-game Logos has led on to Lexicon, Kan-U-Go and of course Scrabble. The best-known of children's card games is Happy Families invented in 1861.

A Tiffany lamp.

the gold has rubbed away, leaving the ugly surface of the glue, a sure sign that it is poor stuff – but it is still collected.

Naturally there is good-quality cranberry glass, blown not moulded. Wine glasses were made with cranberry bowls and clear stems. The most spectacular cranberry ware for the upper end of the market was the epergne, which was described variously as a flower-stand, a fruit and flower glass and a bon-bon stand. It was designed as a centrepiece for a table, and could combine candleholders, lustre drops, hanging baskets and a variety of vases. The most common type consists of a range of fluted glasses fanning out from a central base. These vases, because of their fragility, were usually set in metal holders.

It is remarkable how many of these epergnes have survived intact, though naturally there has been some jiggery-pokery, with broken elements replaced and nibbled or chipped rims filed off. One of the reasons for the high survival rate is that, as with very large mirrors, many dealers would rather not have anything to do with them on account of their vulnerability, and those who do, bearing in mind an investment of at least £150-£200, take special care with them. Taking into account the value of the Victorian pound against ours, epergnes are cheaper now than when they first were retailed at up to £25.

Some of the most attractive cranberry comes in the form of oil-lamp funnels and shades, and gas-light shades, where the rich colour produces pleasing lighting effects. Some of the novelties have a certain charm, and the hats are pursued with vigour. Bowlers, top-hats, clown's hats, witch's hats with an added band of clear glass, all were made in England and America, and moulds intended for ink-wells were brought into service for the hat-making industry.

Cranberry glass is being produced today, and it is often difficult to ascertain whether a piece of cranberry is modern or not. And the same applies to a kind of glass called Mary Gregory – supposedly named after a spinster who loved children and worked for the Boston Sandwich Glass Company of America. She must have had a very high work rate, turning out tens of thousands, maybe hundreds of thousands, of jugs, vases, dishes, plaques, tumblers and indeed anything with a surface, painted in enamel with young children cavorting about, catching butterflies, flying kites, playing ball and behaving in a typical mid-Victorian manner. The truth is less romantic. The glass was produced in bulk in Bohemia and exported to Britain and America, where it was taken up at about the same time as cranberry glass made its appearance. There are two kinds of Mary Gregory glass; either the enamelling is in plain white, or further colours are added, giving a minimal flesh tone. Sets of glasses were made, each one bearing a different decoration.

Unlike cranberry, the creation of a Mary Gregory piece needs a certain amount of expertise, someone who could enamel a life-like picture. So collectors should ignore the glass, and examine the enamelling closely with the help of a magnifying glass. If it is well-modelled and good quality, does it matter whether it was produced in Bohemia in the mid-nineteenth century or Tyneside fifty years later?

Mary Gregory glass is a finite field. This cannot be said of what was called art glass. By the last quarter of the nineteenth century glass technology had reached a high pitch. Almost any colour could be made by introducing foreign substances into the mix, and glass could be moulded, forced and contorted into every imagined shape. Coloured glass was imported from most countries in Europe; British glass was sent there and to America; and America, which had the largest glass industry in the world, was sending glass back, glass which was good enough to be identified on the base with a paper label. Otherwise most of it was anonymous, especially that at the bottom of the market, the pressed glass made in ill-fitting moulds and gaudily coloured – the carnival glass made for fairs, usually a vivid orange but in most other colours too (purple being a favourite), and the Vaseline glass (which was oily, hence the name).

Carnival glass is extremely popular. It is still very cheap. Even elaborate pieces such as boats retail at less than £20; simpler items can be bought for £5 or so. Carnival glass is what it purports to be. It has its collectors, its collectors' circles, and its newsletters. The same interest is not excited by some of the other coloured glass. Agate glass, also called slag glass, mosaic glass or end-of-day glass, is purple with white or grey veins running through it. It is sometimes called end-of-day glass because it was popularly believed that it was made from waste materials collected up at the end of the working day. One manufacturer decided to call it vitro-porcelain for reasons best known to himself.

Amberina glass is two-toned with air bubbles; bronze glass is as one would imagine; Burmese glass is greeny-yellow shading to pink and favoured by Queen Victoria (so the makers called it Queen's Burmese); candy stripe glass has bands of alternating plain and coloured glass; cobalt-blue glass is so dense that it can be mistaken for porcelain; iridescent glass has the sheen of a soap bubble; and opaline glass could be opaque white, semi-opaque 'milk-and-water' or the palest of pastel pinks and blues. All these, and more, could be decorated, enamelled, pinched, pierced, cut and crimped. Sometimes they were painted with unfired colours, which over the years have shown a tendency to chip off. But it is a very wide, uncharted and interesting area, because some of this coloured glass is very good indeed, and it can be displayed in a number of ways, contrasting it with clear glass, spotlighted, mingling the opaque with the transparent. The plain glass is probably of better quality than the decorated, being intended for the more refined home. The larger items such as plant-holders are more desirable than the novelties or the ordinary vases. A preponderance of vases can drag a collection down.

The best of this coloured glass is layered, i.e. made in two or more layers of different colours. Sometimes the top layer is cut into to reveal the second layer. The ultimate in layered glass (or cased glass) is cameo glass. This is art for art's sake with a vengeance. Choice pieces could take years to complete, and might never leave their place of origin, being retained by the manufacturers to show what they could do and that they did not always bow to commercial pressures. A quality dealer could go through his or her working life without coming across a piece of top-quality

French art glass by Daum and Monart.

Pin-ups padlocked

In 1974 Christie's sold a set of ten Pirelli calendars, noted for their array of pin-ups. In 1964, 35,000 were issued; in 1974 43,000 (using a total of sixty models). One man was so concerned about the security of his 1973 calendar that he kept it in a padlocked glass-fronted frame.

Sports memorabilia

Apart from golf and cricket what other sports are rich in memorabilia? Surprisingly, material relating to football is thin, except for programmes, especially those of Cup Finals. Modern football began in 1862; thirty years later attendances at Cup Finals were approaching fifty thousand. Many toys and games were made with a footballing interest, the most popular being blow-football. Novelties were made but were of poor quality, unlike for sports such as tennis and croquet where there are fine-art objects – statuettes in Parian china, glass vases with enamelled tennis players, pendants in the form of rackets, and silver cutlery with the handles in the form of rackets.

Early rackets were collected, but 'early' is relative as lawn tennis, then called 'Sphairistiké', was not invented until 1873. The games of rackets and real tennis have great antiquity. The long-handled racket was invented in about 1500, and until about 1700 the stringing was diagonal. Only in 1875 were rackets strengthened by threading the cross-strings through the main-strings.

There is a big demand for croquet sets (mainly to play with) and also equipment used in the Scottish sport of curling, sometimes made in miniature as ornaments, whisky advertisements and paperweights. Rowing memorabilia is considerable, ranging from presentation oars and sculling blades, which at £50-£200 must be undervalued, to Royal Doulton three-handled loving cups, drinking vessels, Coalport commemorative plates, and a wealth of material related to the Boat Race and the social side of rowing.

Boxing memorabilia includes posters, statuettes and signed photographs. Early contest bills were on printed silk, and ▶

cameo glass – just as a picture dealer could spend a lifetime in the trade and never handle a Turner.

But cameo glass is really what the antique trade is all about. There is no substitute for quality, and as in many other types of antique there is a chasm between the first-rate and the second-rate pieces, even though the second-rate are still a world away from the ordinary mass-produced work.

What exactly is cameo glass? In its simplest form, cameo glass is a relief carved in glass through a surface layer of white fused onto a darker ground. The most famous example is the Portland Vase, made at Alexandria in about 50BC, brought to England in 1770, lent to the British Museum in 1810 and smashed by a lunatic in 1845. Fortunately Josiah Wedgwood had made copies of the vase in the years 1786-90, and with the aid of one of these copies the original Portland Vase was restored.

Wedgwood's copy was not glass, however, and for workers in this medium the Portland Vase was a challenge. One glass-maker offered a prize of £1,000 to anyone who could produce the Wedgwood replica in glass. The challenge was taken up; it was completed in 1876. In 1975 the replica was sold for £30,000 ($52,500), then the highest auction price on record for a piece of glass.

Many of the important pieces of cameo glass are signed and dated. The most famous maker was Thomas Webb, and in 1887 he applied for a patent 'to produce a novel and highly ornamental effect in glass, viz. an imitation of old carved ivory'. This was a retrograde step. To simulate ivory the glass was tinted, and the stark purity of the white glass was lost. Short-cuts were sought to reduce the hours of work necessary for the production of just one piece, but the old craftsmen disdained the use of acids, one of the new aids.

Bohemian glass-workers were persuaded to come to England to assist in the cameo-glass industry, and many of the workers at Stourbridge, the centre of cameo glass in Britain, went to America, where the glass-works were operated on a scale unknown to the natives of Worcestershire.

The Portland Vase was both an inspiration and an inhibiting factor. Many of the cameo-glass makers concentrated on classical themes, Venus and Cupid being especially popular, and the designs were tight and academic, classical sculpture in miniature. 'Tight and academic' would be the last description to apply to the new adventurous glass-makers coming to the fore in France, masters of improvisation, exploiting imperfections such as crazings, air bubbles and cloudings, and evolving new techniques, such as glass marquetry in which hot pieces of coloured glass were imbedded in the object being made, rolled into the body until flush with the surface, then carved. Fragments of gold, silver and platinum were sandwiched between layers of glass. Anything went in art-nouveau glass; a quiet revolution had taken place. In Britain there was aghast astonishment. Art nouveau was 'the result of a self-conscious struggle after novelty'; the movement was 'the outcome of diseased minds'.

There are three big names in art-nouveau glass, two Frenchmen, Gallé and Lalique, and an American, Tiffany. Gallé had made himself known in 1878 as a skilled though conventional glass-maker, but found his true *métier* in about 1884, and by 1890 was running a large factory producing a stream of glass vessels, all of which were signed and no two of which were identical. Many were retailed through Samuel Bing's shop 'L'Art Nouveau' (which gave its name to the movement). Gallé demonstrated that there was a market for the unorthodox, the top-heavy and the downright weird, and other glass-makers took their lead from him.

Gallé died in 1904, but the firm carried on, and although the products were still marked with the founder's name there was now a star beside it to differentiate it from the earlier work. Fake Gallé pieces have been produced for many years; sometimes the star on the later products was ground off to make the pieces appear earlier and more valuable. One piece with the Gallé signature at the base in clear glass relief did not look right to an expert. It turned out that this signature had been applied with glue.

Lalique made a reputation as a jeweller before turning to glass in the 1900s. He was fascinated by moonstones, and evolved a characteristic opalescent glass. He was the antithesis of Gallé, favouring geometric uncompromising forms, and was so successful that he went into mass-production, producing a range of toilet bottles and receptacles for the firm of Coty, with a consequent loss of distinction. Most of his early glass was signed with diamond point and numbered, but later his signature was stamped into the mould.

During the nineteenth century America had built up a massive glass industry and pioneered mass-production techniques in the important coloured-glass market. When the reaction against this occurred it was with a breathtaking effect. Louis Comfort Tiffany was a painter, interior designer, architect (he redecorated the White House in 1882-3), mosaicist and, above all, glass-maker. He is best known today for his gem-like treatment of window glass for lamps, but he was renowned in all the areas of the new glass and was widely copied and imitated, especially by the Bohemian glass-maker Loetz.

In 1969 when the author was living in Sussex he was called on by a knocker who, after realising that he would have no success at this house, showed what he had bought in the village for £5 – a large Tiffany lamp. It was astute of him to recognise something that was only emerging as a valuable antique. Of course there were dealers then who realised that there was a boom ahead in art-nouveau glass, that it was worth while speculating £50 on something that looked like a vase that had gone wrong.

Even auctioneers today can be caught on the hop by the immense demand for top-class art-nouveau glass. In July 1987 a clear and black globular glass vase by Gallé was sold at Christie's for £50,000, over ten times what the auctioneers had predicted. If auctioneers are unable to keep in touch, the market is indeed in a state of flux. For some time, the Japanese have been the strongest buyers of French art glass, which is appropriate as Japanese art was unquestionably a great influence on Gallé and his contemporaries.

British art-nouveau glass does not figure very highly in all this.

▶ material related to pugilism is highly desirable, as are winner's belts.

Skating has always been a favourite subject of artists, and there is a special interest in matters related to speed skating in East Anglia, but the sport most associated with art is horse-racing – not only pictures and prints, but statuettes in all materials including solid silver, though the silver trophies are mostly in the general silver market. There are ceramics with horse-racing interest, such as commemorative ware. The opening of the new main stand at Epsom on Derby Day 1847 resulted in some fascinating plates.

Angling is rich in material, the most spectacular being the stuffed fish in glass cases, still a major decorative item in country pubs. Sometimes the real fish is replaced by a wooden replica. Reels are a major collecting category; the most celebrated maker is Hardy, whose fly-reels were patented in 1888. A complete set of all ages and sizes numbers about 160. These were all-brass until about 1900, when an alloy was used, sometimes with brass. Depending on rarity Hardy reels range from £30 to £600, much less in the shops or on the stalls of general dealers. Boxes of flies are sought after, and are sometimes seen for £1 or £2 and fly-cabinets can be fine pieces of furniture.

There is a challenge to collectors in all sports memorabilia. What is a German alarm clock worth with the movement activating a group of gymnasts? (£40 at auction). Or a set of three trick billiard balls (£20), or an old boxed table-tennis set (£18)? Would there be any interest in a pair of microphones used at the opening of the Melbourne 1948 Olympics by King George VI? Someone thought so, and paid £110 for them.

No doubt there are unsung heroes amongst British glass-makers who were adventurous, and who are waiting to be discovered. British art-nouveau glass has been described as looking like 'an exploded dum-dum bullet'. Typical is the brightly coloured glass vase with blobs of a contrasting colour adorning it; or a vase circumnavigated by a spiral of clear glass. By and large, it is timid, as though the makers thought that if they produced bolder designs they would have nowhere to sell them – probably untrue as Liberty's of Regent Street was selling adventurous pewter and furniture. British glass-makers were still living in the great age of cut crystal.

To many, art-nouveau glass is still ugly; to many others it is still in advance of its time. It is the equivalent of Debussy in music, and early Picasso in art. Unlike, say, cranberry or carnival glass, it does not ask to be put in a cabinet or stuck on the mantelpiece. It is a field where the adventurous and perspicacious collector should venture forth. It may languish unobserved in a cardboard box in a jumble sale or at a car-boot sale. It does not have the look of being immensely valuable. And, unlike true cameo glass, a lot of it was made for the ordinary commercial market, for the new mobile middle classes in the suburbs, for those who were reacting against Victorian values and objects.

Of course there was a reaction against art nouveau. It is called art deco, known in its time as 'jazz modern' or 'modernistic'. For some time the two styles co-existed in glass. This is not surprising as many of the glass-makers of the art-nouveau period were still working – Lalique did not die until 1945. How could glass be made modern? Geometric forms could be used, and new techniques could be evolved to mirror the age. Glass-makers noticed the new materials being used in jewellery and decorative art – rock crystal, jade, obsidian and especially onyx. There was an emphasis on the dynamic and on reconciling art and industry;

Four fine eighteenth century wine glasses.

it was seen clearly in architecture, painting, furniture design, ceramics and even book-jacket design.

A group of enchanting Victorian bottles of top quality.

The glass-maker of the early twentieth century who adapted best was Lalique, and his car mascots (now fetching more than £2,000 at auction) typified the new glass – streamlined and uncompromising. The high prices achieved for Lalique are surprising, for the pieces were not individual, though signed. The car mascots were produced in editions. Lalique had many imitators, good, bad and indifferent, some signing their work and some not. As a result much of the 1920s and 1930s glass is anonymous, and no makers can be assigned to the attractive crackle-glass vases, bowls, chunky decorative objects and satin-smooth statuettes that weave their way through the trade and obtain prices that are probably no more than their cost when new.

This has an advantage, for if anonymous art-deco glass was highly collectable it would be faked. At present it is simply not worth-while doing this, so a collector who has a feel for what can be delightful underpriced art objects can be satisfied that he or she has the genuine article.

The influences on art-deco glass were many and various. There were fads which had an effect on everything – furniture, buildings, ceramics. There was a fashion for all things Aztec, the result being step motifs (as in some radio designs). There was a craze for Egyptian ornament (it can be seen in cinema design). There was a longing for novelty of all kinds, not so different from today, and there were people with the money to indulge their tastes, not necessarily the rich but the comfortably off at £10 a week.

There was something new about the 1920s and 1930s. The interior designer appeared, and art objects were related to a scheme, seen as parts of a whole and not as individual items. We are fortunate in having a wealth of information about the art-deco interior and its contents in the movies of the period.

Art-deco glass can sometimes be confused with 1950s glass, particularly if it is heavy, angular and has a Scandinavian feel (very chic in the 1950s). This does not really matter. Twenty or thirty years in the antique time-scale is not very much.

139

TRICKS OF THE TRADE

At a car-boot sale recently a dealer was moving around, peering under the trestle tables as well as on top, for sometimes items are too bulky for a table-top, and came across a trader unpacking. He knew it was a trader rather than a private seller because it was a typical trader's van, and there was a rapidity in placing the goods for sale on the table, as though the action had been carried out thousands of times. Emerging from a box came an Edward VII coronation mug, and he reached across and picked it up, finding it unchipped and very clean, with the transfer picture of the king and his queen in mint condition, without a scratch. 'Three quid, guv,' said the trader. It was much too cheap, even at a car-boot sale, and as he watched the dealer brought out another, and yet another, and yet another, until there were a dozen King Edward VII coronation mugs on the table.

The trader followed this up with battered old copper candlesticks with snuffers, each battered to the same extent. Two members of the public bought candlesticks. Gradually the dealer realised that everything on the man's stall was reproduction. Was it intended to deceive? He did not think so, for otherwise the man would have brought the items out one at a time. Did the manufacturers of these reproductions intend to deceive? Who knows, but who would want an Edward VII coronation mug but a collector, and if an ordinary candlestick was wanted a clean specimen without damage would surely have been preferred?

One advantage of new categories of collectables is that they have not been accepted into the canon and that they therefore have not been faked. If anything is worth collecting then someone somewhere will make an effort to reproduce it, unless the amount of work involved is out of proportion to any profit. Unfortunately not all quality items are intricate and need a great deal of hand-work, and some of the most collectable of items were amateurishly made and shoddily finished.

There is a distinction between faking, and doctoring or improving. If a 'long' set of chairs is bought, and some are damaged, it is quite in order to spread the imperfect pieces around between the chairs so that the damage is less obvious, or to cannibalise other chairs to make up a presentable set. If a dealer buys a set of five chairs he or she can either reject one and have a set of four, or dismantle the five chairs and cleverly build up six by introducing outside parts that will not be noticed. A set of six is far more desirable than a set of four; not merely 50 per cent more desirable, but maybe three or four times more valuable.

Reproduction furniture, often of sterling quality, is usually sold as such, but even then the manufacturers often introduce period overtones by using a faded polish, and by mellowing the wood by 'distressing' it – though perhaps not to the extent of the deliberate fakers who make up a coffer of reasonably seasoned wood and leave it outside for a year or two until it acquires the three-hundred-year-old look. People have carried out what they have considered to be improvements to furniture for generations. During the nineteenth century fragments of early oak panels were built into contemporary sideboards, and plain old oak long case clocks were carved to suite the current fashions. And it has always been popular to convert something out of fashion into something in vogue by slicing off a chunk of it, adding an extra storey, or making two things out of one, or one thing out of two. That, briefly, is how furniture and types of furniture evolve.

The favour in which some types of furniture are held today would appear strange to their first owners. Pine furniture was invariably painted or stained to imitate a more desirable wood; when the price of furniture was governed by the cost of the materials rather than that of labour, cottages were mostly fitted out with pine. Pine wardrobes imported from Bavaria bear traces of the paint-work, and as painted pine seems to sell better than stripped pine the dealers are beginning to paint their stock, then sanding it down so that the decoration looks old, though many do not realise that their naive attempts at floral painting are quite anachronistic.

Deliberate fakes of small items have been made for very many years. Just before World War I a dealer went to Meissen, 12 miles from Dresden, and looked over the old pattern books which even then were over 160 years old. He ordered a pair of figures, which cost him £70, and as Meissen was using not only the old pattern books but also the original moulds, and as the dealer borrowed two old figures to use as models, with some staining and scraping he managed to produce very good replicas. He sold them for more than £2,000. What chance would even an expert have today of picking out these two figures as not quite what they seem? If the highest-quality porcelain can be manipulated, how about the humbler Staffordshire pottery.

Shortly before World War I 'old' Staffordshire was being imported from Holland and France, at a cost of ninepence (4p) apiece. Toby jugs were a particularly popular line; beer was simmered in them, and then the jugs were wrapped in raw hide and buried in the garden. They deceived the Edwardian collectors, and no doubt they are deceiving us three generations later. Wedgwood was also faked on a large scale as early as 1840, and the continued use of old moulds by the firm of Wedgwood itself served to confuse the issue. One of the few ways in which the counterfeiters gave themselves away was by carelessness, by marking their wares 'Wedgewood' with an extra 'e'. The factory producing 'Imperial Vienna' closed down in 1864, but products bearing the firm's beehive trademark were imported from Austria well into the present century.

Sometimes fakes are more evident now than when they were made, because there is more specialised knowledge available. Around 1910 there was a craze for oriental shams, Benares brass trays made in Birmingham, bronze Japanese candlesticks that were not bronze, ivories that were moulded celluloid, seen today as grubby rubbish, but not then. Netsukes made from fishbone (as they are today) were imported from Japan by the crate, as well as tsubas (sword-guards) stamped out by machinery and sold by the gross, bronzed, and retailed as paperweights.

Bronzes have been artificially aged for centuries, and the Chinese were expert in this process, painting on copper carbonate mixed with lacquer, or immersing the object in a chemical solution, though this spreads the patina (the incrustation on old bronze produced by oxidation) too evenly. Clock movements have often been taken from mean settings and placed in better cases, and at one time car clocks, which had a high-quality movement, were put in antique cases. Victorian bracket clocks were skeletonised and put under a glass dome, thus increasing the value fourfold. The abilities of clockmakers are such that they can

Educative bricks

Alphabet bricks with letters on one side and pictures on the others have been used for centuries as teaching aids. In the 1830s the kindergarten movement encouraged the use of brightly coloured shapes of wood, still a basic plaything in the nursery. In the last century German toymakers introduced building bricks of compressed clay. These led on to linked bricks using metal rods (Bako), rubber bricks which plugged into each other (Minibrix) and to the most versatile of them all, Lego.

An antique shop in Burwash, Sussex, in 1970. All dealers in business at that time will remember the stock they had, and what they paid for it!

study drawings of rare clocks in museums and make up half a dozen to subscription. These copies have been produced for enthusiasts well aware that they are modern, but when put on the open market they may well confuse, though, because of the work involved, even the replicas are expensive.

In the early 1900s there were a thousand fakers at work in Florence, providing reproductions and reconstructions. Fifty Florentine dealers were involved in the business, which came to light when the Italian government clamped down on the export of original works of art.

Is the collector completely at the mercy of the faker? No, not if he or she has had the opportunity to examine unquestionably genuine objects, for the real usually has an aura, a feel, an unmistakable something, lacking in the imitation. With china and pottery the tell-tale sign of the fake can be too much regularity in the crazing, the wrong texture, colours too bright or not quite in keeping, the identifying marks too assertive or too mechanical. If, in a series, such as Pratt pot lids, certain subjects are more valuable than others, these will be the ones selected by the fakers – greed sometimes works to the disadvantage of the dishonest.

It is often the case that reproductions of, for example, Victorian

cast iron or old brass and copper have been carried out to order in countries with a strong metal-working tradition and whose work is as good as that of the original makers. Their labour just happens to be cheap.

If a collector is confronted with something that may not be what it seems, the first question to ask is whether it is economically possible to make it and sell it at the price asked. A skeleton clock at £100 is an absurdity; so is a mahogany break-front bookcase at £500; not so a mahogany tripod table at £20 – five pieces of wood, a top, a pillar and three legs, each piece readily turned out by simple machinery. Furniture made of the expensive woods – rosewood, satin-wood, walnut – is less likely to be suspect than that made from the lesser woods.

It is also important to make certain that what appears to be a fake is not a straightforward revival. And alterations were made to improve certain objects, such as cameras, without intent to deceive. Bellows of pre-1895 cameras may have been replaced at a later stage because of wear, and certain early cameras were modified to take a different film, and may thus be confused either with rare prototypes or clumsy fakes. If an apparently old brass candlestick is turned upside down a pattern of fine concentric circles will be seen.

A Victorian interior about 1860, demonstrating the love of clutter and the juxtaposition of the old and the new. Observe the hanging display shelves, a favourite piece of furniture.

142

Ah, it might be thought, the fakers are covering their tracks; the candlesticks have been rudely cast, and this is the way they get rid of the extra metal: these are the 'fins' that betray hasty work. Not so – the eighteenth-century makers removed rough metal and casting marks on a lathe using a chisel.

It may seem a paradox that the best fakers are collected in their own right. The prime example is Samson, who imitated fine continental china figures with exemplary care, and from about 1860 forged Battersea and Bilston enamelled boxes. At first he signed his work with a monogram, but he later dropped this to increase de-mand and cause confusion. He can be caught out by experts because of pictorial detail that does not belong to the eighteenth century, the period of classic enamels. Transfer-printed enamels cannot be laid at the door of Samson; if these are examined with the aid of a magnifying glass the tiny dot pattern will signify that these are prints.

Of all the areas where the fakers operate, probably the most rewarding is silver, where marks are taken off and applied ad lib, monograms and crests are added to plain flatware (knives, forks, spoons), 'old' Apostle spoons have had saints (especially St Andrew, the most salesworthy) soldered to the top, and three-pronged forks, probably the rarest of table ware, have been made from spoons, either by adapting the bowl or taking off the bowl and adding prongs. Common shapes of table ware are filed down to make more desirable patterns.

Here, as elsewhere, let the buyer beware! But knowledge and the ability to pick out fakes and the not-quite-right come more quickly than you may imagine. And part of the joy of antiques is getting to grips with the problem and outwitting the fraud. The fewer people the faker misleads the sooner he or she goes out of business.

SCIENTIFIC INSTRUMENTS

Scientific instruments are collected for a wider variety of reasons than perhaps any other kind of antique. Some collectors are fascinated by the romance of science and technology; others are scientists who understand the instruments and wish to compare them with those used today, or are surveyors, engineers or medical practitioners who can also see a connection between the work tools they use today and those of yesteryear. There are weekend sailors who like to be reminded of the days before radar. And, of course, there are those who simply like things of beauty around.

The instrument-makers were an elite, and even in periods (such as the time of the Great Exhibition of 1851) when the accent was on extravagance they continued to produce their instruments in the time-honoured manner aloof from the frenzy of progress, though the future was anticipated in 1855 when the first telescope factory was opened in the north of England. Production in quantity was obliged to wait for technical developments. The large-scale manufacture of microscopes and telescopes was not possible before the provision of sufficient quantities of high-grade consistent optical glass. Where there was a commercial spur, research into scientific instruments leapt forward. Where there was none, it languished.

Map-making was vitally important. Accurate knowledge was essential for the construction of roads, canals and the railway; and it was important for the purposes of taxation, rates, property sales and a multitude of other reasons to know who owned exactly what. Land surveying dates back to at least 3000 BC. The Romans systematised surveying, and in the Middle Ages surveyors used instruments adapted from those used in navigation and astronomy.

These instruments were not very accurate. More efficient methods were used by the Arabs in their pioneering sea voyages. If mapping land was important, mapping the seas was vital. The main aid was the compass, in use in Europe probably by about 1400 and among the most familiar scientific instruments. The earliest compass was a magnetised needle on a pivot or floating in water, but soon the mounts were made in gold and silver, elaborately chased, and between about 1650 and 1800 magnificent examples were produced.

The biggest problem the compass-makers had to contend with was the coming of the iron ship, which could throw the compass into chaos; the problem was solved between 1800 and 1803 by magnets and iron strategically placed relative to the position of the compass. Compasses had more than one needle to counter 'moments of inertia'.

144

Rough weather also affected the compass. The liquid compass was proposed in 1779 but not used until 1830. The compass card floats on a bowl filled with two-thirds water and one-third alcohol (to prevent freezing). Gimbal-rings were provided to keep the bowl and card horizontal in all circumstances. Liquid compasses were provided for the Royal Navy in 1845, but it was not until 1906 that all Royal Naval vessels were equipped with them. Until about 1820 mariners' compasses were set on a tripod and moved about as necessary, but then a permanent pillar of brass or wood was introduced, the binnacle. The gyro-compass dates from 1906.

The modern compass dates from 1876, when Sir William Thomson used eight light needles secured to silk threads radiating from a pivot to the rim of the compass. The lighter the weight of a compass the more sensitive it is; this compass was only one-eighth of the weight of the traditional Admiralty compass of 1837. Land-surveying compasses and military compasses were of sturdy construction, and were often fitted with sights. Most were in metal, but in America where wood was plentiful and metal was scarce beautiful hand-crafted compasses were made from hickory, maple, cherry, pine or indeed any wood which happened to be handy.

A group of rare dials with two astrolabes.

The simplest way to measure distance on land is to push a large wheel; this wheel is connected to cogged wheels. The principle was known two thousand years ago, and the instrument has been variously known as a hodometer, waywiser, perambulator or surveyor's wheel. Waywisers could have one or two wheels, and there was a dial so that the operator could read off the distance. The best examples had inner and outer dials so that the distances could be expressed in miles, furlongs, poles and yards.

In surveying it is necessary to measure horizontal and vertical angles. There are many different instruments for doing this. The circumferentor is a calibrated circle made of brass, over which an alidade (revolving index) moves. Invented in the sixteenth century, it was often beautifully engraved and is one of the most collectable of all surveying antiques. With the aid of the sights and the circular scales it was used on a stand to measure horizontal angles, or, suspended from a shackle, vertical angles. This type of instrument was made in various versions, under different names, but it was superseded by the theodolite, the most important surveying instrument.

In appearance the theodolite looks like a small telescope on a complex stand. Immediately beneath the telescope is a spirit-level and an open brass wheel on a central axle, which can be tilted. The base unit contains another level and a number of adjusting screws so that the instrument can be set absolutely horizontally. From the collector's point of view the most desirable theodolites are those made between 1730 and 1850, and the presence of a famous maker's name such as Ramsden adds great value.

There was a need for good instruments. If you look at early county maps you find them very inaccurate. Using circumferentors and similar tools surveyors made errors of the order of 3 miles in 18. Even with sophisticated instruments there was some error due to the limitations of the human eye in reading the tiniest of graduations. This was overcome with the invention of the Vernier scale in about 1631; this was a small device which slid over the measurement scale and split already small sections into intervals yet smaller.

Some surveying instruments were circular; some (called graphometers) were semi-circular; the latter were easier to make and use and were in operation long after the circumferentor was obsolete. The surveyor's quadrant was merely a brass plate with an alidade. It was a quarter of an arc, half a graphometer, and was useful for measuring the height of buildings. How was this done? How would a surveyor – or, indeed, anyone – find the height of a cathedral without going up it and trailing a tape measure behind him?

He would first of all carefully measure the distance to the cathedral from where he was standing. He would then line up his quadrant with the top of the spire, and obtain the angle. He would then read off the height from a mathematical set of tables, often glued inside the lid of the instrument box. These quadrants were used by artillerymen to help adjust the angles of their guns. The quadrant itself was halved to make an octant.

A substitute for the theodolite was the reflecting circle, widely used on the Continent. In appearance it is a more elaborate cir-

Nautical sextant, a compass, a ship model, a marine painting, and a military figure.

A George III orrery by Benjamin Martin c 1770.

A fine plate camera.

cumferentor, i.e. a brass calibrated wheel, but the circle incorporates a mirror and a telescope. Like the theodolite it had a complicated base and stand, with adjusting screws. The repeating circle uses two telescopes.

A mathematical instrument used in surveying was the sector. This looks like a slide-rule, and consists of two equal flat arms bearing various scales, hinged together as in a joint-rule. These were made in brass, wood, bone and ivory, and because of the delicate engraving they are collected.

Many instruments were used both for surveying and for navigation, and the astrolabe is the ancestor of many of them. It is a heavy pierced disc with a suspension ring; around the edge of the rim were engraved scales of degrees, and there was an alidade. They were used extensively up to 1670, made of tin or copper.

The instruments of the time of Columbus helped him to find his way about, after a fashion. By taking bearings on the sun or the stars he could work out his latitude. There were a variety of tools, such as the cross-staff, two battens fitted at right angles and made to slide up and down. The battens had sights, and one had a scale. By aligning the sights and moving the scaled batten up and down the navigator could measure the angle of the sun above the horizon. It was dangerous to use, as it meant staring into the sun, so the back-staff was invented in 1590, used with the back to the sun.

In 1731 Hadley introduced his reflecting octant. Before that navigators were obliged to look in two directions at once. This was difficult even for merchant adventurers. Hadley solved the problem by the use of mirrors.

The octant and its family are the most desirable of nautical antiques, though those bearing a famous maker's name are becoming increasingly expensive. A Ramsden sextant was recently sold for £2,200 ($3,850), three times the estimate. In the same sale an eighteenth-century silver and silver-gilt nocturnal estimated at £500 – £700 ($875 – $1,225) because of a missing dial and pointer, went for a lively £2,000 ($3,500).

The nautical octant was first made of wood, usually rosewood or lignum vitae. It consists of an arc, which is calibrated on ivory if wood, and by engraving if brass. Two struts connect this arc to a pivot, from which the alidade descends to the arc. At the top of the alidade is a small mirror, and at the bottom a slot through which the details on the arc are read. On one of the struts is a sighting telescope, and on the other a second fixed mirror. The height of the star is measured by noting the position of the alidade when the image of the star, reflected from pivoted to fixed mirror, and thence into the telescope, coincides with the horizon seen through an unsilvered portion of the fixed mirror.

Navigation was much simplified with the arrival of the chronometer. In ancient times people got up in the morning when it was light and went to bed when it was dark. The hour-glass and the sundial helped divide the days. The sundial was a fascinating subject; in 1612 one book devoted eight hundred pages to sundials. The pocket sundial was a fashionable accessory in the seventeenth century; many were hinged (these are known as diptych dials) and they often carried complicated tables. One of these sold in 1968 for 4,800 guineas.

The development of surveying instruments and navigational instruments was encouraged by government and commerce, but there was no profit (only prestige) in looking at the sky or at tiny objects invisible to the naked eye. The world of the telescope and the microscope was alien to the ordinary person, until it was realised that the telescope would be useful in war. It was invented by accident in 1608 in Holland.

A high-quality theodolite by one of the great names in scientific instruments, Troughton.

There are two kinds of telescopes, refracting (the 'ordinary' kind) and reflecting. The latter are the kind used in serious astronomy. They are wider in diameter than the refracting type and are open at the front end, with an exposed and vulnerable mirror at the back. They were considered better than refracting telescopes because the light did not have to pass through thick glass – which produced aberrations in the form of colour-fringed images – but merely fall on a mirror. But if good glass was hard to come by so were good mirrors.

In the seventeenth century there was an increasing demand for simple telescopes or 'perspective glasses' as they were called. Most were imported from Holland and Italy but soon British instrument-makers mastered the art. These telescopes command very high prices. Some have one tube; others consist of different tubes fitting together telescopically. The tubes are usually of card and covered with shagreen, silk, leather or parchment, with wood and ivory fittings – because of their length they are kept light in weight.

Much research was devoted to devising a good mirror for reflecting telescopes; more than 150 different alloys were tried. But even the brightest metal mirror tarnished in the atmosphere. In 1729 the achromatic lens, which was free from colour distortion, was born, though the name was not applied until 1766. It was now possible to produce an image the right way round; in 1783 brass draw-tubes replaced vellum.

The most beautiful telescopes are unquestionably the splendid mounted telescopes of the eighteenth and nineteenth centuries, with bases that reflected furniture styles. Sometimes these were regarded as furnishing pieces in the same way as globes were, and they stood in the library to indicate that the owner was a person of culture.

Many scientific instruments were in one way or another visual aids, aimed at improving the range of operations of the human eye, whether it was the telescope, spectacles or perhaps the most perfect, the most collectable, of them all – the microscope. The telescope brought things nearer, but the microscope brought things into existence.

The two instruments have much in common, in particular their problems – the difficulty of finding suitable glass and of getting the individual parts to fit properly. There are two kinds of microscope, the simple and the compound. The first has a single lens, or a lens combination acting as one, positioned between eye and object. The second has two distinct lens systems.

The first microscope with any power (x270 magnification) was made in about 1660, and consisted of a single lens between two brass plates riveted together. The tube became the obvious form for the instrument to take, but a variation was the compass microscope, consisting of a pair of compasses, one leg carrying the lens, the other the object, which was impaled on a point or gripped by forceps. Microscopes were of brass, with fittings of wood and ivory, or of cardboard covered with parchment or a similar material.

Focusing was improved in the screw-barrel microscope, but many microscopes were vertical, making it difficult to light specimens. In about 1693 the body was mounted on a ball and socket joint so it could be tilted; if the body was tilted a lamp could be placed beneath the specimen, illuminating it. John Marshall (1663-1725) was one of the first to use a fine adjusting screw to move the body up and down.

By the end of the seventeenth century microscopes were made with six lenses; spherical lenses were tried without success. In 1725 Culpeper introduced an upright microscope, set on a double tripod. On top of the first tripod was the stage, where the object was placed; the stage was perforated to allow light from a mirror placed on the second tripod to pass. This mirror could be swivelled for the best effect. This was a beautiful instrument, sturdy, reliable, efficient; it was followed by the Cuff microscope in about 1745.

The Cuff microscope featured an upright pillar, beside which the microscope body rode, together with the stage. On the wooden base was fitted a swivel mirror, and an auxiliary mirror for extra light could be fitted to the side of the stage. The Cuff microscope was all brass except for the base, in which accessories were stored. Focusing could be exact. It was the best instrument yet made, and was copied throughout Europe.

However, it was not until 1830 that lenses were finally perfected, and from then on the microscope became a masterpiece of the instrument-maker's art.

A contemporary illustration of the revolutionary microscope invented by John Marshall.

IOHN MARSHALL'S
New Invented
DOUBLE MICROSCOPE,
For Viewing the
CIRCULATION of the BLOOD
Made & Sold by him at the Archimedes &
Golden Spectacles in Ludgate Street.

Pulp?

Experts rummaging through rubbish destined for pulping found the Caxton translation of Ovid. It sold for £94,000.

In many types of antique the same price pattern applies: pre-1600, scarce, rarely found outside museums or private collections; 1600-1700, available, expensive; 1700-1830, classic period; 1830 onwards, decline, cheaper. But this is not so in microscopes, simply because Victorian microscopes were so good. Recently an 1884 instrument, with a large collection of accessories, sold for £3,800 ($6,650). In the same sale a solar microscope by a well-known eighteenth-century maker, Martin, sold for £1,600 ($2,800). It must not be supposed that all Victorian microscopes are top quality; thousands were made for medical students, and many more for home amusement, and these are inferior to modern instruments.

Amongst the most decorative and useful scientific instruments are barometers. There are two kinds of barometer, the mercury and the aneroid, the latter using a metal drum, and patented in 1844. Before the end of the seventeenth century barometers were inefficient; most makers did not use a graduated scale but preferred to indicate changes in the weather.

The first commercial barometers, the stick type, date from about 1670. The mounts were made of walnut; subsequently mahogany, pearwood, satin-wood, rosewood, maple and ebony were used. Lacquering appeared in about 1710 and was fashionable for about thirty years, and marquetry, inlay, brass and other materials were used, reflecting furniture fashions. Because of the difficulty of reading a barometer, a dial was brought in as early as 1665, but it was a century before it was used on a large scale. It changed the appearance into the familiar banjo shape.

The basic shape of barometers, stick and banjo, altered little throughout the nineteenth century. They were a little more ornate, with fancy pediments, carving and mother-of-pearl inlay. Victorian barometers of high quality are readily available at quite modest prices. A good late eighteenth-century stick barometer recently sold for £1,200 ($2,100); an early nineteenth-century instrument with a swan-neck pediment by the well-known makers W. & S. Jones sold for £1,600 ($2,800). As in most scientific instruments a good maker carries a premium.

The aneroid barometer was surprisingly accurate – surprisingly because the aneroid is widely regarded as the poor person's barometer. Invented in France, patent rights there expired in 1859, and there was a free-for-all, with a great quantity produced by many makers. A pocket version was produced in Britain in 1861 by the well-known maker Negretti & Zambra. The better ones are similar in shape to banjo thermometers; the mass-produced version was circular in a carved oak frame, and these were made well into the present century and can be seen everywhere at very modest prices. Some were made for mantelpiece or table and were set on a plinth like a clock.

We pass now from one of the cheapest forms of instrument to one of the most expensive – the orrery. The first was made by the clockmaker George Graham. The orrery demonstrates the movement of the celestial bodies, using spheres connected to a central axis by rods. A drum-like base conceals extremely complex machinery. Fifteen years ago there were two dismantled orreries in Plymouth, much coveted by local dealers. Orreries were made in various forms, including a small table model.

Globes were sometimes fitted out with clockwork, which looked impressive but did very little, though anything to do with globes was of interest, for they were compulsory furniture in a gentleman's library, usually in pairs, terrestrial and celestial. The celestial globe was the earlier, because more was known about the heavens than the earth, and it was self-evident that the stars were fixed to the surface of a revolving sphere. So putting them on a globe was the best way to demonstrate their position, though it was, as it were, inside out.

One of the most attractive types of globe is the pocket globe. A terrestrial globe is contained in a spherical case, usually covered with shagreen, while on the inside cover of the case is pasted a map of the sky. Two examples of about 1790 recently sold for £1,600 ($2,800) and £1,800 ($3,150) respectively. Fifteen years ago the price range was £100-£200 ($175-$350).

Dozens of scientific instruments were invented in the eighteenth and nineteenth century for the most diverse of purposes. Few would be recognised. The acetimeter (1875) measured the amount of acetic acid in liquids, the aerometer measured the weight and density of air and gases, and the altiscope developed into the periscope, a simple arrangement of lenses and mirrors widely used in trench warfare in World War I. Some instruments, such as the seismograph for recording earthquakes, are well known but were made in too small a quantity and with too little variation to be considered collectable. This might appear to apply to the spectroscope, for spectrum analysis, but recently two made by John Browning, the principal maker, turned up in auction. One sold for £1,400 ($2,450) and a very superior specimen sold for £5,000 ($8,750). Both were purchased by the Science Museum, so it is hard to say whether they can be considered 'trade goods'.

Many inventions were variations of instruments already in existence, and some, such as the telemeter, were adapted for military use. The telemeter is better known as a range-finder.

In many categories of antiques, and especially in scientific instruments, there is a wide divergence between London and provincial prices. Good scientific instruments are, on the face of it, expensive. But what is 'expensive'? Certainly it would cost more to make some instruments than to buy them at auction. As the better-known instruments became out of reach, so attention has been turned elsewhere, and prices for the hitherto neglected have soared, but only relatively.

The examples below serve to give some idea of current London prices. The highest price ever paid at auction for a scientific instrument was recently given for a large seventeenth century diptych dial – £165,000 ($288,750). A high-quality silver microscope made by one of the greatest makers, George Adams, made £20,000 ($35,000). A globe dated 1815 sold for £1,300 ($2,275); a table-top orrery made £3,200 ($5,600); an 1836 theodolite once owned by the railway engineer Brunel sold for £2,200 ($3,850). Some of these prices took the auctioneers by surprise.

There is no field more open to adventurous, even brave, collectors than scientific instruments. Knowledge is needed, hard work is needed, but massive scientific expertise is not.

A fine compass on a gimbal mount.

The big sleep?

What is the largest bed ever made? A likely candidate is that made in Bruges in 1430 for the Duke of Burgundy so that he could consummate his marriage with Princess Isabella of Portugal in a satisfactory manner and still have plenty of room to play a round of golf. It measured nineteen feet long and twelve and a half feet wide.

CHILDREN'S CORNER

Everyone *has been* a collector – pebbles from the beach, cards featuring famous footballers in packets of tea-bags, or the accessories for Action Man or Cindy. So *everybody* has the potential to be a collector. Even the line-up of romantic paperbacks on the shelf behind the television is a kind of collection.

Perhaps there are children who collect things with the object of eventually making money, but most get a pure pleasure from accumulating little odds and ends.

These starter collections may have no intrinsic value, or they may by accident contain valuable items – for example an old stamp album of 'standards' which happens to have just one stamp of great value. As children today have more pocket money they are in a better position to collect things where a nominal amount of money, perhaps 10p or 20p, changes hands.

What is there available for the young collector? There are of course things that have established themselves as collectable items not only for children but also for adults – postage stamps, coins, picture postcards. But then there are the unconsidered items, dropped into cardboard boxes for the hopeful buyer to browse through. These include odd beads from necklaces, and fragments of broken costume jewellery. Beads have a lot to commend them. They were made in hundreds of shapes, sizes and colours from almost every conceivable material and now cost almost nothing, often being given away by friendly dealers.

Alongside the boxes of beads and bits and pieces are often boxes of buttons. Buttons come in thousands of varieties and do have serious collectors.

Another collecting field in which items are readily available at knock-down prices is the jigsaw puzzle, seen in their hundreds at car-boot sales at prices that range from 25p to no more than £1. These are not only worth collecting for themselves, but they are collectables that can be used.

Although picture postcards are an established collecting field, there are picture postcards in which serious collectors are not interested. Cards from about 1950 are available in large numbers at 5p or 10p each. Cards posted abroad might be a promising area in which to start, or those dealing with the collector's town or locality.

An investment collection for young people is possible in the field of die-cast model cars and other vehicles. Despite the popularity of plastic, die-cast models have never lost their appeal, and as the model cars of the 1950s are now much in demand among serious collectors it is clear that in twenty or thirty years time those being produced today will have their enthusiasts.

There is always a rapid turnover in toys of all descriptions, including board games, which can be immensely expensive when bought one year, perhaps £10–£15, but the year after turn up at car-boot sales for £1 or so, often unused. Card games can also provide a very fruitful field, for use and for collection.

The habit of collecting can result in nothing but good, introducing a concern for the past and an interest in objects and events of

A typical late Victorian toy relying for its effect on the phenomenon of 'persistence of vision'.

bygone times. And from a concern for the past must follow concern for the future. Also, collecting is a prompt to activity rather than passivity. A young collector will naturally go through various phases, maybe becoming attracted down some obscure byway of collecting, perhaps in due course becoming a specialist in some field hitherto disregarded. And another collection, no matter what it is, of beads, toy soldiers, maybe little china animals, will be dispersed, to go on its rounds again for the edification of a new generation.

ONLY A PENNY! A SENSIBLE AND INGENIOUS TOY FOR CHILDREN.

An amusing cartoon from an 1840s Punch *depicting early mechanical toys.*

Not a children's toy, but a George III doll from about 1800 in original clothing, sold in June 1986 for £2,400.

155

MECHANICAL ANTIQUES

Why was America so predominant in the production of mechanical antiques? Why were British and Continental ideas and inventions not followed up in their countries of origin? There is a clear answer. In America labour was scarce and expensive; there were not enough clerks, there were not enough seamstresses, and there was an enormous demand for labour-saving devices. In Britain and the Continent advanced technology was given over to toys for the rich such as automata, firearms, and clocks and watches.

The first domestic mechanical aid to be produced on a large scale was the sewing-machine, though it was not until 1830 that a French tailor made machines which actually worked.

In the United States a professional inventor turned his attention to the sewing-machine and invented a machine which would make a lock-stitch, the first stitch which did not seek to imitate a hand stitch. He did not follow it up, but others did, and in 1851 Isaac M. Singer patented the first practical sewing-machine which would be recognised as such today. It was widely advertised and the industry was the first to promote instalment purchase. It was soon seen in Britain where it was predicted that the 'iron seamstress' would do needleworkers out of a job, and they would all starve. A seamstress took fourteen hours to make a shirt; with the aid of a sewing-machine it was claimed she could make one in one hour and sixteen minutes.

In America the potential of the sewing-machine was immediatley seen, and a patent war broke out, the results being a wide and eccentric variety of sewing-machines aimed at avoiding break-

A Wheeler & Wilson sewing-machine of the early 1850s before manufacturers closed in the moving parts. Most sewing-machines on the market today date from the 1870s onwards.

ing patents. They could be shaped like dolphins or cupids, or fitted with massive Grecian pillars, but the basic design was a base plate, an overhanging arm carrying the needle, a continuous supply of thread from a spool and a handle to turn or a treadle to pump with the feet. Some were very elegant, black-japanned, with floral hand-painting and often mother-of-pearl inlay, and the wooden cases they were contained in were frequently inlaid.

The story of the typewriter was along much the same path as that of the sewing-machine, and a patent for a writing machine was applied for as early as 1714, though there was little need for one when ill-paid clerks wrote precise and legible hands. The basis of early machines was one-character-at-a-time, and the first typewriter-like object was not developed until 1829, William Burt's 'typographer' or 'Family Letter Press'. The original was destroyed in a fire in 1836, but a replica was made from the original papers in 1892. The typographer was a lettering device, with the letters on the rim of a wheel. By turning a dial pointer the required character was brought into position, and the impression was made by depressing a lever. The types were inked by hand beforehand.

In 1833 the 'Machine Kryptographique' was invented by a French printer. It had typewriter elements – the type was on separate bars arranged in a circle and each type struck upon a common centre. One disadvantage was that the type struck downwards instead of upwards, and could not therefore return to their original position by gravity. The Italian 'Cembalo-Scrivano' of 1837 was 'up-strike', but the inventor had not hit upon the basic principle of the successful typewriter – a cylinder holding the paper moving from left to right to space the letters and rotating to change the lines, though he did use an inking ribbon. He also redesigned the keyboard, so that the letters were not alphabetical.

Many attempts were made, and each inventor added something. By 1860 all the elements for a successful typewriter were there, but no-one managed to bring it all together, with the exception of Sholes, an American printer, who made forty separate and distinct machines, no two alike. In 1872 a factory was opened in Milwaukee, and the present-day 'QWERTY' layout of a typewriter was evolved – the first typewriter that really looked like one was born. There were just two improvements to make – the provision of a shift-key to provide lower case as well as capital letters and a front-striking movement so that the operator could see what he or she was doing.

These typewriters were hand-made. The task of mass-producting them was given to E. Remington & Sons, gunmakers. At first it was not a success, and other makers were entering the field – Yost with his keyboard with seventy-two characters, Hammond with a type-wheel rather than individual type, and Crandall with an extremely sophisticated machine, patented in 1881, that anticipated the IBM 'golfball'. All these typewriters are collectable; a Hammond is in the price range £300–£400.

In 1893 the first mass-produced front-striking typewriter was made by Underwood. In 1889 a machine using differential spacing was invented, but it was too expensive to produce and never came to anything. A curio was the Yost Typewriter No 1 of 1889, in

A Polyphon disc musical box. The disc reads 'Christians Awake!' Very appropriate, as these marvellous instruments emitted a high level of decibels.

which the makers discarded the ribbon and returned to the ink pad. Large numbers were imported into Britain, and are still about. However, the most pleasing of the typewriters was the 1894 Oliver, in which the type bars are set in two banks, one on the left and one on the right, giving the impression of a miniature cinema organ.

The problem of the automatic ribbon reverse was solved by Remington in 1896 with their No 7 model, and in 1898 they evolved tabulator keys. British typewriters such as the Waverley, the Moya and the Salter are very collectable but they are not produced in the quantities in which American machines were. The first portable was the Blick of 1893, the first successful portable the National of 1916 and the best-selling one the Remington Portable of 1920. The first noiseless machine came out in 1910.

The kitchen offered great scope for mechanical innovation. One of the most time-consuming jobs was laundering. In 1780 a patent had been taken out in Britain for a 'machine called a laundry for washing and pressing apparel' but it was not proceeded with.

In 1851 a cylindrical washing machine was evolved in the United States, the basic element being a revolving perforated cylinder. It was horizontal and not very effective, but in the 1860s the familiar vertical-cylinder washing machine was introduced with rotation and agitation carried out by means of a foot treadle or a handle. It was realised that such a machine could also serve as a spin-dryer using centrifugal force, and in 1878 a two-speed single tub washer/drier was introduced, using a four-bladed rotor. The market for washing machines was fully recognised; in 1873 there were two thousand American patents relating to them.

Further development was held up by the absence of a compact power unit, the electric motor, and this applied also to the mechanical dish washer, first made as early as 1865. The principle was the same as for the washing machine – agitation of water provided by rotating blades.

There is potential in early electrical products for the home, one of the first being the electric saucepan – heated by current from a battery – invented in 1887. There is probably more variety in electric fires than in any other electrical domestic aid, and the early ones are extremely ornate with a frame of cast iron often in the fashionable styles of the time.

Some electrical gadgets came in at a surprisingly early date. A patent was taken out by a Halifax man in 1913 for an electric razor, and by the 1920s electrical gadgets of all kinds were being used, especially as the electricity suppliers charged less for appliances than for electric light – two-thirds less. Toasters, hotplates, kettles, meat-covers, coffee mills, coffee percolators, egg-cookers (in which the egg was steamed instead of boiled), curling-tong heaters, combs, dryers – there is almost no end to the useful and useless articles provided for those who were fortunate enough to be on mains electricity.

Most of these articles were intended to be useful. Some were, or, if they fell short, anticipated more successful products. Automata were never meant to be useful. They were amusements to puzzle and delight the spectators – who were mostly rich. They

Not so plain

In September 1987 a three-hundred-year-old doll nicknamed Jane by the auction-room staff sold for £24,000. The vendor was 'absolutely astonished'. She had paid less than £100 for it.

were not intended as toys, though naturally toys developed from them, for the motive force of most automata was the clockwork spring, (though water, sand, steam and compressed air were all employed). Automata were fathered by the clockmakers and watchmakers, and the earliest simple examples are to be found in clock accessories, such as striking jacks or revolving skeletons brought into play by the clock movement.

A battleship with clockwork mechanism by Georges Carette about 1908.

What is an automaton? It is defined as 'a mechanical figure which moves and acts as if alive'. Perhaps this is too narrow. It certainly does not cover mechanical pictures, immensely intricate and made with the precision of a clock. One typical picture has fifteen distinct movements activated by a strong spring connected to a wooden cylinder in which are set pins and staples which engage levers with rods; with the aid of these mechanisms a laundress washes linen, a girl makes butter, two cocks fight, a fisherman lifts and lowers a rod, a carriage crosses a bridge, a bell rings in a church tower, soldiers make merry and clouds scud across the sky, occasionally allowing a shaft of sunlight to light up the hectic scene. However, the most common automaton was the single figure doing something, often a very elaborate task.

Typical of these is the 'Lyre Player' of about 1870, 2ft (60cm) tall, seated on a platform which contains a Swiss musical movement playing two tunes. She is made of papier mâché, and when she is set in motion the arms move, the fingers appear to pluck the strings in time to the music, the head, set with realistic glass eyes, turns from side to side, and the eyelashes flutter. For quality automata such as these the heads were often made of porcelain and the glass eyes by the paperweight factories of Clichy and Baccarat. The 'Smoking Dandy' smokes a real cigarette. The cigarette is lit by the spectator, the figure looks around, brings the cigarette holder to his lips, pauses to inhale the smoke so that the cigarette end glows, then tilting his head back he puffs it out, all done with cleverly arranged clockwork, tubing and bellows.

Tiny automata were made as jewellery, such as articulated caterpillars made of gold, enamel and pearls; gold and pearl-encrusted mice with eyes made of rubies; and rabbits emerging from lettuces. Miniaturisation reached its peak in automata in watches and snuff-boxes, the best-known being the singing-bird type, which uses a tiny bellows and a whistle, the pitch of which is altered by a sliding piston.

Towards the end of the nineteenth century the automaton merged into the toy, a move that was greatly assisted by the widespread use of tin-plate. Walking animals were very popular around the turn of the century, with articulated legs and neck. These may sometimes be found amongst ordinary animal toys at modest prices.

Clockwork was often used in the production of music and the best example is the musical box, invented in 1796, in which a revolving barrel set with pins and powered by a spring acted on a series of tuned teeth set on a comb. The tips of the teeth were set vibrating by the passage of the pins, and a sound-board amplified the delicate music. By staggering the pins a large number of tunes could be put on one cylinder.

The first musical boxes were in plain boxes and were operated by a key; later ones were operated by a lever. Various refinements were added such as tissue paper to imitate the sound of a zither, and drums and tuned bells were also incorporated.

The main deficiency of the musical box was its inability to sustain a sound, even though repeated notes could help fill a gap, and more successful in this respect was a mechanical organ operated by the transport of a perforated paper roll. When there was an aperture in the paper, sound was produced; otherwise not. These organs could be small such as the Organette of 1878 or massive, such as the Orchestrion of 1887, which, as the name implies, was a band in itself. The Organette was intended as a substitute for a harmonium, and had a monotonous tone, but it could have an endless repertoire, unlike the musical box.

In 1886 a second type of musical box was invented which would play discs. The disc revolved on a central spindle, and notches cut in it operated on tuned teeth in the same manner as the cylinder version. Cardboard discs were first used, but these were replaced by metal discs which did not wear out, and have proved almost indestructible. Made in Germany and later in America, many disc musical boxes (known as Polyphons, the name of the principal maker) were imported to Britain, mostly for pubs, hotels and other public places, and purchasers recouped their capital cost by installing a penny-in-the-slot mechanism. These disc musical boxes were very large, up to 10ft (3m) high, and sometimes they were incorporated in a long-case clock. Smaller table-top versions were made for domestic use.

Records of musical boxes of both kinds are often used as background music for period films for the cinema and television, in an attempt to make us believe that the music of the Victorian period was either a tinkle or a jangle, which is quite untrue. Another evocative sound much used by film producers is that of the barrel piano. The same principle as the musical box was used – a revolving barrel, this time of wood, set with pins which acted against tuned wires. No clockwork was involved; it operated by direct drive worked by the turning of a handle. The barrel organ, also known as the Dutch organ, the street organ, the grinder

---

At a Car-Boot Sale

Although he was only a middle-range dealer, he at first thought that it is was infra dig to do a boot sale, though he had bought well at them in the past. But over the months he had accumulated a lot of stock that had either stuck in the shop or was not good enough. There were also mistakes, especially reproduction china taken as genuine, the worst thing to have in an antique shop as buyers see it and are then suspicious of the real thing if it happens to be there.

Realising that image, or lack of it, is important, he put on an old anorak and bundled his stock anyhow into the boot of his car, leaving a picture half-in half-out of a pile of blankets which he normally used to wrap up good-quality furniture. The picture, although on canvas, was modern though dirtied by some previous owner to simulate age.

The boot sale was being held on the car-park of a pub, and although it was advertised as starting at ten he arrived at nine, only to find that it was already in full swing, and that he could only just squeeze into the last parking bay available. He imagined that it would be all very leisurely, as it was at an antique fair or even a flea market, everybody watching him politely as he unwrapped his goods. He had hoped to do the round of the other cars before beginning to sell. ▶

organ and the hand organ, had roots in the fifteenth century. A revolving barrel set with pins opens the valves of organ pipes, admitting air from a wind-chest. Each revolution of the barrel played one tune, but by shifting the setting of the barrel several tunes could be played. Barrel organs could be portable and primitive, or as sophisticated as manual organs.

Clockwork was also eventually to be the motive power of the phonograph and the gramophone. The principles of these two are the same, except that the phonograph used a cylinder and the gramophone a disc. Edison invented the phonograph in 1877 as an aid to business, but it was not successful. The idea was taken up in Britain and the graphophone was born. In 1888 Edison returned to the problem of the talking machine, choosing electricity as his motive power, though until the arrival of mains electricity it was never truly viable. Phonographs were hired out as dictating machines, but increasingly they were used for entertainment. Operators hired them and then put as many as seventeen listening tubes on one machine. Recordings were one-offs, and the artist or artists were obliged to perform to a battery of phonographs over and over again to get enough copies. Eventually it became possible to record a master cylinder.

In 1894 the Columbia company became the first to market a spring-drive cylinder machine, and Edison followed in 1895 with his version. Competition was fierce, and the new disc gramophone was a formidable competitor. For a time it was difficult to see which would triumph, and large numbers of phonographs were sold in Britain. Most of those seen today are of this period. The phonograph with a segmented horn supported with a crane was introduced in 1908. Later models had the horn enclosed in a case. As recently as 1929 cylinders were being sold for phonographs. In 1977 an Edison phonograph was sold for £1,300, an auction record, but similar instruments are appearing on the market ten years later at much lower prices.

There are still a lot about. If you buy one listen to it several times before making a decision, and bear in mind that although spares are available they are mainly for the most popular kinds, such as the Gem and the Standard. Check the motor for rust and see if there are any signs of repair. If it is an uncommon specimen there may be difficulty in finding suitable cylinders for that particular model. The surprise about phonographs is that, despite

▶ There was no chance of this. As soon as he had parked, even before he had applied the brake, faces three-deep appeared at the window, peering in. As there was nothing in the car but a torch and a Thermos flask the owners of the faces were disappointed. The dealer got out of the car, opened the boot, and began taking out his wallpapering table – the usual type for boot sales, flea markets, and other places of ill-repute. That was as far as he got, for the 'snatchers' were at him, reminding him of a wild scene of revelry in an old Dutch painting. His cardboard boxes were wrenched out, and busy hands unwrapped the treasures. A box of junk jewellery was snatched from one woman's hands and taken by a sour-looking woman of the jumble-sale brigade to the bonnet of the car for close examinaton. 'How much, mate?' 'What you got there, then?' 'How much is your picture? . . . Four quid? You must be barmy!'

'I said fourteen', said the dealer, feeling that matters were getting out of control. There was a choice between retrieving his jewellery and making certain that his precious china, priced at between £1 and £5 per item, was not stolen. 'Give you twelve', said someone. 'What?' asked the dealer. 'The picture, you said the picture . . .' 'All right.' ▶

A very superior typewriter of the nineteenth century. Notice the type-head anticipating the IBM 'golf-ball'.

their dumpy primitive look, the reproduction they offer is really very good. There is something of a ceremony in setting them up and starting them, but no more so than with early gramophones. They certainly have a more antique look about them than gramophones, and their repertory, not usually transferred to modern discs or tapes, has a period charm. It was a large repertoire; by 1893 Columbia had a catalogue of thirty-two pages. One band alone had recorded eighty-two marches.

In 1887 the gramophone was invented; it was at first regarded as a toy and was so marketed in Germany, but when the project was taken to America its potential was realised. A satisfactory clockwork motor replaced the direct drive, and the new machine was advertised as 'The Talking Machine That Talks Talk!' Shellac took over from vulcanised rubber for the discs. In Britain the Gramophone Company began operations in 1898, using discs stamped in Germany, and within two years was advertising 5,000 different records. In 1900 the familiar paper labels appeared on records. In 1903 12in (30cm) records were introduced, and this type of record survived until 1948 and the coming of micro-groove records. Between 1900 and 1925 records revolved at between 74 and 82 revolutions per minute; electrically powered turntables set the norm at 78rpm.

The early years of the century saw further development, especially in the size and design of the horn, which in 1906 was incorporated into a piece of furniture by the Victor company of the United States. This design was known as the Victrola. In 1914 in America dance mania gave a massive boost to the sales of gramophones, and by 1919 American companies were making two million machines a year. It became more and more fashionable to enclose gramophones in cabinets with splendid names such as the Duncan Phyfe, the Aeolian Vocalion, the Deccalion and the Oranola, and superb Georgian furniture was converted to house the gramophone.

The coming of the radio shook the gramophone industry to the core, but electrical recording, which introduced high fidelity, came to its aid, though true reception needed a horn at least 9ft (2.7m) long, which was ridiculous. The problem was solved by folding the horn back on itself, and in 1925 the Orthophonic Victrola was introduced in a blaze of publicity. However, the huge trumpet horn became a feature in itself, and 1920s gramophones fitted with these are among the most sought-after today. At about the same time the first all-electric gramophone was introduced by the firm of Brunswick. The giant combine R. C. A. Victor was on the verge of introducing the $33\frac{1}{3}$rpm record, and the future looked rosy. The slump destroyed the American industry; gramophone sales dropped from 987,000 in 1927 to 40,000 in 1932. Britain survived better, and there was a boom in portable gramophones.

Gramophones are still not collected to the same extent as phonographs, and except for the long-horned freaks are not at all expensive, splendid cabinet pieces in full working order being available in the provinces at less than £100. Although it is no longer possible to get portables at £5 each, as it was four or five years ago, they are still common. It is rather sad that cabinet

▶ Surprisingly the woman with the jewellery spent £15 with him, and as the various objects disappeared money was pushed at him. Some of the faces were familiar. They were dealers he had dealt with in the past, seen and chatted to at fairs or who had visited his shop – and not so long ago either. Surely they were buying things they had actually seen in the shop and rejected, and at more or less the same price. And they were buying the mistakes he had made. How would they sell it on? The blue-and-white 1920s willow-pattern bowl with a chip in the foot, surely nobody would give more than £5 for *that*.

The arrival of more cars, although there was nowhere for them to park, encouraged a stampede away towards the newcomers, and the dealer, his pocket full of coins and crumpled notes, wondered how much he had taken. The notebook he had bought to jot down receipts was empty. He realised how much he had disliked the stock he had got rid of. Why had he bought it in the first place? And he knew. It was because it was cheap. And that is why it had sold, because it was still cheap. He supposed that so long as the ghastly ornaments he had got rid of were cheaper than similar items in supermarkets and chain stores, there would be some demand for them amongst people who did not buy things because they liked them but to fill a space in a cabinet or on a shelf. ▶

gramophones are increasingly bought as furniture and modified, the gramophone being taken out and thrown away.

The old 78rpm records are much collected, to be played rather than stored away, and it is odd that present-day manufacturers of record-players are no longer fitting a 78rpm playing facility. Much of the music once available only on 78rpm records has been transferred to long-playing records, but it would be impossible to transfer it all, and the oddities remain untranscribed. It is a specialised field. The early one-sided records are much sought after, as are records by such artists as Caruso. Dance-band and early jazz records are energetically collected, and 1950s rock 'n' roll records can change hands at very high prices, with Bill Haley and his Comets being in the top bracket. There is also a demand for quite recent vinyl records, such as those featuring the Beatles and other pop idols, and the magazines devoted to this field can be a source of amazement and disbelief.

Auctioneers still catalogue early gramophones along with sewing-machines and typewriters as collector's items. If two determined collectors are present at a sale the result can be startling. In August 1987 an early gramophone with a hand-drive, dating from around 1893, was finally sold for £1,300 against the auctioneer's estimate of £400–£600. Although the horn was missing, it did have three contemporary records, including 'God Save the Queen'. The price range for an early hand-driven Edison phonograph of the 1877-88 period would probably be very much higher than this, but for unusual items there can be little accurate prediction. A gramophone of the early 1900s driven by hot air generated by a spirit burner recently appeared at auction. Estimated at £700 it fetched £1,150, but could have failed at £300.

It is doubtful whether the radiograms of the 1930s will ever achieve worth-while prices, unless the cabinet happens to be of extreme period interest. But there are certain areas of collecting where there is scope for adventure, as in early tape-recorders, which date back to the telegraphone of 1899, leading to the magnetophone of 1935. During World War II many nations experimented with tape-recording, though the British were more interested in wire-recording. In 1944 the Allies captured Radio Luxembourg and with it perhaps the finest tape-recorder made to that date, a German machine playing 14in (35cm) spools at 30in (76cm) a second. With knowledge gained from this machine the Americans started a tape-recorder industry in 1947.

Vintage radios appeal to the same type of person as gramophones. The cabinet gramophone is not so different externally from the radio, with cases of widely different quality. Radio design became more progressive than gramophone style, and the radio manufacturers Ekco & Murphy employed leading furniture-designers of the day such as Gordon Russell and Serge Chermayeff to design modernistic cases. Bakelite proved to be an ideal substance. Such cases with their strong 1930s flavour have recently been reproduced with modern transistor radios enclosed. The expertise involved in putting an old radio in working order is far more demanding than that required for a gramophone. Today the radio valve is an alien as the gas-mantle or the 3 amp electric plug, and there is as good deal of trafficking in spares.

A singing-bird snuff-box of high quality.

▶ It was a salutary experience for him. When he got home and found that he had taken £80 he was astonished. If someone had asked him for the stock he had taken to the boot sale for a jumble sale or a charity stall he would gladly have handed it over. He would have to do it again sometime. But he later realised that to sell cheaply one has to buy cheaply. And that the goods he had sold for £80 – mistakes, errors of judgment, unsaleable rubbish bought for the sake of buying – had almost cost him that much.

Later in the year when he went out looking at boot sales for the odd bargain he saw the old familiar objects on the trestle-tables, and behind the tables the dealers, like him in the middle-range, to whom he had sold them. And the prices had not gone up either. Mistakes were mistakes no matter who bought them.

ON THE TRAIL

A collector coming to Britain for the first time might very well be confused by the variety of goods offered at the hundreds of outlets – shops, fairs, antique markets, street markets and sale rooms. There are far more shops and fairs in Britain than on the Continent, where the emphasis is on huge once-a-year events. Many foreign dealers make their money doing just one fair a year, spending the rest of the time looking for stock.

Americans will find prices cheaper in Britain whatever the dollar is worth against the pound, simply because antiques from Europe (including Great Britain) have to be shipped, usually in containers, and this cost is added on in America to the normal wholesale price – and transport can be expensive. There is no sense in looking for large furniture, for although it may appear cheap, if private buyers have to bear the cost of transporting it they may find the item rather more expensive than they had at first imagined.

Many antique shops have opened up in towns popular with visiting Americans, just to cater for them. These include Stratford-on-Avon, Windsor, beauty spots within easy reach of London such as Petworth, towns in the Cotswolds such as Stow-on-the-Wold, and Bath. There are towns such as Brighton with a remarkable number of antique shops, and the Sussex and Kent coasts are well-geared to the needs of continental buyers, especially the trade. Continental dealers often arrive at Dover or Folkestone, take in the towns down the coast as far as Eastbourne, and return, loaded up. This is their standard run.

The American collector who wants to steer clear of the traditional tourist route should study the various books listing antique dealers in the United Kingdom. It is very easy to get the feel of the antique shops in a specific town by reading about them and their specialities; one even gets some idea from the names of the shops. Sometimes it is a good idea to strike off towards a town of a good size which seems to have only a couple of shops. The antique shops will be there, even if they are not in the reference books.

For those for whom money is no object there is generally not much need to leave London, where the very best is always available in all the main categories. But for those who are looking for unusual or specialised items, it may be necessary to cast around. Maritime instruments, for example, are often to be found in cities such as Plymouth which have strong naval connections. If a collector is interested in acquiring items related to Queen Victoria where would he or she go? It would be logical to go to Windsor, taking in as well the antique shops of Eton, or Osborne in the Isle of Wight, where Queen Victoria had a residence.

It is also a good idea to frequent the English auction rooms. There is not a lot of difference between English and American auction rooms. Perhaps English auction rooms are conducted at a quieter tempo; when large bids take a particular prize there is not usually prolonged applause, though this is changing. The American way of bidding with 'paddles' (implements with numbers on them) has been tentatively taken up by some

When on the road it is easy for a dealer to buy without really examining his purchase. This George III armchair was actually made about 1900.

larger auction rooms.

Local auctions are always advertised in the regional newspapers, usually in the Friday or Saturday issues, or in the local weeklies. These include not only antique auctions, but those of household goods and farming items (in which there may be something of interest as well as cows and pigs and perhaps a combine-harvester).

Just as continental buyers find items from their own country at a fraction of the price they would expect to pay at home, so Americans often find objects from their own country in the British antique shops. It is sometimes surprising how they got there. Although the item will be recognised for what it is – for example, a distinctive American patchwork quilt – it may be priced in relation to its British equivalents, and thus undervalued.

It is always tempting to exploit current economic conditions and travel to areas of high unemployment and deprivation in the belief that there are antiques there going for the proverbial song. This is not so. The people who are deprived have never had antiques and in the event of their being exceptions to the rule anything at all desirable has long been sold. British dealers have often set out for the Welsh valleys or the mill-towns of Lancashire in the belief that they can load up their vans and cars by shaking a £5 note at the natives, only to return sadder and wiser. They have found that even in the most unlikely places there are select antique shops with prices on the level of the shops in their own localities.

Where should collectors from overseas head for? The answer is, to those places a little off the beaten track, towns which do not fit into the normal antique dealer's run, which relies on motorways or arterial roads. A collector can afford to do a detour of fifty miles or so on the off-chance of coming across something, whereas a dealer, for whom time is money, may have rejected the idea. If a likely town

Old pictures and engravings often give a wonderful idea of the furniture that was actually used in humble homes. Notice the ladder-back chair with pad feet, and the three-legged 'cricket' table, known as such for no very clear reason.

is found, head for the older part or the area near the railway station – because these parts are frequently due for redevelopment and shops are on a short lease and are often taken by antique and junk dealers for a year or two.

The outlying areas of large seaside towns are often worth a visit for those on the lookout for antique shops that have not been recorded in any guide book. Typical of such towns is Weston-super-Mare on the Bristol Channel; it has a very large number of antique shops within about a mile of the railway station, which, as in many seaside resorts, is situated a good way from the beach and the shopping areas. The reason why antique shops are so common in seaside towns is that they have a population with a high proportion of elderly people who have retired there. When they die, their goods are dispersed, often locally, and help to build up the stock of the local antique shops.

Another point about seaside towns is that they are usually off the main dealers' runs; roads often go to such towns and then stop because of the sea. This is particularly true of resorts with rocky coasts, such as Padstow in Cornwall, where there is basically one main road in and the same road out again.

When venturing into the regions there are two basic courses to pursue – to map out an itinerary, or to trust to the impulse of the moment. A good modern road map is essential. Towns near a motorway within say 80 miles of London will be commuter territory, meaning a good deal of wealth and a steady private trade for antique shops, with maybe a price range above the average. Villages and small towns with more antique shops than one would expect are worth looking at, as competition means that prices are not silly. And as they are surviving it means that they are worth buying from; antique shops which charge too much have a short life-span. Villages which are not recognised beauty spots rely more on mundane trade than on tourism.

A village with just one antique shop may mean that others have tried and failed. It may be that for some reason it is in a bad area, not necessarily poor, but lacking in sparkle, and it is very easy for a dealer to fall in with the general mood of the place. In the early 1970s the author visited a village in Cornwall, reached by a narrow lane, and only then by skirting holes in the road due to mining subsidence. It was a small village, yet there were seven antique shops there. There was something wrong about the place. Amongst the shops was a very high-class establishment specialising in good furniture. It did not fit in. There was only one shop which did, tiny, with a set of shelves filled with rubbish, presided over by a young man who did not bother to lift his eyes from the newspaper he was reading. Three years later there were no antique shops there at all.

For those who do not mind adventuring into unknown territory,

A charming papier-mâché tray. This one is undamaged, but it is a material apt to get nibbled and difficult to repair.

the suburbs of large industrial towns and cities are well worth a visit. These suburbs were once individual villages before they were swallowed up in urban sprawl and often possess traditional-type shops.

Visitors to Britain should never neglect the long-established street markets. These are rarely advertised; they are just there. In market towns which look as though they should have an open market there is no substitute for going into a shop and asking. It may be asking too much for visitors to undergo trial by jumble sale, where the unwary are lucky if they can escape with merely an elbow in the ribs, but car-boot sales are open house for everybody. Maybe they are not the place to find the treasures of a kingdom – but one never knows.

A magnificent piece of furniture into which an entire family would fit. Not something to be picked up by a tourist on the trail.

MILITARIA

In the early 1950s a good armour (the true term, not suit of armour) could have been obtained for under £100. Twenty years later this would have appreciated at least ten times. A half suit (i.e. no leg armour) was sold in about 1952 for £55; the same item reappeared in 1971 when it fetched £1,700 ($2,975). In 1972 a full suit of armour for man and horse made to special order in about 1840, no doubt to fill a space in an ancestral home, sold for £5,000 ($8,750). No-one had worn that kind of thing in anger for hundreds of years.

Where armour does turn up at auction it is often a composite set, with different parts mostly dating from the seventeenth century from diverse suits, and falling in the price range £4,000–£12,000 ($7,000–$21,000). At one time Japanese, Indian and Middle Eastern armour was not highly regarded, but this has increased in value despite the fact that much is quite modern.

The invention of the pistol rendered the heavily armoured man-at-arms obsolete in about 1530, and only the heavy cavalry were well protected.

Many of the armour pieces and accessories on the market today date from the English Civil War (1642-8), and are still within reach. These include the lobster-pot helmets, called burgonets, which look like jockey caps with an angular tail to protect the neck.

With the advances in firearms helmets went out of use for more than a century, reappearing in the Napoleonic Wars when decorative helmets of burnished steel, brass or copper were worn by the cavalry.

The pickelhaube or spiked helmet introduced by Prussia in 1846 was widely copied by most armies including the British. In World War I the French wore a crested helmet and the British revived the sallet of the fifteenth century, with its low crown and broad brim. The Germans replaced the pickelhaube in early 1916 with the familiar steel helmet. The French, British and Germans continued to use World War I helmets in the 1939-45 war. The Americans used the British helmet until 1942.

The most collectable of the helmets are the German, though there is an interest in Japanese helmets in America. All helmets should have their liners and chin-straps intact. Millions of British 'tin-hats' were issued not only to fighting men but to air-raid wardens, fire-fighters and a host of others. They sometimes bear initials and emblems, sometimes not.

At one time it seemed that every provincial antique shop had a military uniform gathering dust and largely unwanted. No uniforms, despite appearance and the ravages of moth, are of great age, for it was only during the English Civil War that soldiers

Election collection

General Elections always bring their novelties in the form of badges and stickers and souvenirs, but those produced today are not likely to have a future antique interest. Perhaps an exception may be made in Shropshire where it is traditional to order commemorative items from Coalport – if the Conservatives win all four seats. When Labour won the Wrekin seat in 1966 the pottery lost their privilege for the nonce. Amongst the earliest pieces of electioneering pottery were plates of Bristol delftware issued on the occasion of the Taunton election of 1754. The man who was named lost. No doubt he had placed his order when full of confidence, or drunk. Not every electioneering souvenir was complimentary. In 1886 the Beleek pottery of Ireland produced a chamber pot with Mr Gladstone's likeness on the interior. Mr Gladstone was not the Irishman's favourite person at that time.

began to wear clothing different from their everyday garb. There was little standardisation until 1742 when the first official clothing book was compiled.

Most uniforms, for both officers and men, remained cumbersome and constricting, and it was not until the early years of the nineteenth century that there was a distinction between full dress and service dress.

All ranks wore bright easily muddied colours, and until 1836 even the ordinary soldier wore gold and silver lace trimmings. In the 1830s it was decided that most soldiers would wear red, though certain regiments were exempt. In 1878 regimental buttons for other ranks were replaced by a standard pattern; this fact is a useful dating guide.

In India and other foreign countries white uniforms were worn (providing excellent targets for enemy sharpshooters) and then khaki was introduced. The use of khaki died out in the 1850s, but was revived in 1878. In the 1870s the Sam Browne belt was introduced for officers. In 1902 khaki became the accepted colour for uniforms except for ceremonial purposes, and it is likely that uniforms that have survived are dress rather than working uniforms, and that their age is overestimated.

Unless a collector has a great deal of space at his or her disposal the difficulties of displaying a collection of military costume are obvious. It is much easier to display items associated with uniform such as cloth or metal badges of rank, regimental or divisional insignia, armbands and sashes.

Soldiers' headgear is more easily displayed than uniforms, ranging from the sombrero-type wide-brimmed flat-topped hat used by soldiers in the English Civil War, through the three-cornered hat known as a mitre cap, on to the shako, a tall cylindrical leather cap with a small peak which survived in one form or another until it was replaced by the German pickelhaube. During the Crimean War supplies of the shako ran out, and both officers and men resorted to what might be termed casual headgear, including the shako without a peak, now worn by page-boys.

The cavalry and the prestige regiments wore grand exotic creations, often with plumes. The brass helmet with plumes introduced in 1846 is still in use for ceremonial occasions.

For off-duty wear other ranks wore forage caps. In the eighteenth century this was a stocking cap with a tassel at the end. It was replaced in the nineteenth century by a 'pork-pie' cap, and from 1874 by the Scottish glengarry, complete with trailing ribbon. This lasted until 1890 and the introduction of the folding field cap, a kind of Balaclava helmet. A curious short-lived forage cap was the 'Broderick' cap of 1902-5, named after a war minister.

In World War I the familiar peaked khaki cap was worn by both officers and men, and the only further developments lay in the other ranks' envelope-type forage cap and the beret. There is much to be said for collecting a series of military headgear. There is nothing in recent history so rare as to be solely a museum piece. Much the same is true too of military uniform, kept for sentimental interest, though the value here may lie in any badges or insignia which the uniform bears.

Although this illustration is of a French soldier, the kind of equipment he has is of great interest to the collectors of militaria.

The most plentiful and diverse of all badges are the pin-on or clip-on cap badges of World War II, less interesting if they were made into brooches for loved ones. Those of highly specialist regiments or regiments since abolished are the most desirable, and officers' badges in silver or silver-gilt carry a slight premium over those of other ranks. The German Army did not take to cap badges with as much enthusiasm as the British, but they made up for it with tunic and collar badges. Regimental insignia in wire on a fabric backing are not of great interest, as they were made for the blazer trade, ex-soldiers who looked back in nostalgia.

The first medals to commemorate a particular event were struck at the time of the Spanish Armada, and although many medals were struck during the time of Cromwell and Charles II, all are rare to the point of being unobtainable. The East India Company also issued a large number of medals (51,065 for one minor engagement alone), but these medals too are rarely found. For some wars, such as the American War of Independence, no medals were issued at all.

The first general medal was the Waterloo medal of 1815, awarded to both officers and men, and in the nineteenth century the little wars of Queen Victoria inspired nearly forty different medals. Some were issued long after the war had ended and most of the participants were dead.

Most medals had clasps or bars denoting specific campaigns and battles, and the combinations of these clasps are endless. The Naval General Medal can have 231 clasps, some associated with major engagements, others for minor incidents involving a handful of sailors.

There is a belief that medals from World War I are valuable. The three standard medals, known as Pip, Squeak and Wilfred after the cartoon characters, are almost valueless. Good-conduct and long-service medals are of less interest than gallantry medals, and those issued to officers are more collectable than those issued to other ranks (so a Military Cross ranks above a Military Medal). The Defence Medal and the War Medal of World War II were awarded to millions, many of whom were hundreds of miles from any fighting.

Of foreign medals, the best-known is the Prussian Iron Cross, introduced in 1813, revived in 1870 for the war against France, and issued in great numbers in both world wars. During World War I many new medals were issued including the Croix de Guerre.

Medals and badges can be displayed in many imaginative ways, and non-military badges, such as those issued for minor sporting victories, are ideal for starter collections. Very many handsome bronze medals were issued by agricultural and horticultural societies and these circulate at £2 or £3 each.

One of the most important areas of militaria is weaponry. The two major divisions are weapons such as swords and daggers, and firearms. The principal edged weapon is the sword, in ancient times made from copper, and later from bronze, iron and steel. Early swords still come onto the market, usually in what is known as 'excavated condition'. These were basic swords consisting of the blade and the crosspiece (or quillon) between blade and grip (the tang), and on the end of the grip was a decorative device, the pommel. Swords were made in two types, two-handed weapons with blades 3ft (90cm) or more long and smaller swords for hand-to-hand fighting. These were of two kinds, slashing weapons with a sharp broadish tapering blade, and piercing weapons such as the rapier.

The main development of the sword was in protection for the hand, first of all by extending the crosspiece and twisting it in the shape of an 'S', providing internal spokes to further protect the user. The cup-hilt was an improvement, with the hand protected all the way round by sheet metal which lent itself to decoration, piercing, engraving and added insignia. Long after the sword was obsolete this type was made for ceremonial purposes, and it still is – it is the traditional officer's sword, not expensive, and cheaper to buy than to make. The grip was often of shagreen, bound with silver wire. If the sword seems light, it is probably a theatrical prop.

In the sixteenth century it became fashionable to wear a rapier as a normal part of male civilian dress. Fencing became a fashionable sport, and the rapier became lighter, and the guard had been reduced to two solid oval shells and a 'knuckle-bow' (a curved arc of metal between the bottom and top of the grip). This was the smallsword, the badge of the gentleman until the end of the eighteenth century, and hardly ever used in anger except to batter a servant about the head.

The decoration of the smallsword reached such an extraordinary level that it could almost be a piece of jewellery. The metal parts of the hilt could be inset with intricate gold and silver inlay; the pommel could assume the most fantastic form; the guards could be most delicately shaped in filagree or composed of thousands of tiny steel beads threaded on wires. Even the blades were etched. The grips were sometimes made of solid gold with enamel inserts, or of porcelain. The knuckle-bow was also subject to treatment, the unyielding metal replaced by strings of beads.

Swords with slightly curved blades were used for hunting and naval service, and in the form of the sabre were used in the cavalry. The sabre was originally an Eastern weapon similar to weapons used and made today such as the Persian scimitar. Because of the problems of dating, Asiatic weaponry is a difficult area. Often the hilts were fitted with a very simple guard, or had no guard at all, and it is not easy to trace a historical progression, so explicit in European swords.

Of all the swords ever made, those of Japan are the only ones that have semi-religious overtones, existing almost unchanged from the eighth century until the present day. The Japanese sword had a long wooden grip bound with cord, a guard (or tsuba) consisting of an oval or circular plate, and a slender curved single-edged blade. The blade was a masterpiece of dedication, bars of iron and steel hammered together, repeatedly folded over, and forged fifteen or twenty times. By the time the blade was complete there could be thousands of layers of these metals, which when polished had a wood-grain effect all over the surface. But so far as collectors are concerned, the glory of the Japanese sword lies

A Victorian presentation sword by Mappin, Webb and Company, London 1886.

in the tsuba, which was detachable, and the owner of a sword could have as many as thirty tsuba to swap around. Tsuba were made in all metals – gold, silver, iron and various alloys, a favourite being copper with silver. They were subject to all forms of decoration – engraving, piercing, enamelling, stippling and inlaying – and the tsuba itself could be in the form of a coiled dragon or a frieze of animals. High quality tsuba are still being made today.

Daggers do not enjoy the same prestige as swords. The various types include the rondel dagger, with guard and often pommel formed as a disc, obsolete by the sixteenth century; the ballock knife (sensitively retitled the kidney dagger), with a guard formed of two rounded lobes, the classical killing instrument of Shakespearian times; the Scottish dirk, derived from the ballock knife; the baselard, a long dagger halfway to a sword, named after the Swiss city of Basle, with a hilt in the shape of a capital 'I', and favoured by bellicose civilians; the stiletto, short with a thin blade of triangular section; the cinquedea, wide-bladed, with a sloped-down quillon; the ear-dagger, which has a pommel made from two discs set at an angle to look like ears; and the most decorative, with ornate guards and quillons often curving outwards, the left-hand dagger, used in fencing to parry rapier attack. Some left-hand daggers had a comb-like back edge for trapping an opponent's weapon.

The most collectable daggers belong to two opposing groups – Nazi ceremonial daggers, and the diverse types of commando daggers of World War II. To give some idea of contrasting values, the Nazi and commando daggers would fall within the price range £150–£400 ($262–$700), while a continental ballock dagger of the sixteenth century would be in the £1,000–£2,000 ($1,750–$3,500) bracket. Beware of daggers made for theatrical purposes, though a lot of these have trick blades, spring-loaded so that they slide inside the hilt.

Unquestionably authentic are bayonets, made for work not display, and inexpensive so not worth faking. If the armies of the world are considered, there are hundreds of different types, and for collectors on a limited budget yet who want a challenge it is a rewarding field. The name is derived from a dagger formulated in Bayonne in France, and by 1640 it referred to a weapon that could be pushed into the muzzle of a gun converting it into a spear. This is the plug-bayonet and was used until recent times by hunters in France and Spain.

Reloading a musket could take several minutes, giving the opposing forces time for a counter-attack, and the fixed bayonet gave the musketeers some protection. First used by the French from 1642, it was taken over by the Saxons in 1663 and by the end of the century was being used by most European armies. The main disadvantage of the plug-bayonet was that the musket could not be fired while it was in place, and it was superseded by the socket-bayonet, consisting of a slender blade usually of triangular section fastened by an angle bracket to a tube which fitted over the end of the barrel, held in place by a lug on the barrel engaging in a slot in the socket.

Although the socket-bayonet continued to be used – and was

Armour was very much collected by the American millionaires who entered the buying market towards the end of the nineteenth century. Much was faked and altered for their benefit.

the standard spike bayonet of the British Army in World War II – a new kind of bayonet, the sword-bayonet, was also in use during the Napoleonic Wars. The hilt was grooved and was slipped onto the barrel and held in place by a spring catch.

Naturally the shape of bayonets depended on the weapons on which they were fitted. Some were aesthetically pleasing, such as the Brunswick sword-bayonet, based on ancient Roman designs, or the naval cutlass-bayonet. Some had a saw-back to help clear undergrowth. Many bayonets were engraved with the manufacturer's name, details of the regiment, and other interesting data. Early bayonets have a low survival rate and are likely to be worn and pitted.

Weapons such as spears and lances are likely to be in excavated condition, if found at all, except for African hunting spears for which there is no great demand. Bridging the gap between throwing spears and firearms is the crossbow. The military crossbow has long been a museum piece but surprisingly Elizabethan sporting crossbows still turn up occasionally, and later ones quite frequently, often ornate, with ingenious levers to draw back the bow. They are not overly expensive for what they are, obtaining at auction £400 ($700) and upwards for seventeenth- and eighteenth-century specimens. The ordinary longbow is purely a sporting item.

Of all forms of militaria firearms are the most diverse. The first hand-gun was a miniature cannon, as capable of killing the users as the enemy, but in the fifteenth century the matchlock appeared, followed by the wheel-lock, the snap-lock and the flintlock. These were all variations on the same theme, involving striking a piece of iron pyrites or flint sharply with a piece of metal to produce a spark, which ignited powder to propel a missile. The gunmaker belonged to the craftsman elite, and from the sixteenth to the nineteenth century all the finest firearms were elaborately decorated, with engraving, etching, gold and silver, inlay, chiselling and enamelling, a tradition that was carried on with the sporting shot-gun, and is continued to this day.

Various ways were found of increasing the efficiency of the gun, from extending the length of the barrel to rifling, first recorded in the sixteenth century but adopted generally only in the nineteenth century. Rifling is a series of spiral grooves inside the barrel which causes the projectile to spin in flight and thus improves the accuracy of the shot; rifling also ensures that the projectile is a close fit, so that the explosive force of the powder is utilised to the full.

Before the rifle, and later competing with it, the standard infantry weapon was the musket fitted with a flintlock. The British had found out the value of the rifle in the American War of Independence; the continental mercenaries the British employed had been equipped with rifles. The first British regiment to be equipped with rifles was the Rifle Brigade, formed in 1800. Flintlock muskets were supplanted in 1830–40 by the percussion musket, patented in 1807, in which a chemical detonating compound struck by a spring-actuated hammer ignites the charge of gunpowder in the barrel. This opened the way to modern rifles, but it was not until the 1860s that breech-loading was introduced,

Militaria

Writers on antiques often get themselves into a great deal of trouble. A description of a Grenadier Guards cap as displaying a badge in the form of a thistle resulted in a flood of angry correspondence, especially from ex-Guardsmen. The symbol is in fact a flaming grenade (thus the name of the regiment). The expert in question should perhaps have been doubled round the parade ground in full kit and equipment. If he had referred to the cap as a hat it would have been even worse; that might have got him Field Punishment Number One.

and it was no longer necessary to ram a bullet down the barrel. In about 1886 the magazine rifle was born, the ancestor of today's automatic and semi-automatic weapons.

Pistols work on the same principle as the guns, flintlock superseding wheel-lock and so forth, and were essentially the weapons of the cavalry. Early pistols had short barrels, with a stock set at right angles, but later the barrels were lengthened and the stock was set almost as a continuation of the barrel. Many pistols had silver mounts, and hall-marking carries a considerable premium. They were provided in pairs and, if cased and with all the accessories, they are valuable – £3,000 and upwards. Barrels became shorter in the eighteenth century, and earlier pistols had theirs truncated, thus losing the front-sight. When this has happened, unscrupulous dealers extend the barrel, for the early long-barrelled specimens are worth more.

Eventually the revolver superseded the pistol, and with the revolver comes involvement with the Firearms Act. The wording of the Firearms Act 1968 Section 58 has caused problems in the antique trade: 'Nothing in the Act shall relate to an antique firearm which is kept as a curiosity or ornament.' However, an antique firearm was not defined. Certain weapons over a hundred years old, and therefore considered antique for Customs and Excise purposes, are chambered for cartridges which are available today. It is an area where collectors should walk carefully.

Probably the best-known of all antique firearms is the blunderbuss. It was used both in pistol and gun form, and its main characteristic was its short barrel and wide bell-shaped aperture. It was a general-purpose weapon used by coachmen, innkeepers, the vaguely defined peace-keepers of the eighteenth century, the navy, the general public and highwaymen. The barrels were mostly of brass, and it seems that the bell-shaped end of the barrel was not to increase the efficiency but to enable the blunderbuss to be reloaded in difficult conditions – on top of a swaying coach, on deck in a gale, or when beleaguered by a mob. It is often believed that anything was poured down its gaping muzzle to serve as ammunition – nails, gravel, broken glass – but it is more likely that it was small shot.

Blunderbusses were mostly flintlocks, and they were mainly used in the eighteenth century. Sometimes the furniture – i.e. the trigger-guard, butt-plate and side-plate – is made of silver and engraved, and occasionally de-luxe specimens were made for noble families, but essentially it was a frightener, ineffectual at anything above close range, but formidable close-to as the user could hardly miss. It was such a basic weapon that many were cobbled together using any old equipment that happened to be around. This was also true of many Asiatic and African firearms, and long-obsolete weaponry such as the matchlock was in production at a time when the Europeans being fought were equipped with magazine rifles and Maxim machine-guns.

The most collectable firearm accessory is the powder horn or flask. To start with, any suitable hollow object was used, with a suitable plug, the most common being a cow's horn, the wide end capped, the sharp end nipped off. The horn could be softened and flattened by boiling, making it more convenient for carrying,

Danger on display

In 1972 a new owner took over Potter's Museum in Bramber, Sussex, famous for its tableaux of stuffed kittens and other furry mammals playing games and having tea-parties. He began to clear out the collection to make room for his display of pipes. On display was an assortment of militaria. There were six shells, a Mills grenade, and a gas bomb dating from World War I. They were all fully armed and lethal. Hurriedly a bomb disposal unit was summoned to render them safe.

The new owner said, 'I didn't think anybody could be such a fool as to put live bombs on public display'. He did not quip that, had the shells been there much longer, more than his pipes could have been smoking.

and the more sophisticated were fitted with a metal nozzle, often sealed by a spring-operated cut-off comprising a disc held against the open end and released by pressure on a spring-held arm. Sometimes there was a double cut-off at the bottom and top of the nozzle so that the powder could be measured out in even quantities.

Britain thirteen-piece Royal Lancaster Regiment set of 1907.

Some horns were engraved with battle or sporting scenes, and were fitted out with carrying rings or fixed to a strap. Sections of antler were also used, stoppered and decorated. All are rare, all are valuable, and all are faked. More attractive are the wooden flasks enclosed in a pierced and highly ornate metal frame, and shaped like a cut-down triangle with protruding nozzle; these are also faked.

From the eighteenth century copper pear-shaped flasks were produced in quantity, often decorated, with telescopic spouts to give a graduated amount of powder, and these were employed well into the nineteenth century. Powder flasks made in India paralleled musket design – fanciful, curiously shaped and exotic, using ivory and silver.

European sporting powder flasks were made in a variety of materials and shapes, becoming something of a fashion accessory.

The most common military object has nothing to do with swords or firearms. It can be seen at car-boot fairs and jumble sales priced at between £2 and £5, more if it is extra large This is the shell-case, polished and used as a vase, or fitted with handles. Many people do not realise what it is; to them it is just a brass vase. But all the details of date and origin are on the base. To connoisseurs World War I shell cases are preferable to those from World War II, and more plentiful, as many more millions of shells were fired. It is strange what souvenirs soldiers bring back from the war; the British soldiers of World War II were more astute. They bought back cameras and binoculars.

BARGAIN BASEMENT

No matter how lordly and disinterested even the most elevated antique dealer may appear, it must never be forgotten that his or her aim is to buy goods at less than the going rate and sell at a profit. Sometimes this profit may be small, perhaps no more than 5 per cent on an item costing several hundred pounds, and maybe even less if the purpose is to ingratiate the dealer with a special customer.

What is the going rate? This varies from district to district, even from month to month. A sensational and widely publicised auction in London may upgrade a type of antique, and make nonsense of price guides and previously recorded prices. Prices also depend on fluctuations in the dollar, and it is often believed that the world of antiques sways alarmingly when the dollar suffers, though with items such as top-class porcelain hardly a ripple is felt.

In 1980 the dollar stood at $2.48 to the pound; in February 1985 it went to $1.12, with 'parity' the vogue word at the time. In some parts of the country the Americans are never seen and wonder is expressed at their influence on the antique scene; they are a mysterious X-factor, and if few London dealers are around the country buying, their absence is put down to the disappearance of Americans in London.

In 1985 the strong dollar did influence prices in areas where there was a major American interest. The prices of Pembroke tables, at one time modest pieces everyone could afford, rose more than 50 per cent in a year. At the same time prices for old oak were stagnant, even going down. So a dealer who had bought a Pembroke table at more than the going rate the previous year and still had it in stock had got a bargain, not because he had been particularly perspicacious but because events had oc-

Once dismissed as of no interest, early vacuum cleaners are now being sought as curiosities and as examples of primitive technology.

A quiet time in the Newton Abbot Racecourse antique fair, the largest in the south-west.

curred which turned a bad buy into a good one.

When prices drop, private collectors come forward, and in their own specialities they are often more knowledgeable than general dealers. The best way to keep in touch with prices is to buy the *Antiques Trade Gazette* (generally on subscription only, from 17 Whitcomb Street, London WC2H 7PL, though single copies can be bought at one or two selected outlets in London). If the collectables belong to a recognised category and are disposed of at auction at specialist sales at Sotheby's, Christie's, Phillips and Bonham's, the catalogues of these sales should be subscribed to. There are other auction rooms which specialise in certain types of antiques. There is one known for its concentration on Royal Doulton figures, and Onslow's hold regular sales of railwayana, motoring antiques, aeronautica etc, usually on-site at establishments associated with these fields.

Many of the auction rooms outside London have an enormous turnover, and prices achieved are often in excess of those obtained in London, and are duly reported in the *Gazette*. Branches of the large London auction houses often specialise in locally remunerative fields – Phillips of Glasgow, for example, has a well-deserved reputation for its sales of golfiana.

It is easy to scorn the items that new collectors feel are within their scope, and it is useful if these objects are looked upon as exercises, trying the water, even training the eye to pick out certain objects from the many thousands of items a visitor can see in just one day at an antique fair or flea market. A run-of-the-mill dealer with a medium-sized shop once exerted himself to do a stock-taking, rather than casting an eye over the shelf and saying, 'Well, that lot has to be worth a couple of hundred'. He bought himself a notebook and began religiously to note down every item

with its buying price, real or assumed. By the time he had finished, many hours and a headache later, he had found that he had over a thousand different objects.

Many of them were 'old friends', items that had been around a long time and had been bought because they were cheap, not because the dealer liked them in any way. Almost every general dealer falls to this temptation, and although everything does sell in the end, these not-very-likeable objects represent money spent that could have gone elsewhere to better effect.

177

One million pounds

In 1970 the first picture to top £1m was sold at Christie's. It was a portrait of the artist's mulatto slave by Velázquez.

Most dealers have pet aversions – items or even a group of items that they have been tempted to buy on price considerations alone. Sometimes they learn by their mistakes; sometimes they are hell-bent on repeating them. Dealers new to the trade often find that certain kinds of pottery and porcelain are extremely cheap and cannot be resisted. If they are initially short of stock and want to make some kind of display they will soon find to their horror that they are inundated with:

- Odd cups and saucers.
- Small vases with a chip 'that really you don't notice'.
- Purply slag-glass vases that were bought as Victorian but are not.
- Egg-cups (only blue and white are ready sellers).
- Pretty flowery plates of the 1920s, often chain-store art deco.
- Large white meat-plates.
- Pottery vases encrusted with big flowers, mostly chipped.
- Small china animals, often dogs with spots.
- Single candlesticks.
- Earthenware jam-pots.
- Armorial miniatures not by Goss.
- Salt-glaze ink-bottles.
- Plain 1950s ware by top makers such as Spode and Wedgwood.
- Boring 1930s one-colour teapots.
- 'Amusing' 1950s animals, usually cross-eyed cats and dogs.
- Modern commemorative ware such as Charles and Diana wedding mugs.
- Late nineteenth-century bisque figures with bits knocked off.
- Jelly moulds with bad crazing.
- Crackle vases of glass of indeterminate age.
- Home-made table lamps made from vases.
- Part tea-services (five cups and saucers instead of six).
- Matt green art-deco vases, sometimes with a supernumerary handle.
- Single soup dishes, even from famous makers (Copeland etc).
- Small 1930s cute plaster figures.
- Coffee-pots from the 1920s and later.
- Book-ends.
- Japanese egg-shell china cups and saucers (or, woe upon woe, a complete service).

If dealers, who should know better, have this detritus on their shelves, so have collectors. Of course, many are aware that these miscellaneous objects have little intrinsic merit; they have been accumulated rather than consciously sought after because they remind owners of objects associated with their youth. They are therefore in the nature of stage props or items of interior decoration.

Not surprisingly both dealers and collectors are caught between buying items that appeal to their current more educated taste and those that hark back to younger days. For dealers who have come from working-class homes this can be confusing, for articles associated with the happy times can also be unsaleable rubbish.

If new dealers have an accumulation of undistinguished glass, china and pottery, they will also have acquired in moments of ignorance or aberration items which are far more unwieldy and cannot be hastily thrust away into a dustbin. These can be articles that once had some resale value but have deteriorated to such an extent that they are not only ugly but a danger to life and limb.

Amongst these are old tins. There is a theory that old tins are worth something, but the ones that go the rounds are rusty and battered, with designs much the worse for wear. Old farm implements come under the heading of bygones; they are often made of iron, and become rusty. True they would look nice cleaned up and hung up in some cottage by an open fire, but who will take the trouble?

Amongst the more cumbersome items that stay around with an uncanny persistence are 1920s and 1930s wooden folding screens, wooden fire-screens (glazed to contain an embroidery or print), large

Bing tinplate open car about 1902.

brass plaques stamped out to the thinness of gold leaf, and small items of 1950s oak furniture which dealers buy because they think it is useful, though naturally not to them for otherwise they would keep it when it fails to sell.

Surprisingly even the most unlikely candidate will eventually find a purchaser. There is a market for everything; sometimes when the snow lies thick and the antique shop or market might very well be in Omsk this might be doubted – but it is true.

One day a dealer was sitting in his shop wondering how he had acquired thirty white soup plates and, more important, how he could get rid of them. A young man came in and bought them all. What for? asked the dealer. Oh, it was for a game at a charity show in a nearby field, a competition to see who could skim them the longest distance. So the ultimate in the unsaleable had found a home. The broken pieces are probably there now, to provide a puzzle for bottle- and treasure-hunters of the future.

When is a bargain not a bargain? When inflation is not taken into account. It is easy to look at auction reports of eighty years ago and go 'ah!' when reading the prices. Here are some of them from 1902:

Chelsea egg-holder in the form of a goose	£24
Lowestoft bowl painted with flowers	£29
Hepplewhite satin wood secretaire	£50
Pair of Chippendale armchairs	£47
Chippendale stool	£10
Pair of lead garden figures	£200
Limoges enamel plate	£756
French Louis XV gold box	£1,995

It is difficult to relate the pound sterling of 1902 with that of today. But how about the pound of 1938? Is that any easier?

In the summer of 1987 a seventeenth-century Italian oak and walnut chest with marble inlay sold at an auction in Canterbury for £1,600 – not a bad price considering that early furniture prices are fairly static (the pieces are too expensive to be bought as mere furnishings and are not showy enough for the nouveaux riches). This chest had been bought at a house sale in Kent shortly before World War II for £100.

How pleased the vendor must have been! How shrewd the pre-war buy had been! But a thoughtful trade journalist took the trouble to make some rough calculations of inflation based on Bank of England indices. He found that £100 in, say, 1938 was more or less the equivalent of £1,600 in 1987.

LONG AGO AND FAR AWAY

Some antiques do not travel and remain in their country of origin; some are discovered by outsiders hundreds of years after they have been made, and these can make an immense impression, influencing current design and introducing new or previously overlooked materials.

Outsiders take what they want, sometimes ideas, sometimes the articles themselves, often aided and abetted by the resident population who see trade possibilities, often brutally and against the wishes of the natives, as happened in Africa in the nineteenth century. Many of the more outlandish items continued to be regarded as quaint novelties, or converted into something acceptable to civilised life.

Since the Renaissance there has been a general consensus in Europe about what is fashionable and what is acceptable. One of the reasons for a uniformity of taste was that the people who set the tone travelled widely and knew what was going on in the favoured centres of Europe. To adhere to past fashions, not only in clothes, but in furniture, pictures and art objects, was to proclaim oneself uncultured.

The romance of the East meant that objects from India, Japan and China were always given serious consideration. Japanese ceramics were imported to Europe from 1641 by the Dutch. The Dutch traders persuaded the Japanese to use all-over decoration and rich colour based on brocade designs. This was Imari ware (named after the exporting town), which became the favourite. Imari was also copied, not only by Worcester, but by the Chinese, who were quick to note its popularity. Cheap Imari of the nineteenth century is known as Nagasaki ware.

An 1880s interpretation of primitive African artifacts, when their history was little known and understood.

Satsuma was pottery, a crackled cream ware with at first sparse decoration, developed in about 1795. As the nineteenth century progressed the ornament and gilding became profuse, smothering the body, and the finished product was gaudy, believed by fans of *The Mikado* to be the essence of the Japan of the time as lacquer had been earlier.

Although probably invented in China, lacquer was the prime art form of Japan. Lacquer is sap from the lac tree. As many as three hundred coats of lacquer might be applied to one object. Lacquer could be carved; painted; encrusted with mother-of-pearl, shell, coral and metal. A characteristic item was the *inro*, a miniature medicine-case consisting of up to five compartments, worn on the girdle.

Mainly through the Dutch trading companies, consignments of lacquer screens, chests and cabinets began to reach the West, and the lacquer was duly copied, the process being known as japanning, a name it bears to this day. Imitation Japanese decoration was applied, either in low relief or painted. Panels were made to fit into furniture, and furniture made in the Chinese taste under the influence of Chippendale and others was often japanned. Japanned articles were very popular in the 1870s and 1880s.

Buddhas in bronze and other materials, sometimes gilded or painted, were brought in bulk to Britain from all over the East, as were objects in soapstone, a form of talc. Soapstone is found all over the world, but most of the items found in antique shops are oriental or pseudo-oriental. They are usually cheap, which is rather odd, because the quality of the carving can be high; the prejudice against soapstone probably arises from its name and texture.

Jade is another matter. Venerated by the Chinese, it comes in a variety of colours from a pearly white to a greeny black, 'cabbage' green being the most common. Too hard to carve, it is shaped by abrasives, and the Chinese produced animal and human figurines, relief panels, seals, snuff-bottles, belt buckles, ritual objects, and jewellery. As with soapstone, jade is found all over the world, with the largest deposits in the United States, which periodically has 'jade rushes'.

Jade jewellery and figurines were accepted without question into the West, as were bronzes, whether Buddhas or the imposing 'archaic' bronzes. The thick-pile Chinese rugs were welcomed unreservedly – so much warmer for the toes than the stringy austere products of the Middle East. Although we are so accustomed to them that they do not seem at all out of the way, the netsukes from Japan and the snuff bottles of China must have seemed alien when they were first imported. The netsukes were perhaps regarded as malformed carvings making use of odd lumps of ivory, wood, horn and metal, rather than as belt toggles, and as for snuff *bottles*... what was wrong with the good old English way of using a box?

Tobacco was introduced to China from the Philippines in the sixteenth century; it was probably not taken as snuff until the seventeenth, and it was not until well into the eighteenth that the aristocrats began to use small bottles up to 3in (7.6cm) in height

Although of European manufacture, these quadrants owe much to the pioneering navigation of the Arabs.

to hold the snuff. These bottles were made of every conceivable hard stone, porcelain, glass (sometimes painted on the inside), lacquer, ivory, horn, wood and coral.

Other objects from the Far East could be easily assimilated into the western home, and the owners were happy to remain in blissful ignorance of what the objects were. In country houses it was usual to have a huge pot inside the front door to hold sticks and umbrellas; these were sometimes used as door-stops or waste-paper containers. No-one really looked at them. If they were knocked over and broken by children on the rampage, a shrug of the shoulders was the only reaction. When in due course a house sale occurred these pots were shaken to get rid of the cigarette-ends and toffee-papers, and put up for auction; they sometimes made as much of the rest of the house contents put together. There are still stories of Ming vases being put to un-natural and unsavoury uses; and many of them are true. However, not all large jars or vases are necessarily worth a king's ransom. Many imposing specimens are still in the £200–£400 range.

Cloisonné vases from Japan and China were very acceptable because they were not so very different from those produced by the same enamelling technique in the West. Tang animals and figures fitted nicely in a gentleman's study, being restrained and discreet. As for Japanese woodcuts, well, they were very colourful and looked nice in the bathroom, but of course, they were only *prints*.

Artefacts from India drifted into Britain along with stuffed heads of tigers shot by sahib. There were fold-up tables with brass tops, ivories (sometimes of questionable taste), bronzes of deities with multiple hands, and over-exposed women, and, of course, there were jewels in abundance. One of the earliest imports was the Indian carpet which then vied with the Persian in quality, but the most significant classes of import proved to be fabrics, the chintzes and the Kashmir shawls, the latter copied by man-ufacturers in Norwich, Edinburgh and then Paisley, who exported them to Turkey and Persia, demonstrating a curious universal taste – that is, until the 1870s when the shawl was démodé.

A certain amount of convoluted teak and padouk furniture found its way to Britain, desks that are too heavy to move, with pigeon holes that trapped the hand, and unbearably uncomfort-able chairs. A piece of undecorated wood was an insult to the maker, and these charmless pieces took their place alongside the gargantuan follies of the 1850s and after. Often there was not much discrimination in what was brought back, because the taste of many of the empire-builders was suspect. But sometimes ob-jects specifically made for the British and tailored for their level of appreciation proved enormously popular in England and were reproduced by the thousand. Particularly suitable was brass ware, whether it came from India or the Middle East, complete with authentic-seeming patterns and calligraphy.

If Europe was open to the British aristocrats in the eighteenth and early nineteenth centuries on account of their wealth and their ability to profit by other nations' misfortunes, the world was open to the nineteenth-century soldier, trader and man of fortune.

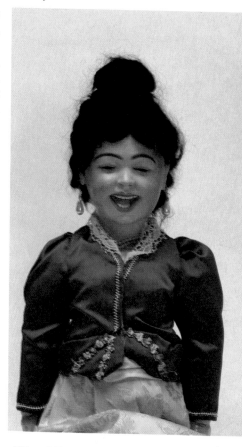

Although French, English and German dolls are frequently seen, this high-quality Japanese doll is something of a rarity.

Large Canton vase of about 1750, the kind of object found in large country houses open to the public for the disposal of sweet-papers and often worth many thousands of pounds.

183

A Regency simulated bamboo chair on turned legs, very much influenced by Chinese mannerisms and motifs.

At first glance this might appear an ancient Spanish chair with its leather seat and back of brass studs. Actually it was made about 1870. With intent to deceive? Who knows?

Of course most European nations joined in the quest, but Britain was supreme as she had the largest empire to quell. Weapons, jewellery, ritual objects, magic items, art works and unknown curios, all were taken. It was believed by the native inhabitants that if they had an image of their enemies they would be able to control them, so carvings of European soldiers appear alongside masks, totems and clubs.

It was not long before the so-called barbaric races realised that the white conquerors would be taken in by anything that appeared genuine and they began making tribal art for systematic export, which they still do.

In the provinces ethnographica is still an uncharted area. In London, though demand is erratic, it is a formidable collecting area. Africa has always been a major supplier, and since the Spanish Conquest curios have been brought to Europe from the Americas, including carvings and what was regarded as quaint pottery. Although much tribal art is sophisticated, there is a curious absence of elegant pottery or porcelain, accounted for by the fact that the potter's wheel was not known and the high temperatures needed for firing porcelain were not available. Nor were glazes to make products waterproof widely used.

Amongst the most widely collected are the art and artefacts of Oceania. An interest in this area was established many years ago when the wooden club which killed Captain Cook in Hawaii in 1779 was sold for 1,000 guineas (£1,100). Recent prices for Oceanic art include £6,000 ($10,500) for a Marquesas Islands wooden figure from a canoe prow and £3,200 ($5,600) for a crescent-shaped bowl with mother-of-pearl inlay from the Solomon Islands.

To illustrate fluctuating prices in tribal art, an Angolan mask brought back in the 1930s by a missionary (missionaries were for many years a basic primary source of goods) was estimated by the auctioneers at £300-£400 ($525-$700); in the event it was sold to a Belgian buyer for £4,600 ($8,050). A curious wood and copper-wire construction which might have been interpreted as a night-school collage but was in fact an African reliquary figure made £26,000 ($45,500). It is indeed an area of wonder. An American-Indian antler club, without much decoration and, to an outsider, with nothing much to distinguish it, sold for £5,000 ($8,750).

In the art of China and Japan, in tribal art and in the art of the 'curious civilisations', fakes and forgeries are rampant. There is also the additional factor that artists in Japan and China backdated their work not to mislead, but out of reverence for past reigns and dynasties.

It is impossible to realise today the hold Greek and Roman antiquities had on the upper classes of the eighteenth century, and the reverence and awe reached a high point in 1807 when fragments of statues rescued from the Parthenon in Athens were put on show in a house in Park Lane, London. These were the Elgin marbles, and they were later bought by the British Government and placed in the British Museum, where they are today.

In 1820 the most famous statue in the world, the Venus de Milo, was discovered, and since 1834 generations of schoolchildren have giggled at it in the Louvre. There was a fashion for all things classical. Women took to wearing clothes in the Greek style, and architecture was strongly influenced, as we can see in the giant caryatids (standing female figures) flanking St Pancras Church. When municipal museums, handsomely funded from local rates, began spreading throughout the United Kingdom there was a huge demand for antiquities, and as the Elgin marbles had set a precedent it did not seem to matter if they were damaged. Meaningless fragments of terracotta were regarded with rapture by newly appointed curators.

Unlike tribal art, many antiquities were excavated, and throughout much of the nineteenth century Rome and its environs were like a building site. The excavation in 1763 of Pompeii, destroyed by the eruption of Vesuvius in AD79, had created enormous interest throughout Europe, and when further major excavations were carried out in 1861 there was a fever of expectation.

There are certain materials that do not take kindly to burial. Fabrics disintegrate, iron rusts, and pottery, though not harmed by interment, is easily broken during the digging. Fortunately the interest of, especially, the British and the French, meant that those doing the excavating were more careful than they would have been (it being in the nature of searchers to be more interested in gold and other treasures than in old pots). Foreign interest also meant that certain choice items were wafted away from the site and reproduced or copied by skilled workmen, the products being fed to the market at regular intervals. There are probably more fakes in the field of classical art than in any other branch of collecting; often these fakes have long found resting places in the British Museum, the Louvre and the Metropolitan Museum of New York, and it takes a good deal of courage to expel them.

What is there from antiquity, from the Greek city states, from the Roman Empire (which encompassed not only Britain and Gaul but also what is now Asia Minor, rich in excavated treasures)? The best-known objects are the statues in marble, the most informative the Greek pottery painted by great artists, pottery that included drinking vessels, bowls, wine jugs, water jars, oil flasks, wine and water containers and, the most familiar, the amphora, the storage jar. Oxides of iron in most Greek clays meant that the colour of the untreated pottery was red-brown or black, and there was a natural sheen without glazing.

Much Roman pottery was utilitarian, but they occasionally produced highly decorative jars, though perhaps their most interesting products in pottery are the lamps. Certainly there is nothing to match or even approach Greek pottery. But there is nothing in Greek glass that compares with Roman.

The making of glass dates back to about 3000BC; it probably originated in western Asia. At some point in the century before Christ was born, glass-blowing was discovered, making glass cheap. The Romans exploited all the techniques available to them, which means almost all the techniques that are available today. The supreme example of their skill was the celebrated Portland Vase.

The Egyptians were soon producing drinking glasses with

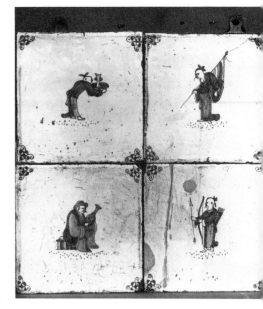

The influence of the orient is well seen in these early Dutch Delft tiles.

Bargain dolls

Doll-collectors, gnash your teeth! In the seventeenth and eighteenth centuries, hand-made wooden dolls were sold at fairs and markets for £1 a half-gross (seventy-two) – less than 1½p each.

The Chinese influence is very evident in this Worcester teapot and cover of about 1758.

wheel-engraved decoration. The Romans made window-glass; in about 1226 the British eventually acquired the skill. The Romans also made mirror-glass; the British consumer had to wait even longer for this.

In remote antiquity silver was more valuable than gold, because silver had to be expensively mined and gold had only to be happened upon, largely in the beds of streams. So gold was more often used than silver in jewellery, though silver plates and other items of household ware were made for the rich, regardless of expense.

A Worcester tea service influenced by Japanese Imari patterns.

The Romans were very skilled in metal-work of all kinds. Bronze was widely used in figure work (especially in Egypt with its multitude of gods) and for mundane articles such as toilet implements, spoons and the handles of knives (the blades being of iron). Bronze mirrors were made in Greece from the sixth century BC, later with a thin sheet of silver to improve the reflection.

An ornate rococo mirror; it does not take much imagination to see the oriental influence in the ornamentation.

Some antiquities are within the range of a collector of modest means. Some are not. The best deserves the best money. An auction of antiquities does not attract attention in the popular media nowadays; still less an auction of ancient glass.

Perhaps the supreme art object of the ancient world is cameo glass. The Portland Vase was smashed, but a piece of the same genus was offered for sale in November 1987 in London. This was a two-handled drinking cup of the type known as a skyphos, with a blue ground, the white cameo decoration in the form of chariots and horses. It made £320,000 ($560,000); the second most expensive piece, a gold glass fragment of the fourth century AD with a gold foil portrait of a family group, went at £26,000 ($45,500). It probably came from the walls of a catacomb, impressed for identification of those interred there. Had it been repaired the auctioneers suggested that it might have made £40,000 ($70,000). It was an odd object to survive for more than a millennium and a half.

Who have we to thank for the existence of so many treasures from the distant past? Certainly not governments. Certainly not individual politicians. There can only be one answer – the entrepreneur and the collector.

HOBBY ANTIQUES AND COLLECTABLES

'What on earth do you want to collect that for?' This might be asked of devotees of nineteenth-century Worcester porcelain or fine Regency furniture, but it is not likely. But it may well be asked of those who have acquired a taste for collecting Beatle ephemera, material relating to Charlie Chaplin, or aeronautica. Recently a collection of Charlie Chaplin material appeared at auction, and the prices realised give some idea of the demand.

It is essential that the subject for a major new personality-collectable should be famous beyond the norm, known throughout the world, loved and perhaps revered – not a character who occasionally needs to be dusted off and re-evaluated. Of course, it can be a category, or it can be a group of persons, but one distinct person on whom the focus can relentlessly fall is best. And so to Charlie Chaplin...

His hat, cane and shoes made an astounding £110,000 at Christie's South Kensington on 11 December 1987. The intrinsic value of these three items is nil; they would have been rejected by Oxfam. Their associative value is another matter, for they were associated with Chaplin's best known persona, the tramp. The hat and cane came with top-class credentials, a letter from a Hollywood costumier associated with Chaplin outlining the history of these articles.

This was the first sale devoted entirely to Chapliniana, though Christie's had previously in one of their ephemera sales sold another hat and cane for £15,000, which was regarded as a considerable sum and unlikely to be repeated. The boots were the only ones selected by Chaplin himself, and the right boot had a special hole in it so that the actor could be anchored to the floor when performing one of his stunts.

Middle-range items, including a motion-picture employee-identification card from 1942, which made £3,500, the original script of 1939 for the film *The Great Dictator* (£1,000) and five albums of press cuttings (£2,400), were just as special and inimitable. Two other canes, without the impeccable provenance, made £5,000 and £1,600. But the bidders were not taken in by boring nothings. A presentation Bible from Lambeth Boys' School not to Chaplin himself but to his cousin failed at a modest £55. Some items have more charisma than others. In this sale the run-of-the-mill material consisted of articles produced by way of commercial exploitation – photographs, postcards, figures in all materials, toys and chocolate moulds, for many of which there

---

Rolling pins

Glass rolling pins have been in use since at least the late seventeenth century, and the early ones were plain and made of ordinary glass. The much-collected blue specimens were made from the last years of the eighteenth century until about 1860, but beware of modern copies. They were a popular love token, given by sailors to their sweethearts. Other popular colours include opaque white, ruby, and green, with the blue and white marbled type perhaps the favourite, alongside the delightful rolling pins with inscriptions and quaint pictures of ships.

was little demand.

This sale is exceptional because of the startling price levels, but it is by no means unrepresentative. And there are other names waiting in the wings, equally loved, especially by the age-group who have the money. These personages do not necessarily have to be real; they can be Walt Disney's creation Mickey Mouse or J. M. Barrie's Peter Pan. A fairly recent costume for an actress playing Peter Pan was put up for sale with an estimate of £1,500 to £2,000. The present demand could not take it, but the costume did reach £650 before it was bought in (bought by the auctioneer on the vendor's behalf because an acceptable price had not been reached). All things considered this might have made Oxfam. But in a year, when the costume may be re-presented, who knows? Peter Pan has the makings of a collecting cult.

To judge by recent events, material related to Sherlock Holmes might well one day be elevated to an arcane level, particularly with the Japanese so active, to whom Sherlock Holmes represents Britain at its best and most characteristic. Sherlock Holmes made his first appearance in *Beeton's Christmas Annual* in 1887. Today this is probably the most valuable magazine in the world. Surprisingly, copies of the magazine in which the Holmes short stories appeared as regularly as clockwork, the *Strand*, are still available at modest prices.

Material related to Sherlock Holmes is fairly extensive. There is associative matter related to the films and plays in which Sherlock Holmes appeared, material connected with his creator, Conan Doyle, and a host of novelties and ephemera, ceramic busts of Holmes and Watson, silhouettes, brooches, cigarette cards, models of hansom cabs, deerstalker caps, Sherlock Holmes brooches, key-fobs and bookmarks, playing cards and games, comic strips, jigsaw puzzles, finger puppets and even a song, published in the 1890s.

Rock 'n' Roll memorabilia has now established itself as one of the major growth areas, but it is still new enough for hitherto unregarded material to creep onto the market. The audiences of the 1950s rock 'n' roll stars such as Bill Haley and his Comets and the 1960s phenomenon, the Beatles, who bought material or acquired souvenirs at the time are only now reaping rich dividends from their enthusiasms. Thirty years ago, a photograph of Bill Haley and his Comets signed by the band would have been modestly cherished, and in due course swapped for something else on the same level – a ticket for a pop concert perhaps. Today such a photograph, plus one other, unsigned, can be worth at auction £300. Suits worn by Beatles John Lennon and Paul McCartney have been recently sold at auction for £1,500 and £2,000; a first draft of a chapter from Lennon's *A Spaniard in the Works* was bought in at £13,500, having failed to reach its ambitious reserve.

To those nurtured on the traditional antiques these prices are astonishing, especially to those dealers who were practising their trade in the 1960s. Postcards now selling for £10 each, and medium-range ones at that, seem positively cheap, as do the items in many an old-established hobby-antique category, such as aeronautica.

There has always been a demand for anything in the nature of even mildly saucy, and amongst the most collected artists of the genre is certainly Raphael Kirchner, the master of art nouveau naughtiness.

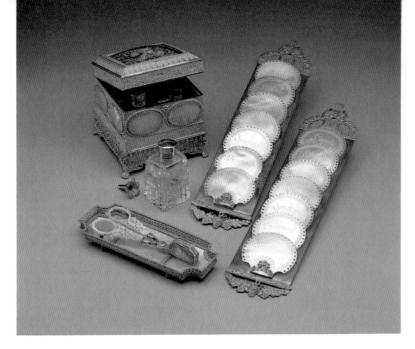

A fine selection of French mother-of-pearl items of about 1820.

Two fine nineteenth-century pendants.

Is it a bargain? Is it collectable?

The first class of aeronautica is associated with ballooning, which was very fashionable between about 1783 and 1830. The most common items are prints (some of them reproduced so beware) but ballooning designs found their way onto snuff and other boxes and pottery and porcelain.

The successful flight of the Wright brothers was commemorated by souvenirs, but not in the quantity one would have predicted considering the epoch-making event it was. Many of the early flights carried mail, and picture postcards 'despatched from the clouds' can be worth several hundred pounds. One of the most valuable of these early cards was that carried by balloon post in 1903 to raise funds for the lifeboat service. In top condition one of these cards can be worth £1,000. The concept of flight was popularised by aviation meetings and their associated items – medals, posters, hand-outs and all kinds of advertising material. Apart from ephemera, there were tin toys, usually out of scale.

Prior to World War I, aircraft were basically box-kites with an engine. There were virtually no instruments. During the war there was constant development, and by 1918 aircraft had reached a high level of efficiency. Instruments, equipment, fabric and propellors of World War I aircraft are very much collected, together with log-books, manuals and Royal Flying Corps memorabilia. Aviation meetings between the wars brought a new range of posters, invitations, and advertising material. Travelling by air was expensive and restricted to the rich, and this phenomenon was used by the makers of totally irrelevant goods to promote their products.

Aeronautica from World War II includes uniform insignia (but hardly the uniforms as they were so common), model aircraft, (including Dinky models and brass and chrome miniatures made in aircraft factories when the operatives were out of sight of prying eyes), instruments and aircraft parts (including relics of German aircraft which were shot down during air-raids), and a wealth of paper items – log-books, diaries and other personal items.

Motoring collector's items are well established, and range from early magazines (such as *the Car Illustrated*), programmes (such

A rare tinplate limousine by Georges Carette, sold in September 1987 for £5,500.

One of a pair of fine hand-painted nineteenth-century French panels.

as that for the thousand-mile motor-vehicle trial of 1900, value £100-£150), books (especially those of a technical nature) and sales leaflets and handbooks (particularly if they are associated with prestige cars such as the Hispano-Suiza, Alfa Romeo, Rolls-Royce or Aston Martin). Amongst the most valuable magazines is the *Brooklands Gazette*, a short-lived monthly the first volume of which (twelve issues 1924-5) is worth about £450.

Among the most collected items are badges and mascots, the most valuable being the glass emblems of Lalique, the easiest to recognise the Rolls-Royce 'Spirit of Ecstasy'; the chromium-plated version of the latter is valued at £150-£250. The mascots varied greatly, probably the most common being Mercury, and almost all are chromium- or nickel-plated.

Cars spawned a mass of novelty items, such as cigarette- and match-holders in wood and brass modelled on specific cars, often with rubber tyres; silver ashtrays; chromium-plated decanters in the form of car radiators; pewter dishes in art-nouveau style embossed with a car design; and silver cigarette-cases. And of course the makers of accessories were not slow in promoting their wares in the novelty market. Collectable accessories include rubber-bulb horns, dashboard instruments (particularly if they can be associated with a specific car or are sporty, such as revolution counters), lamps of all kinds, sparking plugs, veteran carburettors of the 1900 period (value £150-£200), and even high-tension coils of the same era. These are much in demand, not to display, but to use in veteran cars. There is also a trade in old petrol- and oil-cans, which has led to some dealers speculating in rusty specimens which have no value. More interesting are the enamel petrol, oil and garage signs, many in remarkably good condition considering their years of travail.

Prices and collecting levels are not yet stabilised in motoring memorabilia, and posters selling at no more than £50 at the time of writing will almost certainly have appreciated four times within the next year or so. Early AA and RAC badges are due for upgrading; outside specialised motor auctions they make £4 or £5. Interested collectors should keep an eye on autojumbles (an

Who can resist the appeal of a well-stocked antique shop?

ugly portmanteau word) for likely items.

Sportiana is a very wide area, but the attention of collectors is particularly concentrated on two sports – golf and cricket. Cricketana is dominated by one man – W. G. Grace. There is more memorabilia associated with his name than with all the other cricketers put together. These range from plates made by Coalport commemorating Grace's hundredth century in first-class cricket, through transfer-printed handkerchiefs bearing his portrait, to a rare three-handled Doulton jug of 1882 with Grace in action illustrated on the side.

The one great advantage of Grace was that in appearance he was thoroughly distinctive; no doubt there were other cricketers with beards, but no-one was so bushy, and he was also big, even portly. This was a help to the makers of novelties; there was no question who a cricketer with a beard was, even if badly modelled. And there were novelties in abundance – cast-iron book-ends, desk-pieces with Grace flanked by inkpots, Grace ashtrays, and Grace brooches and tie pins.

There are many items in cricket that lend themselves to commemoration, and there is a sharply defined history: early cricket, up to 1865 when W. G. Grace entered the game; the period to 1895 when cricket became thoroughly organised with fourteen counties in the county championship; the golden age to 1914; the period 1919-39; and the post-war age.

The earliest bat in existence dates from about 1750; it was more like a baseball bat than anything else, but by the end of the eighteenth century the cricket bat was taking on the familiar shape. Bats are often signed by teams or famous players; one signed by Grace would be valued at £200-£300, one by a lesser man at a tenth of this. Early photographs are much valued, and early prints and paintings fetch prices quite out of proportion to

An early rock 'n' roll photograph of the type fetching large amounts at auction.

their artistic merit.

Many manufacturers used cricket and cricketers to promote their products, and these included Fry which put out advertising sheets depicting Grace and entitled 'The Finest Cricketer and the Finest Cocoa of the Century'. Landmarks such as certain cricketers' 'century of centuries' were commemorated by potters, especially Coalport.

Amongst the more substantial cricketana are the cast-iron pub tables bearing portraits of W. G. Grace on the legs; inscribed silver mugs and tankards; silver trophies; cast-iron cricket-bat gauges; cricketing craftsmen's tools; bronze, silver-plated and spelter figures; cast-iron W. G. Grace doorstops and the various games based on cricket from simple table-top toys in cardboard to the massive pier-end arcade games with a penny-in-the-slot facility.

Smaller items include paper-knives in the form of a cricket bat; miniature cricket bats in all materials; cricketing tablecloths; ties, badges, ashtrays in all materials; match-holders; wine and liqueur glasses with enamelled or painted cricket scenes; sweet containers in the shape of a cricket bat; condiment sets; cricketing buttons; copper plaques; snuff-boxes with cricket motifs; belt buckles; tiles; and pipes with the bowl moulded as the head of Grace. This gives an indication of the range available, and although the prices are at present modest it is a collecting field where values are sure to rise.

The number of books on cricket and the amount of ephemera is immense – scorecards (including silk replicas), autograph albums, posters and advertisements, letters, diaries, menus, programmes, brochures, cigarette cards, and promotions. There are the oddities – the leather ball coming apart at the seams which *may* have been a Victorian cricket ball, and the brass-coated cricket stumps, the purpose of which must forever be in doubt. One of the most interesting and valuable items sold at auction was a cricket bat bearing the signature of sixty-five cricketers of the golden age. This was originally auctioned at Christie's in 1915 for 70 guineas (£73.50) in aid of the Red Cross 'in memory of those thousands who were playing cricket at the front'. It was sold in 1986 for a sum well in excess of £1,000.

Golfing memorabilia fetches much higher prices than cricket items, especially as there is very strong American, European and Japanese interest. Early 'official' golf was contempory with early cricket; club golf, from which evolved rules and the established layout of a course, came into being in 1744; St Andrews was founded in 1754; and the first club ouside Scotland, Blackheath near London, started in 1766. Equipment associated with golf pre-dates existing cricket relics. Very long heavy clubs have been found that date back to at least 1714; they were probably used with boxwood balls, though early golf balls were made of feathers in a hide case. Gutta-percha balls ('gutties') were introduced in 1850; being smooth they flew badly, but when it was found that the performance improved with wear they were dimpled.

The gutta-percha balls ruined the wooden clubs then in use, and golf clubs were redesigned, using leather facings and softer woods for the heads, such as apple and pear. The standard wood

An Edwardian mantel clock of modest quality surmounted by a golfer addressing the ball, while the base is held up by a pair of clubs and an assortment of golf balls.

for the shafts was hickory. A challenger to the guttie was the 'putty', made of a secret composition believed to consist of cork chippings and india-rubber, but it did not fly far. In 1902 the rubber-cored ball was introduced, known as a Haskell after the inventor. Again clubs were remodelled, persimmon being used for the club-head with faces inset with ivory, bone and metal. Irons came into their own. The steel shaft ousted hickory in about 1929.

Feathery balls and early golf clubs can be worth well over £1,000, sometimes much more, but it is a very specialised and expert field, and rusting clubs dug from the back of garages are not necessarily worth very much.

As with cricketana, there is a vast quantity of golfing items and memorabilia – the mass-produced novelties and the one-offs. There is nothing in golf literature to compare in value with a complete or near-complete run of Wisden's *Cricketers' Almanack* (£3,000 plus) though certain rare books such as Kerr's *The Golf Book Of East Lothian* are valued at about £800, and books which were once ordinary stock in second-hand bookshops priced at £1-£2 are now much sought after.

Amongst the commercial items are lighters, sometimes disguised as golf balls; biscuit tins in the form of golf bags; biscuit barrels with golfer finials; desk-sets; tie pins in the form of clubs; cutlery; pocket watches in silver with dimpled backs; clocks with golfing motifs on the dial; enamel and silver cigarette-cases; match-holders; and many ceramics, among the most interesting being Royal Doulton ware decorated with 'Crombie' figures. Charles Crombie was the author of *The Rules of Golf Illustrated* (first edition £250-£300), a very amusing series of cartoons sponsored by the mineral-water firm Perrier.

Anyone who tries to compile a price guide for sportiana is not to be envied, for prices fluctuate wildly depending on who is bidding against whom, though there does seem a distinct general re-evaluation of major sporting figures. And there is no comparison between the prices obtained at specialist auctions and those in the provinces. To give some idea of the uncertainty, unavoidable with so many imponderables: in 1985 a bat inscribed and signed by Jack Hobbs, 'I used this bat in the Surrey v. Middlesex match at Kennington Oval, August 9th 1930, when I passed W. G. Grace's aggregate record of 54,896', was auctioned in London; the estimate was £100-£150 and the bat realised £1,200.

Sportiana is a world away from the field of picture postcards; in the latter there are yearly catalogues, price guides and magazines, dozens of specialist dealers and prices ranging from 20p to £20 and upwards – something for everybody, and only a few items rare enough to be out of reach. The first postcard dates from 1869, Britain began issuing uninteresting General Post Office Cards in 1870, and only in 1894 were privately printed cards allowed through the post. Between 1895 and 1900 a squarish card, known as a court card, was used, and two firms, one in Edinburgh and one in Leicester, began printing view-cards of local scenes.

The golden age for the postcard was between 1902 and 1914. The most desirable are art-nouveau cards, probably the best-

---

What is a dissected puzzle?

A jigsaw (the jigsaw is a tool invented in the 1870s, thus the name). Early jigsaws have survived because they were made of wood, were mainly religious or educational, maps first of all, and were cut in a few simple shapes. Towards the end of the nineteenth century the lid of the box began to be printed with the final picture. In the 1920s photographs were first used as subjects.

known artists of the period being Raphael Kirchner, who designed about 630 cards, and Alphonse Mucha, whose posters have been reproduced for the bed-sit trade in huge numbers. There are dozens of collecting fields in postcards – trams, trains, buses, motor-transport, post offices, shop-fronts, military subjects, crashes and exhibitions – and the postcard dealer is never short of custom.

At one end of the collecting spectrum, coins can form a starter collection; at the other coins are a serious study, valued for their historical interest and as mini-sculptures in relief. It is likely that coinage of some kind has been used for three thousand years, and Roman coins are fairly common, the oldest antiques likely to be bought for a very modest amount. Coins are struck, not moulded; a heated metal disc is placed between two dies, and is struck with a hammer or subjected to mechanical pressure. Until the sixteenth century all coins were made by hand, and were irregular and open to 'clipping' and forgery.

Coins are modelled large, and reduced on a device called a pantograph to the proper size. Condition is of prime importance, though it is in the nature of things for coins to be well handled and therefore to some degree worn. With postage stamps, coins have been a favourite collectable of schoolchildren and how disappointed they have been to find that their thick Georgian pennies, with the date just discernible, and the Victorian 'bun' pennies, often wafer thin, are worth very little.

In the long run, it is a matter of chance who or what is taken up, and a collector who invests time and money in the pursuit of some specific and narrow subject must pause to wonder whether the enthusiasm is warranted, and whether he or she will tire or become disenchanted.

It is often easy to forget that not everything appreciates over and above the rate of inflation. Sometimes the market dips, and everyone says 'I told you so!' If the objects involved are classic antique items the purchaser merely has to wait until sanity returns. In the early years of the present century there was a great demand for drawing-room sculpture, especially the marble statues of Jean-Antoine Houdon (1741-1828) which did not seem to have an upper price limit. In 1915 a bust by Houdon sold for $200,000, then the equivalent of £41,200, around half a million pounds in today's money. Then the demand dropped and, until recently, few eighteenth century drawing-room marbles topped £15,000.

Until recently... Anything with intrinsic value, of superb quality which cannot be forged, will eventually override momentary setbacks. Works of art of superb quality which can be forged are a different matter. It is interesting to look at bronzes, whether they are the signed animal bronzes by a handful of French master sculptors, or Degas dancers. In 1967 a Degas dancer sold for £53,000. There was no certainty that there were no others waiting to go on the open market when the time was ripe, for any number of bronzes can be taken off one master. It is acknowledged that in 1925 twenty-six casts were made from a Daumier plaster model. Daumier bronzes were making more than £10,000 apiece in the late 1960s.

One could write for years without going through all the

Novelty items have always held a strong place in collectors' affections!

Tile collecting

Tiles from a very interesting collecting category, and very early Persian and Syrian tiles are still available at modest prices, sometimes less than £50. Among the most appealing are the blue-and-white Dutch Delft tiles, exported to Britain in great quantities from about 1630, which can be confused with those made in Britain, though in value they are on a par. Most of the tiles on sale today in general antique shops and in fairs and markets are Victorian or art nouveau but beware, these are being reproduced, though not with intent to deceive. Colourful art nouveau tiles were often used on the back-boards of wash-stands, and now fetch more money than the wash-stands themselves did no more than ten years ago. Tiles lend themselves to display, and do-it-yourself enthusiasts often incorporate old tiles with modern ones in the decoration of the kitchen or the bathroom, where any nibbling at the edges can be disguised by cunning grouting. A Victorian tile with a maker's name such as Minton carries a premium. The most sought after of Victorian tiles are probably those hand-produced by William de Morgan, especially the lustre ones.

categories that might qualify as hobby antiques and collectables. Cinema memorabilia began to be popular in the late 1960s, and in about 1970 an auction of 184 lots of Hollywood material was held, including five hundred posters and seven thousand film stills. A set of Greta Garbo postcards was considered wildly over-priced at £80, but twenty rare stills from early Dietrich films made only £7. The most interesting objects appear when studios sell off their stock. In the early 1970s Judy Garland's shoes from *The Wizard of Oz* were sold together with Marilyn Monroe's fur bikini and Pussy Galore's catsuit from a James Bond film. One of the largest props was an 11ft (3.3m) airship for a film of that name. General film material overlaps with cult material related to names such as Mickey Mouse, Snow White, James Dean, and three or four thousand others, many with their own fan clubs and magazines.

Film stills were turned out in millions, as were posters in every language. There were brochures, campaign books putting forward advertising methods, film magazines and fan magazines (the least interesting of ephemera), sheet music, and thousands of novelties, Donald Duck watches, Shirley Temple lookalike dolls, and lead models of Snow White and the Seven Dwarfs.

Much of the memorabilia associated with the cinema has a counterpart in that of the theatre – signed photographs, posters and play-bills, the various props used in plays and stage shows, auctioned off at intervals together with costume, promotion material and programmes. Many of the props are extremely realistic and can be taken for the real thing, especially shields, swords and daggers, and the stage crowns and regalia can impress from a distance. Analogous is circus material, with more variety in promotion ephemera, and with the present nostalgia for old music-hall there is clearly potential here.

One of the most important collecting areas is railways, whether it is called railwayana or railway relics or whatever. The end of steam and the closing of inconvenient lines sparked off an unquenchable nostalgia for days gone by, with the desire to have some memento be it ever so humble. The end of an era can similarly be a spur for other collectables.

Perhaps the most highly prized of all railways items is the locomotive name-plate. Those of the famous engines are now mostly in museums or private collections. Early plates bear engraving on brass, later ones were cast in brass with raised lettering and rim. Name-plates are being reproduced – not with the intent to deceive, but time makes nonsense of good intentions. Carriage destination boards are still used on long-distance trains but those painted with pre-BR livery are eminently collectable, as are the maps, advertisements and views slotted in above the seats in the carriages and providing reading matter, information and harmless entertainment for the travelling public.

Probably the railway ticket is the most widespread of railway ephemera. Early tickets were mostly hand-written, and as there was a multitude of self-contained companies there is considerable diversity in ticket design and layout. Those of the more obscure and short-lived companies are naturally of more interest, as are tickets printed for specific excursions. Single tickets are preferable to cut-in-half returns, and there is a modest demand for platform tickets, a once-scorned category.

An interesting class of collectables consists of objects made to while away the time. These can be mundane, but during the Napoleonic Wars French prisoners-of-war, especially those incarcerated in Dartmoor Prison, which was built for them, made the most remarkable objects – exquisite straw boxes, for example – out of simple materials such as straw and bones.

Far more plentiful are the objects made by sailors at sea, the most famous being scrimshaws – walrus tusks, whalebone and whale teeth carved and engraved, sometimes with just a knife, sometimes with a range of instruments. The designs were scratched or pricked out on the tooth, inks and dyes were worked into the lines, and superfluous colour was wiped off. Sometimes the bone was whittled into stiffeners for corsets or stay busks, suitably adorned with designs or messages, and given to wives and sweethearts after the voyage. Scrimshaws are widely forged. A good scrimshaw can be worth well over £1,000.

Other sailors' work is not so amenable to faking. The fine models of ships, correct in every detail, with rigging that defies description, will outwit the cleverest faker. These are the equivalents of the modern scratch-built models of cars, trains and machines. But the sailors did not have lathes and precision instruments. We can only marvel at their expertise. How much has been lost? At the time these models were no doubt cherished, but they were only the by-products of periods of enforced inactivity, not what were popularly known as art-works. And the same applies to prisoner-of-war work. How much was idly tossed aside by the prison warders when their charges were released in the fullness of time?

Some antiques can be converted to modern use, such as early telephones. These are being reproduced, but the National Telephone Service example illustrated is genuine.

GLOSSARY OF FURNITURE TERMS

Acanthus A stylised leaf decoration, very popular in mahogany.
Amorini Cupids or cherubs.
Anthemion A honeysuckle design.
Apron A masking piece under the front edge of a piece of furniture.
Arabesque Fanciful figures, fruit and decorative devices in groups and combinations, largely used in marquetry.
Arcading A line of ornamental arches.
Astragal A type of moulding on the bars of bookcases.

Bail A hanging pull for drawers.
Ball-and-claw A design for a foot on all types of cabriole-leg furniture: a claw holding a ball. Probably derives from a Chinese model.
Balloon back A swelling curved back for chairs, with a nipped-in waist, very much used in early Victorian furniture.
Baluster A turned shape on uprights of furniture, somewhat in the form of a vase. Cut in half lengthways it was fixed to chests etc as decoration.
Banding A border around doors, panels, drawers, tables etc – flat, veneered or ornamented. Straight banding is cut with the grain and cross banding against the grain; feather-banding and herring-bone banding are a sequence of chevron patterns, usually on walnut furniture.
Barley-sugar twist Spiral turning.
Beading A moulding either plain or semi-circular section, or in the style of a string of beads. Where the beads are alternatively rounded and rectangular it is called 'bead and reel'.
Bevel A sloping cut, usually in glass.
Blind fret A fretted design on a solid background, much used as a frieze on tables.
Blister An American term for the marking in certain woods that looks like a blister.
Bobbin turning Turning in the shape of bobbins, a kind of squashed spiral turning.
Bombé 'Blown-out' in French. Furniture with a swelling outline towards the base.
Boulle work A process of inlay, using brass and tortoiseshell, less used in Britain than in France.

Bow front A gentle curve on the front of furniture such as chests-of-drawers.
Bracket foot A shaped foot, projecting slightly, first used in the late seventeenth century and used particularly for chests of all kinds.
Break-front A kind of bookcase in which the central section juts out.
Broken pediment A pediment broken by omitting the apex (the central point) but the symmetry is still kept.
Bulb The bulging shape of elements in old oak-furniture uprights. Later used in walnut.
Bun foot A foot shaped like a bun, largely used on chests-of-drawers and similar articles.

Cabochon A raised oval with a rim often used on chair ornament.
Cabriole leg A leg curving outwards at the top, tapering in a gentle arc to the foot and ending in a pad, hoof, ball-and-claw etc.
Cameo back A chair-back consisting of an open oval.
Carcase The basic frame of the furniture, without veneer or extras.
Cartouche A shield or circular shape surrounded by scrolling, with space for inscription. Often found on the corners of buildings as well as on furniture. Originally meant to imitate a sheet of paper with the ends curled over.
Castors Small swivel wheels on all sorts of furniture, made of wood, leather, metal or porcelain.
Chamfer A bevelled edge on square-section furniture, giving a less austere impression.
Channel moulding Grooved decoration.
Chip-carving Faceted surface ornament mainly on oak using gouge and chisel.
Cleat A strip of wood applied to the end of a flat surface to give strength.
Cockbeading Bead moulding used on drawer fronts from 1725 onwards, and much used in chainstore Edwardian and 1920s furniture.
Column turning Turning producing the effect of a column.
Cornice The uppermost horizontal member of a piece of standing furniture, a term taken over from architecture.
Countersink To make a hole to accommodate a 'countersunk' screw – meaning that the top of the screw is flush with the surface.
Cresting rail The top rail of a chair.

Cup-and-cover Bulbous decoration, often highly ornate, used on Elizabethan furniture and on chain-store tables of the 1930s.
Diaper Diamond shapes with dots or interior decoration.
Dished corner A table-top corner with a depression in it; sometimes on gaming tables to take counters, sometimes to hold a candle.
Dovetail A joint in which wedges interlock with a series of corresponding wedges.
Dowel A wooden peg holding timber members together.

Ear A block of wood at the top of a cabriole leg, giving strength.
Egg-and-dart A moulding in the shape of alternate wedges and open-centred ovoids.
En suite In a matching set.
Escutcheon A shield-shaped surface on which a crest, monogram or other device is displayed. Also a plate pierced for a key-hole.

Fall front (or drop front) A writing surface of a desk or similar piece of furniture which has to fall or drop for use.
Fielded panel A panel with the edges bevelled.
Figure The name given to the pattern in timber.
Fillet A narrow strip of wood.
Finial A turned knob (usually elongated), a spike or an ornamental design used to top off a clock or section of a piece of furniture.
Fluting Grooving, either in the legs of furniture or on the flat.
Fly-leg A table leg without stretchers which swivels to support the top. A truncated gate-leg.
Frets Fretwork.
Frieze A thin rectangular section, usually decorated, running horizontally beneath the top of a table or below a cornice or on any piece of furniture needing such decoration.

Gadrooning Decorative moulding consisting of curved shapes, either concave and convex, or just convex.
Gallery A low railing in metal, wood or some other material.
Gesso A plaster used as a base for painted or gilt decoration, usually applied on wood as in picture frames.
Guilloche An incised pattern of interlinked circles, often used in a frieze.

Hipping A method of chair construction in which the top of the leg is carried above the corners of the seat-rail.

Hoop back A chair-back in which the uprights merge into the top rail to make a hoop.

Husk A decorative bluebell-like or corn-husk design, used end to end or in clusters.

Inlay Material of all kinds such as brass, mother-of-pearl etc let into solid wood to form a picture or other design.

Key pattern A geometric pattern of key shapes.

Ladder back A chair-back with horizontal rails, slightly curved or straight, like a ladder.

Latticework A kind of fretwork in the Chinese style.

Linenfold Carved imitation, mostly on early oak, of folded linen.

Lining The sides and back of a drawer interior.

Lion mask Self-explanatory – a popular form of decoration, dating from the early eighteenth century and persisting throughout the Victorian period on oak (known to the trade as 'pussy-cat' oak).

Loper Substantial pull-out wooden runners supporting the fall front of a bureau or similar piece of furniture.

Lozenge An incised diamond pattern, often with interior design.

Lunette An incised fan-shape with interior detail, often used on friezes.

Marquetry Different veneers glued to the surface of wood to present a picture or other design.

Medallion An applied device on almost any surface, usually circular or oval.

Mitre joint Two surfaces fitted together at an angle of 45 degrees.

Monopodium A support with a lion-mask top.

Mortise-and-tenon A joint in which the tongue (tenon) slots into a rectangular hole (mortise).

Moulding A shaped length of wood, sometimes substantial, used as decoration, or to mask joints.

Muntin A vertical wooden piece separating two panels.

Ogee An elongated 'S' shape used in mouldings etc.

Ormolu Gilt bronze, often applied to gilt or lacquered brass.

Ovolo A moulding with a quarter circle section, often used on drawers.

Oyster veneer Circular forms created by using cross-sections of branches of walnut or other woods.

Pad foot A rounded foot akin to a club foot.

Parquetry Geometric marquetry.

Patera An oval or circular design depicting a flower.

Patina The surface acquired by wood or other materials after polishing, wear and constant rubbing plus changes in the texture due to age.

Paw foot Self-explanatory – a foot popular in the eighteenth century and the Regency.

Pediment A prominent moulding used to top a bookcase or similar piece of furniture.

Pie crust The scalloped rim of a round table.

Pilaster A flat-sided column.

Plinth A rectangular or square base.

Quartering Four pieces of veneer of identical figuring symmetrically opposed to each other, giving a mirror effect. Used on table tops and doors, and very popular on 1920s and 1930s glossy furniture.

Ram's Head Self-explanatory – a popular device for decoration on the same level as the lion's mask.

Rebate A groove cut to receive an edge.

Reeding The opposite of fluting – raised semi circular beading usually on uprights such as chair- and table-legs.

Roundel A circular ornament of any kind.

Rule joint An ingenious joint allowing a table-leaf to fold without leaving an ugly gap.

Runner A strip of wood to facilitate the smooth running of a drawer.

Sabre leg Introduced in the Regency period, a leg of square section curving outwards in a gentle arc.

Saltire An 'X' shape formed by stretchers of tables and chairs, usually with a finial at the intersection.

Scroll A curved or spiral decoration, often used as the foot of a cabriole leg.

Serpentine An elongated 'S' shape used for the fronts of chests-of-drawers and similar furniture.

Shell Self-explanatory – a very common motif used on almost everything, very popular in the eighteenth century.

Shield-back A chair type made famous by Hepplewhite and his followers, self-explanatory.

Shoe-piece A wooden section at the bottom of the back of a chair in which the central splat was fixed.

Skirt A name applied to the apron beneath the front of the seat of a chair.

Spade foot A tapered rectangular section terminating the legs of fashionable furniture, particularly chairs.

Spiral twist Another name for barley-sugar turning.

Splat The central piece between the seat and the top of a chair-back, plain or ornamental.

Spoon back A type of chair-back in which the splat gently curves.

Squab A thick soft cushion, from a Swedish word meaning flabby.

Stile An upright member in framing or panelling, from a Dutch word meaning pillar.

Strapwork Carved decoration representing leather straps.

Stretcher A horizontal connecting strut between the legs of tables and chairs to give added strength.

Striation Fine streaks or thread-like parallel lines in timber.

Stringing Narrow inlay of contrasting wood or a metal such as silver or brass.

Sunburst A design of radiating lines used as a decorative feature in the eighteenth century; revived in 1930s.

Swag A hanging festoon of husks or floral motifs.

Swan-neck A gentle curve, applied to certain drawer handles etc. A swan-neck pediment is a broken pediment in which the two sides are curved instead of straight.

Tambour Narrow strips of wood placed side by side on canvas and glued, forming a flexible sliding door or a roll-top for a desk.

Terminal The end of the arm of a chair.

Turning The use of a lathe to shape and decorate free-standing lengths of timber.

Under-brace Another name for a stretcher.

Veneer A thin sheet of wood glued to a base to make a design.

Volute A spiral scroll, much used to finish off a design.

Wainscot Timber used for panelling; originally a general term meaning timber from the Baltic.

GLOSSARY OF ANTIQUE-TRADE JARGON

As bought Without guarantee, relieving the vendor of all responsibility.
Aggro A piece of ugly furniture or one which has been badly repaired.

BB Dealer's name for a bureau-bookcase.
Bent gear Stolen property.
Biddy The little old lady of legend, believed to be an easy target for the unscrupulous, but often shrewd and knowing.
Bought in Purchased by the auctioneer on the vendor's behalf when a lot does not reach an acceptable price.
Boys, the The regular dealers at a sale, often in the ring.
Breaker An unsaleable or damaged article from which elements can be taken for use elsewhere. Often applied to books.

Call-out A request by a potential vendor to a dealer to see goods for sale in a house.
Chairman The leading figure in a dealer's ring, often appointed because he or she is the most powerful or richest dealer present.
Clearance A house clearance, undertaken by the dealer or junk-collector who offers the most for the entire contents.
Collector's item An ironical term applied to items no-one could possibly want.
Commercial An item of little importance or beauty but saleable.
Cost As in, 'You can have it at cost.' Sometimes true, more often cost plus a small margin.
Cut down Used of large item reduced in size to make it more saleable. Sometimes a comment made of chairs with legs which seem too short.

Down to me An expression used by dealers at markets or fairs, expressing a commitment to buy and pay and collect later.
Drink in it, a Payment for passing on useful information or acting as a go-between.

Estimate An auctioneer's idea of what a certain item will make.

Flea-market Not quite a junk market, not quite a collectables market, but something in between, organised to provide self-evident bargains.
Folky Used in respect of country furniture. Quite saleable. By extension, double folky or triple folky. Somewhat outmoded expression.
Follower An amateur who keeps an eye on a specialist dealer, knowing that when the dealer stops bidding he or she can still buy profitably.
Fresh Used of goods new to the area.
Furnishing piece Something that is not what it seems to be, or is too modern to be reckoned of antique calibre.
Hammer price The price at which an object was sold at auction.
Honest Used of something which is unpretentious and straightforward.

Inner ring The ring within a ring at an auction, where items bought by the ring are put up again for a select group of more prosperous dealers.
Investment Used by dealers to possible buyers to describe something which is perhaps overpriced.

Jockey A courier employed by a foreign dealer to line up trade calls, and sometimes accommodation and entertainment.

Kite A bad cheque.
Knocker A dealer who goes from door to door offering to buy antiques.
Knocking down The selling of an item at auction.
Knock-out The settle-up of a dealers' ring, where the highest bidder acquires goods bought on behalf of the ring by the spokeman.

Leave something in it Used in the context of a deal within the trade which enables both parties to make a profit.
Line, the The dealers' routes from London far into the provinces.
Looker A window-shopper at an antique fair or market.
Lumber, to To saddle a disliked dealer or collector with something suspect or too expensive.
Lump A large piece of unwieldy and awkward furniture.
Lyle's Lyle's price guide.

Made-up Used of a piece of furniture constructed from different items or from scratch using old materials.
Marriage A uniting of two different items to make a convincing whole.

Megadealer A large-scale dealer, probably a shipper.
Miller's Miller's price guide.
Moody Used of an item that is not what it pretends to be but there is some doubt why.

Off the wall Used of a non-existent bid at auction to boost the price.
Old friends Goods which repeatedly go the rounds without leaving the area.
Out of the air See 'off the wall'.

Period Used in such a phrase as 'It's period,' implying that the person being addressed may think it more modern.
Pull, to A term used by knockers and low-grade dealers. To pull from a house or crib – to buy cheaply from a naive householder.
Punter A private buyer.
Pussy-cat oak Heavy Victorian oak furniture with lion's-mask adornment on terminals.

Repro Reproduction furniture.
Right Used of something which is what it purports to be.
Ring A gathering of dealers at auction, who arrange not to bid against each other, and appoint a spokesman to act for them. The acquisitions are later auctioned among the dealers.
Rooms, the A term for auction rooms, used by dealers anxious to impress.
Rough In damaged or distressed condition.
Run, the The route or road system to antique-worthy areas away from the big cities.
Runner A dealer with a van or lorry who touts goods from shop to shop, or who buys for the shippers.
Run up, to To put in bids at auction to raise the price, either by a dealer to push up his or her own goods, or to annoy someone.

Sclenter, to To fake a picture or give false authentication.
Screw up, to Similar to lumbering, to make a buyer pay too much for something in the saleroom.
Settle, to To pay up at the knock-out of a ring.
Shipping goods Items bought for export, usually for container shipment, most often furniture with 'smalls' in drawers and cupboards.
Sight unseen Bought on description only.

Six and two Pertains to a set of chairs (six ordinary, two carvers). Can be four and two, eight and two etc.

Smalls China and small items, valuable and otherwise – used contemptuously by runners and furniture dealers.

Snatcher An over-eager dealer at open-air antique markets who buys from the back of vans and lorries, and whose sole aim is to get first pickings.

Speculative buy Something which may or may not have a future potential.

Spokesman The dealer who makes bids on behalf of the ring at auction, usually chosen because he or she is local and knows the form.

Suss Suspect, applied to a possible fake.

Tight wad A mean buyer.

Tinker An itinerant dealer.

Touch, a Sometimes a 'cheap touch'. A good buy.

Totter A street trader.

Trade, the Antique dealers.

Vicky Victorian.

WAF With all faults (an auctioneer's term) thus guarding against any comeback from a disgruntled buyer.

Wrong 'un An article, especially furniture, that is in some way suspect.

GUIDE TO VICTORIAN REGISTRATION MARKS

Registration marks were introduced in 1842 to safeguard designs. They were not successful and were discontinued in 1883.

Four types of goods were marked – metal, wood, glass and ceramics. These classes were shown in Roman numerals in the circle at the top of the diamond.

The other details were changed in 1868. Up to that date the letter beneath the class number gave the year of manufacture. The left-hand letter of the diamond showed the month of manufacture. The right-hand letter gave the day of manufacture in that month. The figure at the bottom of the diamond is unimportant. It denotes the manufacturer.

In 1868 the class number remained. There was now a figure instead of a letter immediately below the class number; this was the day of the month of manufacture. The month is shown at the bottom of the diamond. There was now a letter on the right-hand side, denoting the year. On the left-hand side was a number denoting the manufacturer.

See the table for details of classes, year of manufacture, and month. The example given shows that the class number is IV (ceramics) the year is J (1854). The month and day are of little significance to anyone. The 'RD' in the middle of the diamond means 'Registered'.

CLASSES

The Roman figures in the top circle refer to the class of goods as follows: I, metal; II, wood; III, glass; IV, pottery.

YEAR LETTERS

1842	X	1853	Y	1864	N	1874	U
43	H	54	J	65	W	75	S
44	C	55	E	66	Q	76	V
45	A	56	L	67	T	77	P
46	I	57	K	68	X	78	D
47	F	58	B	69	H	79	Y
48	U	59	M	70	C	80	J
49	S	60	Z	71	A	81	E
50	V	61	R	72	I	82	L
51	P	62	O	73	F	83	K
52	D	63	G				

MONTH LETTERS

January	C	May	E	September	D
February	G	June	M	October	B
March	W	July	I	November	K
April	H	August	R	December	A

BIBLIOGRAPHY

Andere, M., *Old Needlework Boxes and Tools* (Newton Abbot, 1971)

Andrews, J., *Price Guide to Antique Furniture* (Woodbridge, 1969)
  Price Guide to Victorian Furniture (Woodbridge, 1972)

Angus, I., *Medals and Decorations* (1973)

Armstrong, N., *A Collector's History of Fans* (1974)

Ash, D., *Dictionary of British Antique Silver* (1972)

Aslin, E., *Nineteenth Century English Furniture* (1962)

Baines, A., *Musical Instruments Through the Ages* (1961)

Barilli, R., *Art Nouveau* (1969)

Barnes, R. M., *History of Regiments and Uniforms of the British Army* (1950)

Battersby, M., *The World of Art Nouveau* (1968)
  The Decorative Twenties (1970)
  The Decorative Thirties (1972)

Beard, G. W., *Modern Glass* (1968)

Bedford, J., *All Kinds of Small Boxes* (1964)
  Paperweights (1968)

Bemrose, G., *Nineteenth Century English Pottery and Porcelain* (1952)

Bernal, J. D., *Science and Industry in the Nineteenth Century* (1953)

Bickerton, L. M., *Eighteenth Century English Drinking Glasses* (1971)

Boger, L. A., *The Complete Guide to Furniture Styles* (1961)
  A Dictionary of World Pottery and Porcelain (1972)

Boothroyd, A. E., *Fascinating Walking Sticks* (1973)

Bradbury, S., *Evolution of the Microscope* (1967)

Bristowe, W. S., *Victorian China Fairings* (1971)

British Optical Institute, *Dictionary of British Scientific Instruments* (1921)

Britten, F. J., *Old Clocks and Watches and Their Makers* (1973)

Bruton, E., *Clocks and Watches* (1968)

Buchner, A., *Mechanical Musical Instruments* (1921)

Butler, R., *Arthur Negus Guide to Antique Furniture* (1978)

Calvert, H. R., *Globes, Orreries and Other Models* (1967)

Chapuis, A. and Droz, E., *Automata* (1958)

Clifford, A., *Cut-Steel and Berlin Iron Jewellery* (1971)

Clutton, C. and Daniels, G., *Watches* (1965)

Colby, A., *Samplers* (1964)

Cooper, D. and Battershill, N., *Victorian Sentimental Jewellery* (1972)

Cooper, G. R., *The Invention of the Sewing Machine* (1968)

Cousins, F. W., *Sundials* (1969)

Cowie, D. and Henshaw, K., *Antique Collectors' Dictionary* (1962)

Coysh, A. W., *Blue and White Transfer Ware* (Newton Abbot, 1970)
  British Art Pottery (Newton Abbot, 1976)

Culff, R., *The World of Toys* (1969)

Cunnington, C. W. and P., *Handbook of English Costume in the Nineteenth Century* (1966)

Current, R. W., *The Typewriter* (1954)

Cushion, J. P., *Pottery and Porcelain* (1972)

Daumas, M., *Scientific Instruments of the Seventeenth and Eighteenth Centuries and Their Makers* (1972)

Davies, D. C., *English Bottles and Decanters 1650-1900* (1972)

Delieb, E., *Silver Boxes* (1968)

Dilby, A. U., *Oriental Rugs and Carpets* (1960)

Dunhill, A., *The Pipe Book*

Elville, E. M., *Paperweights* (1954)

Evans, J., *A History of Jewellery 1100-1870* (1970)

Fastnedge, R., *English Furniture Styles* (1969)

Fleming, J. and Honour, H., *Penguin Dictionary of Decorative Arts* (1977)

Flower, M., *Victorian Jewellery* (1967)

Folson, R. S., *Handbook of Greek Pottery* (1967)

Foster, K., *Scent Bottles* (1966)

Fraser, Lady A., *A History of Toys* (1966)

Garner, P., *The World of Edwardiana* (1974)

Garratt, J. G., *Model Soldiers* (1961)

Gelatt, R., *The Fabulous Phonograph* (1956)

Gernsheim, H. and A., *History of Photography* (1969)

Gloag, J. E., *Short History of Furniture* (1954)

Goaman, H., *English Clocks* (1967)

Godden, G. A, *British Pottery and Porcelain 1780-1850* (1963)
  Encyclopaedia of British Pottery and Porcelain Marks (1964)

Gorden, H., *Antiques. The Amateur's Questions* (1951)

Haggar, R. G., *English Country Pottery* (1950)

Haslam, M., *English Art Pottery 1865-1915* (Woodbridge, 1975)

Hayward, H. (ed.), *Handbook of Antiques Collecting* (1960)

Hayward, J. F., *English Cutlery* (1956)

Hill, H. and Paget-Tomlinson, E., *Instruments of Navigation* (1958)

Hillier, B., *Art Deco* (1968)
  The World of Art Deco (1971)

Hillier, M., *Dolls and Dollmakers* (1968)

Holmes, E., *An Age of Cameras* (1974)

Honey, W. B., *Glass* (1946)

Howarth-Loomes, B. E. C., *Victorian Photography* (1975)

Huetson, T. L., *Lace and Bobbins* (Newton Abbot, 1973)

Hughes, G. B., *English Snuff Boxes* (1951)

Hughes, G. B. and T., *English Painted Enamels* (1951)

Hughes, T., *Small Decorative Antiques* (1959)
  English Domestic Needlework 1680-1860 (1961)
  Cottage Antiques (1967)

Jervis, S., *Victorian Furniture* (1968)

Jones, M. E., *A History of Western Embroidery* (1969)

Joy, E. T., *Country Life Book of English Furniture* (1968)

Kiely, E. R., *Surveying Instruments* (New York, 1947)

Klamkin, M., *The Picture Postcard* (Newton Abbot, 1974)

Lang, D. M., *The Georgians* (1966)

Larson, K., *Rugs and Carpets of the Orient* (1966)

Laver, J., *Victoriana* (1966)

Lewis, M. D. S., *Antique Paste Jewellery* (1970)

Lloyd, H. A., *The Collectors' Dictionary of Clocks* (1964)

Luddington, J., *Antique Silver* (1971)

Mackay, J., *An Introduction to Small Antiques* (1970)
  Price Guide to Collectable Antiques (Woodbridge, 1975)
  Nursery Antiques (1976)

Marquoid, P. and Edwards, R., *Dictionary of English Furniture* (1954)

Masden, S. T., *Art Nouveau* (1967)

McCausland, H., *Snuff and Snuff Boxes* (1951)

Michaelis, R., *British Pewter* (1969)

Moody, E., *Modern Furniture* (1966)

Mount, S., *Price Guide to Eighteenth Century Pottery* (Woodbridge, 1972)

Murray, P., *Toys* (1968)

Musgrave, C., *Regency Furniture* (1971)

Naylor, G., *The Arts and Crafts Movement* (1971)

Norman, A. V. B., *Arms and Armour* (1964)

Oman, C. C., *English Domestic Silver* (1959)

Osborne, H. (ed.), *Oxford Companion to the Decorative Arts* (1976)

Owen, M., *Antique Cast Iron* (Poole, 1977)

Pearsall, R., *Collecting Mechanical Antiques* (Newton Abbot, 1973)
  Collecting Scientific Instruments (Newton Abbot, 1974)
  Making and Managing an Antique Shop (Newton Abbot, 1979)

Peterson, H. L. (ed.), *Encyclopaedia of Firearms* (1964)

Pevsner, N., *Pioneers of Modern Design* (1960)

Pinto, E., *Treen and other Wooden Bygones* (1969)

Polak, A., *Modern Glass* (1962)

Quennell, M. and C. H. B., *History of Everyday Things In England* (1938)

Ramsay, L. G. C. (ed.), *Concise Encyclopaedia of Antiques 5 vols* (1955-60)

Ridley, M., *Oriental Antiques* (1977)

Roche, S., *Mirrors* (1957)

Savage, G., *Glass* (1965)
  Dictionary of Antiques (1970)

Sevensma, W. S., *Tapestries* (1965)

Singer, C., Holmyard, E. J., Hall, A. R. and Williams, T. I. (eds), *A History of Technology, 5 vols* (1954-8)

Smith, A., *Illustrated Guide to Clocks and Watches* (1975)

Smith, D. J., *Discovering Railwayana* (Tring, 1971)

Spero, S., *Price Guide to Eighteenth Century English Porcelain* (Woodbridge, 1970)

Staff, F., *The Picture Postcard and Its Origins* (1966)

Symonds, R. W., *History of English Clocks* (1947)

Thoday, A. G., *Astronomical Telescopes* (1971)

Toller, J., *Discovering Antiques* (Newton Abbot, 1975)
  Treen (Newton Abbot, 1975)

Turner, H. A. B., *Collectors' Guide to Staffordshire Pottery Figures* (1971)

Wakefield, H., *Nineteenth Century English Glass* (1961)

Wardle, P., *Victorian Lace* (1968)

Webb, G., *Cylinder Musical Box Handbook* (1968)
  Disc Musical Box Handbook (1971)

White, G., *European and American Dolls* (1966)

Whittington, P., *Militaria* (1969)
  Undiscovered Antiques (1972)

Wilkinson, P., *Swords and Daggers* (1968)

Wills, G., *Collecting Copper and Brass* (1962)
  Candlesticks (Newton Abbot, 1974)

Wood, V., *Victoriana* (1960)

Woodhouse, C. B., *Victoriana Collectors' Handbook* (1970)

ACKNOWLEDGEMENTS

A book of this nature is greatly helped by first-rate colour photographs previously unpublished in book form. I am very grateful to the following for allowing me to use their colour transparencies. The figures refer to page numbers.

Michael Asprey Ltd., Duke Street, London SW1: 114

Bearnes, the Rainbow Rooms, Torquay and David Dolbey, photographer, of Totnes: 11, 14, 18, 19, 22, 27, 30, 39, 43, 46, 47, 62, 71, 74, 75, 78, 79, 83, 95, 107, 115, 118, 120, 127, 131, 134, 135, 139, 155, 163, 171, 189, 191

Christie's, South Kensington: 169, 175, 179

Crowther of Syon Lodge: 107

Halcyon Days, Brook Street, London W1: 7, 23, 38, 51, 54, 55, 56, 57, 58, 59, 62, 63, 111, 119, 130

Sean Hickey, photographer, of Torquay: 9, 10, 50, 103, 187, 190, 191

The Parker Gallery, Berkeley Street, London W1: 146

Pennard House Antiques, Shepton Mallet, Somerset: 6, 26, 30, 31, 167

Phillips, New Bond Street: 181

Randolph, Hadleigh, Suffolk: 15

Anthony Woodburn, Leigh, Kent: 34, 35

I am most grateful to the following auction rooms for permission to use the following black-and-white photographs. The figures refer to page numbers.

Phillips: 13, 16, 20, 21, 24, 25, 32, 33, 37, 44, 45, 49, 57, 60, 68, 69, 72, 73, 76, 77, 80, 81, 85, 103, 118, 132, 145, 148, 184, 185, 193

Sotheby's: 35, 164, 184

Christie's: 40

Jacket photographs by Paul Biddle courtesy of H. El Masri, Rooms, Ashburton, Devon.

INDEX